GOTCHA!

GEORGE BAIN

HOW THE MEDIA DISTORT THE NEWS

KEY PORTER BOOKS

Canadian Cataloguing in Publication Data

Bain, George, 1920–
Gotcha!

ISBN 1-55013-555-4 (hc) 1-55013-601-1 (pbk)

1. Reporters and reporting – Canada. 2. Mass media – Canada – Influence. 3. Journalism – Political aspects – Canada. 4. Government and the press – Canada. 5. Television broadcasting of news – Political aspects – Canada. I. Title.

PN4914.P6B35 1994 070.449320971 C94-931237-1

The publisher gratefully acknowledges the assistance of the Canada Council, the Ontario Arts Council and the Ontario Publishing Centre.

Key Porter Books Limited
70 The Esplanade
Toronto, Ontario
Canada M5E 1R2

Front cover photograph: Fiona Spalding-Smith
Cover design: Ivan Holmes Design

Printed and bound in Canada

95 96 97 98 99 6 5 4 3 2 1

CONTENTS

PREFACE

A FUNNY THING HAPPENED TO ME ON THE WAY TO retirement—two, actually, neither of them rollickingly funny, both with an effect on my view of journalism. First, John Godfrey, then the president of the University of King's College in Halifax, now the Liberal Member of Parliament for the Ontario constituency of Don Valley West, asked me to become director of the college's School of Journalism. The original director, David Oancia, another former *Globe and Mail*er, had had a falling out with the management and left, and the new school was quietly foundering. I first said no, was asked again, thought about it some more and said yes.

Several years later, while I was at King's, Bob Lewis, managing editor (now editor) of *Maclean's*, asked me if I would be interested in doing a monthly column as the magazine's media critic. He broached the idea late in the evening, at a decidedly vinous dinner after the 1984 Liberal party convention had chosen John Turner as leader. The next morning I found in my jacket pocket a note that said, "Call Bob Lewis about column," and, having refreshed my memory about just what sort of column we were talking about, and the terms, I called him and accepted the offer.

I would be unfair to myself if I said that while I was in daily journalism, for much of the time as a five-columns-a-week columnist, I did not think about the nature of journalism. I did—but sporadically and in no concentrated way, and with a natural tilt towards the belief that journalists were almost always right. Nevertheless, the difference between looking from the inside at the business I had long been engaged in, and looking at it, not only from the outside, but with a deliberately critical eye, proved to be greater than I would have imagined. I am less sure than I once was, which is a restrained way of putting it, of our essential rightness in all circumstances, or even, at times, of the purity of our motives.

At King's, it quickly sank in that these students I suddenly had in front of me were not insiders of journalism, like the people with whom I was most used to associating, but outsiders contemplating a leap in the dark and naturally anxious to know more about the terrain in which they would land. Therefore it became desirable for me to re-examine that terrain myself, to see if it was quite as I thought it to be. The *Maclean's* assignment encouraged that altered thinking.

I identify four or five eras in journalism in the time I have been in it. (The reason for my hesitation over the number will become evident shortly.) The first of those I saw only as it came to the end of a very long run. That was the era of the wholly dominant publisher, or editor, or editor-publisher; it was not unusual at the time for the two to be combined in one person, who might even be the proprietor as well.

The Toronto *Telegram*, where I began in the middle 1930s, was a paper with a difference. It was so in being the prime asset of a charitable trust, the John Ross Robertson Trust, of which the beneficiary was Toronto's Hospital for Sick Children. Whether or not that is the explanation, the *Tely* had a benign air. It did not fire people during the Depression, and it even hired me, not alone but among not many. It was an unpressured, congenial sort of place in which to work, money aside—and money was very much aside, everywhere in journalism, at the time. But the *Tely*, once the leader, was by then being left behind by the hard-driving and unabashedly sensationalist *Toronto Daily Star.*

The Telegram was Conservative, all day, every day. The *Star* was correspondingly Liberal. Its founder and publisher, Joseph E. Atkinson (sometimes known as "Holy Joe"), was a confidant of the prime minister, William Lyon Mackenzie King. The morning papers, *The Globe* and *The Mail and Empire*, although less aggressive in proclaiming their political loyalties, were respectively Liberal and Conservative. Indicative of the paper's orientation, a big item in the *Tely*'s assignment book was the annual Orangemen's Day parade, which was covered to excess by a small squad of reporters; a standing requirement of the lead story was to include the precise time it took the glorious march to pass a given point in its wandering course through the lower part of the city.

Although the *Star* was the bigger paper, the *Tely* was the power in municipal politics. Before elections for city council, it customarily ran a box containing a list of desirable (i.e., Conservative) candidates, under the no-nonsense heading "Vote for These." By good majorities, the voters of Tory Toronto—heavily British immigrant, Protestant and royalist—regularly did.

Those political characteristics of the press of the era were not unique to Toronto. In Vancouver, the *Sun* and the *Province*; in Winnipeg, the *Free Press* and the *Tribune*; in Ottawa, the *Journal* and the *Citizen*; in Montreal, the *Gazette* and the *Montreal Star*; in Halifax, the *Chronicle* and the *Herald*—all were opposites, Liberal versus Conservative, and not at all reticent about saying so and urging their readers along in their own direction. Such editorializing was not always confined to the editorials; at election times, particularly, it was everywhere. At times of federal and provincial elections, a few *Tely* reporters wrote speeches for Tory candidates, not at all surreptitiously. The term "conflict of interest" had not been invented yet—or, if it had, not a lot of attention was paid to it.

Newspapers of the time projected a distinct corporate personality, much more than they have done since. Often enough it directly reflected the personality of the dominant editor/publisher/owner. A graphic American example was described by Robert Casey in *Such Interesting People*, published in the 1940s, on the bright, the boffo and the bizarre in the Chicago newspaper world, which produced a lot of all three. He told of a paper of a notably irascible nature, which I think may have been the long-defunct *Chicago Inter-Ocean*, whose publisher was known to express his journalistic philosophy in the words "I sit here with a sockful of nightsoil [Casey's euphemism] and sooner or later everyone passes under my window." With large circulations in metropolitan areas, little competition from radio and no television to steal away their advertising, newspapers often swung great weight in their communities.

That sort of newspaper was on the way out in the late thirties, however, and was nearly gone by the end of the Second World War. It was being superseded by a second style of paper, in which the key word was Objectivity, with a capital O. A "church and state" separation came into being between the editorialists and the newsroom. Although the built-in slant in reporting never vanished altogether, now, at least, "slant" had become a bad word. A paper's views on politics were to be confined to the editorial page; reporters' opinions belonged nowhere; reporters recorded the news, they did not make it, and they intruded very little upon it. Newspapers and the rapidly sprouting television were to serve as pipelines, taking in information at one end and delivering it unadulterated at the other.

Not all newspeople or news organizations accepted this austere code as either desirable or achievable. Objectivity was viewed by some as a myth. Journalists could not automatically shed their upbringing, religion, education, cultural background, economic status and various other influences at the moment they sat down at their typewriters, and suddenly become intellectually aseptic. (Whether or not that made a sufficient argument against *attempting* objectivity remains debatable.)

Canadian political journalism, like so much else Canadian, takes its leads, usually with some time lag, from American practice. It was the vicious anti-Communist crusade of Senator Joseph McCarthy of Wisconsin in the 1950s, with its denunciations of largely illusory Communists and fellow travellers in government, that revealed the weakness in an idealistic, wholly hands-off style of political journalism. If a public person said one day something that was not consonant with what he or she had said a month earlier, was it editorializing to retrieve the earlier statement from the files and insert some reference to it as a guide to the reader? If reporters were forbidden to include fresh, authoritative information assembled at their own initiative, would not the public be denied another side to the argument? In such a case, what check was there to the wild career of McCarthy or any other conscienceless demagogue?

The era of pure-pure objectivity was short-lived, and even in its brief time objectivity was more an ideal than a settled practice. In any case, there was more at the time than the McCarthy malignancy to make managements in print journalism think about what they were doing and where they were going. The rise of television from fringe player in the business of news delivery to today's dominance, which seems now to have occurred overnight, actually was achieved over more than a decade; it scared newspaper publishers half to death, and no wonder. Television was the biggest development in the news business in a hundred years, reaching much farther than Paul Julius Reuter's setting up the first agency to sell news internationally in the mid-nineteenth century. There was a lot of sombre pondering over what newspapers could do to justify their continued existence in the face of this new medium that could *show* people the news, hours before journalism could deliver it on paper.

The wise decision that eventually evolved was to go where television couldn't, in part because of its inflexible format of neat half-hour and hour-long passages, from which the minutes of commercials, sign-ons and sign-offs and assorted messages must be subtracted. *The New York Times*'s ancient boast, "All the news that's fit to print," became in the television translation "All the news that fits the time." The magic word in print suddenly became "depth".

In this third style of newspaper, any substantial story, especially on government and politics, would provide not just facts on the news event itself, but reaction from outside parties (frequently lobby groups), a sketch of what lay behind the development, some anticipation of where it might lead and probably some analysis of likely political winners and losers. Investigative reporting, which was not new but a revival of what in the previous century had been known as muckraking, became an instrument in achieving depth. It was essentially detective work—digging into files, finding and interviewing persons with insider knowledge who were ready to talk, even if only on condition of anonymity.

There was more than just extra material in print's adjustment to the threat that it might go the way of the horse. Business and economic news, for example, was raised to new prominence, because such news does not lend itself to pictures, without which TV goes limp. Hard news—pure reports of today's happenings—declined in relation to interpretative news because television almost always would be first with happenings, and also because television, notwithstanding that it is an oral medium, does not handle words well except in short bursts. (Consider how infrequently interviewees in news-related shows ever get to complete a second sentence—assuming, of course, that they got to complete the first.)

In that third period, roughly the sixties and seventies, in which television was taking over and print was struggling to present itself as indispensable to being well informed, readers and viewers enjoyed some of the best journalism of the century. However, at the same time, attitudes were being formed among the young that would profoundly affect the next phase, or phases, in journalism. In the fourth, print eased off in the effort to make itself distinctly different from television and quietly absorbed part of the opponent's philosophy—that the road to the audience's heart (and mind) lies through the emotions. Drama became a more important element not just in action news—crimes, wars, natural disasters and the like—but news of all sorts, including political.

The question is whether there has been a distinct fifth style in news, or simply an enhancement of the worst features of the third and fourth. Interpretative reporting has become more designed to affect people's *feelings* about issues than their understanding. The purpose of investigative reporting has become less to find out than to denounce. The changes of greatest consequence have been in attitude. In recent years, as epitomized by the Ottawa press corps, the media have become less a miscellaneous collection of similarly employed persons competing independently in the same place at the same time, and more a fellowship representing a narrow range of viewpoints. The well-known pack instinct has gone from being expressed in mass attacks and feeding frenzies when scandal occurs to being a sort of systemic groupthink. In the Mulroney years, correctness demanded not just that opposition to the government be maintained but that, like justice in the courts, it be seen to be maintained.

So much for how the trade, and one practitioner, got here from there. Now, before going on to what this book is, a note on what it is *not*.

First, it is not a delicately balanced, clinically objective account. It is opinionated. The opinions are mine, and the bias that infects them is my belief that recent media performance has not been dazzling. I feel no great anguish in saying so, recognizing that the media, unlike most persons and institutions they report and comment on, have instant, unlimited means of reply.

Secondly, it is not about all the news media in Canada, but just the English-language media. If I were offering an excuse, I would say that the English and French media are sufficiently different, not just in language, to deserve separate treatments, which I think is true. Unfortunately, what is truer is that I am incapable of adequately judging the French counterparts.

Thirdly, it is not an equally distributed treatment of all newspapers, magazines, radio stations and television channels and networks. *The*

Globe and Mail and the CBC figure disproportionately, not because they reach the greatest numbers of Canadians, but because they have acquired the mystique of leadership, which, whatever it may or may not do with the public, works well with governments and with other media. On top of that, when the subject is what is wrong with the media, they provide the best illustrations.

Fourthly, this book is not at all intended to say, "See what a good boy am I." If there is a journalistic sin catalogued in these pages that I have not committed sometime in a long career, I can only attribute the omission to oversight.

INTRODUCTION: THEN AND NOW

CANADIAN JOURNALISTS HAVE ALWAYS TENDED TO POOH-pooh their influence on public opinion in matters of politics, not out of modesty, heaven forbid, but so as not to have too much invested in case something or someone whom they incautiously endorsed earlier turns out not quite as expected. It is a species of pre-emptive disavowal. I remember myself saying once in some discussion, no doubt looking for a deathless aphorism as well as a hedge against any future reckoning: "The press have never defeated a good government or elected a bad one." If that was ever put on paper, in the column I was then writing for *The Globe and Mail*, I have not been able to find it. It seems unlikely I would have let go with just one use what appeared to be a good line. But I must admit that the statement hasn't worn well, and now looks unwarrantedly dogmatic and perhaps even slightly fatuous. The Trudeau governments, four of them over a period of sixteen years (with one brief break), could not be called an undiluted boon to the nation—not with the commencement in that era of the steep slide into mammoth national debt that remains Ottawa's most intractable problem. Therefore, they were partly bad governments. I also would be happier with the proposition if the Mulroney governments had been positively *good* governments rather than just—as is my own belief—much less *bad* than they were made out to be over a nine-year career. The press did not single-handedly create either the acclaim which elected the one, or the bile which ultimately devastated the other, although they were superabundant contributors to both. This book is largely about the latter—and the most intense and unrelenting campaign of denigration that any Canadian government has faced at least this side of the Second World War.

The loss in the 1993 general election was of course Kim Campbell's, but she was the inheritor of all that had gone before, as no commentator has failed to say. Even a year after Mulroney had left, when the successor Liberals celebrated their first six months in office, journalists in the capital—Edward Greenspon, for one, the *Globe and Mail* bureau chief, in an orgasmic effusion over Jean Chrétien's leadership to that point—were still going on about Brian Mulroney having been "the most unpopular prime minister in Canadian history." (Perhaps; there was not much polling in our first century.) But public opinion does not come out of nothing.

When newspapers had the business of selling day-to-day information virtually to themselves, editors and publishers were pleased to think of themselves as opinion leaders, and were not shy to say so. That is no longer the case. They prefer now to say that editorial and other commentaries are offered with no intention to tell people what to think, heaven forbid, but simply for their interested consideration. Their news, for its part, is always several degrees purer than the driven snow.

If public opinion in the late eighties and early nineties was correctly identified as being filled with discontent, cynicism and distrust towards Parliament, government, political parties, politicians and all institutions created by or responsible to them—at least as late as the 1993 general election, the media and the polls were still saying it was—all that remains to be decided is to what degree those conditions were caused by the media. It could be no degree at all. It may be that everything Canadians read, see and hear in the media bounces off them like balloons at a kids' party; or that the country's mood was attributable to some mysterious, self-generated, mass psychological disturbance.

But that is not something broadcasting executives or newspaper editors can offer with equanimity in support of a not-guilty plea, because implicit in it lies the admission that their influence on the public for good, bad or anything in between is nil.

It could be, too, that however much the political reporting of the time may have led Canadians to feel sour about government, no such effect was intended, and that people were reading meanings into wholly objective and unslanted news messages innocently delivered. But neither is that a thought with which our media leaders can be comfortable. Not long after the Second World War, Sir Ernest Gowers, a noted

English writer on writing, said, "Writing is an instrument for conveying ideas from one mind to another; the writer's job is to make his reader apprehend his meaning readily and precisely." Broadcasters, so as not to feel neglected, might note the similar observation of the historian G.M. Young that "the final cause of speech is to get an idea as exactly as possible out of one mind and into another." Thus, if the public misunderstood what was being given them by the media, the fault lay with the media.

Another proposition to be taken into account is an old standby of the media—and, as might be expected, one designed to be exculpatory. Whenever a complaint is made against some element of the media for having dangled before the public something that could reasonably be said to engender cynicism, or any of the other listed ingredients of public dyspepsia, the reply (in tones of wounded innocence) is: "We don't *make* the news, we just report it." In other words, "Don't blame us. If people are upset, if they are mad at anybody, that has nothing to do with us. We are but mirrors of the surrounding reality. We just observe and chronicle. The people who are *reported upon* make the news. Take your complaint up with them."

This don't-shoot-the-messenger ploy is more than a bit of a fraud; it is threadbare hokum. For a start, journalists are not in the business of picking up messages here and unquestioningly delivering them there, like Canada Post. They select, from the tens of thousands available every day, those messages *they* decide their readers or viewers should have. Next *they* decide how much or how little information on the chosen subjects can be fitted into the product—how many seconds' worth of television and radio time, how many centimetres of type. Then *they* decide how the information should be interpreted—in what words and with what playing up of this aspect at the expense of that. Then, if the message contains both good guys and bad guys, which is very often the case, *they* decide which are which. In short, the message this messenger delivers is the messenger's.

Whether the media's recent phase of extreme judgementalism, stretched fault-finding, simulated outrage and denunciation has passed or lingers suspended in the pink mist of a prolonged honeymoon, it is too early to say with confidence. Certainly, in the first half-year of the Chrétien government, most reporting of the new government was sympathetic, quite different in tone and substance from that of the beginning period of his predecessor. That and the idiosyncrasies (or, to put it less politely, the biases and prejudices) that influence media image-making—or image-trashing—will play a considerable part in this book. And there are other, deeper influences, notably in Ottawa, that have led to reporting becoming skewed. One is the excess of like-mindedness arising from a new sense of community in the media.

Not everyone in any community—business, professional, ethnic, religious or other—is cut to the same pattern, but obviously all will have some characteristics, interests, enthusiasms and prejudices in common, otherwise there would be no community. While there is a journalistic community in Canada, and a distinct subcommunity of impressive size and immense influence in the capital, the members of the latter do not care for the term "community", preferring to think of themselves (and to be thought of) as sturdy individualists, straight arrows all. The suggestion that reporters of national government and politics might be influenced in their judgements by a group mindset is repugnant, perhaps particularly because there is rather a lot of evidence that it is true.

It is to this community, the largest body of experienced journalists in one place and dedicated to one subject, that most of the characterizations of "the media" in this book relate. That, admittedly, is geographically unfair. The parliamentary press gallery, as it is formally (and inaccurately) called, is mainly composed of persons in bureaus representative of the country's largest news organizations—in television, radio, news agencies, newspapers, magazines, the works—most of which are based in the Toronto-Ottawa-Montreal triangle.

But this disproportion is justifiable, because these are the news organizations which extend the longest reach across the country, have the largest audiences and produce the greatest volume of what is considered national news. It could be said that for any matter of gross error or alleged wrongdoing in government to become a certified national scandal, the story needs to be initiated by a news organization in that group, and immediately taken up and improved upon by (preferably) at least two others. Therefore, if the media exert influence on the thinking of the country in matters of government and politics, the elements of this eastern corps exert most of it. And they do it first by influencing one another.

Some cohesion has always been present in news gathering—or as close to always as I can testify from direct exposure or reading. There once was a practice called "scalping", meaning taking the top off another newspaper's story. As a first assignment of the day, the reporter at an afternoon newspaper might be given three or four clips from a morning paper and told by the city editor, "Gimme about eight inches on this, and about six on that, and just a squib on the other two." If there was time and it seemed worthwhile, the reporter would be expected, with a couple of phone calls, to flesh out the most significant of these with a little firsthand new detail; otherwise simple rewrites would disguise the fact that the items were pure theft.

Scalping was a sort of competitive sameness. Many newspeople were in the habit of saying that competition was the lifeblood of their business; it drove reporters to dig deeper to find matters of genuine public interest that governments, businesses or individuals might have preferred to keep secret. But quite a lot of what resulted was little more than a busy-busy shuffling of feet going nowhere. When I did a series of interviews with newsroom staffs across the country for the Royal Commission on Newspapers—its report was published in 1981—I found some skepticism about the sort of competition that was not to *do* anything, but not to be outdone. One experienced reporter who had worked for both *The Toronto Star* and *The Telegram*, which were fierce competitors, told of being asked at the *Star* one morning to scalp a story in the first edition of the *Tely*; the city editor admired its angle, and preferred it to the story his own paper already had. When the rewrite was done and published, it turned out that in the meantime someone at the *Tely* had admired the *Star*'s version and in turn had scalped that.

The term "scalping", so far as I know, has disappeared from the language. However, followership in large matters has become standard operating procedure. If the story is big enough, the so-called competitor may not even have to wait for it to be published or aired—especially aired—to scalp it; the initiator will often be happy to deliver it in advance, though not so much in advance as to allow the competitor to get it out first. There are two reasons—the additional publicity the initiator will get, and the follow-up needed to establish the original as a bona-fide, first-class, consequential scandal.

The term "pack journalism" used to be applied to the madness that sets in among a corps of otherwise supposedly independent, competitive and relatively sane political journalists, which causes them all to hare off after a scandal with a common purpose—to exploit it as titillating news to which establishing its truth becomes secondary at best. This syndrome showed up in all the main scandals of the Mulroney years. Several examples are included here, beginning with the famous Tainted Tuna Scandal, but with more attention given to the other side of the story. (The currently preferred term for the pack phenomenon is "feeding frenzy", evocative of a school of piranhas threshing the water to a pink froth as they strip a deboated fisherman to the bone. The old term was apparently inadequate to describe the voracity of the devouring horde.)

In everyday Ottawa, routine follow-the-leader(ship) in reporting has gone so far as to produce almost a reverse image of what existed when newspapers constituted "the media" virtually in total, and were unequivocally partisan. If from time to time in that era a political slant sloshed over into the news columns, it was nothing for the reader to be surprised at, or to cause wonderment about the beliefs and political preferences of its sponsors; the latter were routinely on display on the editorial page. Now, if a slant is detected, it can be attributed to no source of inspiration more exact than the conventional wisdom of the moment in the Ottawa media community. The question is whether the news consumer is better off knowing where a slant comes from, or being left to guess. On the rare occasions when slanted reporting is commented on in the media—*The Toronto Star*, with its long-standing economic nationalism theme, has been cited more than once as an offender—a term that regularly crops up is "editorial interference in the news", suggesting a blot on good journalism. Instances in which media groupthink seems the only explanation are more numerous but less commented on—and very much more tolerantly treated, as simple reflections of the thinking of that exemplar of all virtues, The Ordinary Canadian.

The dominant strain of thought identifiable in political reporting in recent years has been that of the generation that was in its teens in the sixties and seventies—now mainly in their own forties and fifties, and established as senior reporters, bureau chiefs, commentators, editors of one sort and another. The generational traits they have brought with them include a vague-ish, vogue-ish leftism; distrust of all things institutional from Parliament to the cop on the beat, and notably government; a general anti-everything prejudice reflective of the belief that all of Western society was a cesspool before their arrival (the trust-no-one-over-thirty syndrome prolonged by thirty years); and a saintly piety founded on fond recollections of press clippings from their time as a generation of idealists. Elements of their creed: To be anti-authority is, in principle, to be on the side of the angels. Merit is immediately translatable into elitism, which is objectionable. To succeed materially is to be suspect. Persons in positions of power need to be watched because they got where they are by looking out for themselves. All rights are sacred, all responsibility optional. And minorities are more moral than majorities.

Some of that, of course, has only reinforced predispositions that have been around in the Ottawa press corps for ever, rooted in the way journalism likes to see itself and would like to be seen by others: as an institutionalized knight-on-a-white-horse always galloping off in pursuit of some noble cause. Journalists have accordingly encouraged a gallant image of themselves, as reflected in the sententious old proposition that goes back to London's Fleet Street, once the home of Britain's metropolitan press, that the journalist's mission in life is to "comfort the afflicted and afflict the comfortable".

The old romantic image fostered in North American journalism, greatly assisted by Hollywood, was of a raffish sort of fellow who knew everybody (had tremendous "sources"), was afraid of nobody, took no guff from anybody and wore his hat far back on his head with a press card stuck in the band. (I have yet to see in real life a journalist with a press card in his hatband.) But behind that outgoing, smart-talking, tough-guy front—so the sanctioned illusion went—there dwelt a crusader, defender of the underdog, corrector of wrongs, attacker of the status quo, smasher of icons and all-round swell guy, who perhaps smoked too much, drank too much and was determinedly cynical, but had a heart of gold.

All of these self-images, including the current one, obviously have points in common. The journalist is a free-thinker, the human counterpart of the dog that wears no man's collar, radical in tendency, an advocate, a reformer (most definitely not of the Preston Manning sort), a person of unfailing compassion for the unfortunate of the world and, perhaps most of all, a person who considers the word "conservative"—adjective or noun, small c or large—applied to himself or herself as highly offensive, if not actually defamatory. I can't say that I have *never* seen a Canadian journalist who admitted to being a conservative, much less a large-C Conservative, but there cannot have been more than four or five, although I have always suspected there were a few more who hadn't come out of the closet.

It ought not to be surprising, given these shared characteristics, that the Ottawa media community and the political reporting and commentary that come out of it have become predominantly from one viewpoint, so that in 1993 we had what came close to being a six-party election covered by a one-party press. And the homogenization of the news has not been limited to national news and commentary or to the reporting level. The media as a whole have grown together. In the list of causes, concentration of ownership is only the oldest. Ten years apart, we had in Canada two inquiries—a special Senate committee led by Senator Keith Davey, and a royal commission under the chairmanship of Thomas Kent, a former newspaper editor and later a senior adviser to two prime ministers, Lester Pearson and Pierre Trudeau. Both inquiries examined essentially the same concern—the concentration of newspaper ownership in fewer and fewer hands. The feared consequence was a loss of diversity in the viewpoints brought to bear on the public business.

In its report, issued in mid-1981, the Kent commission said: "The commission's mandate is broad. It reflects the gravity of the situation within the newspaper industry and the intensity of public concern." Grave or not, public concern or not, the loss of diversity has happened—it was well developed then and has become more pronounced—not through any failure of the inquiries or of governments to do anything in response (though they didn't), but because it was already too late. The concentration of ownership has not continued as it was going mainly because the number of newspapers in most cities had already reached the irreducible (let us hope) minimum of one. Meanwhile—again notwithstanding the gravity of the situation and the public concern—when a television cable channel became available for a national all-news television service, which became NewsWorld, it wound up in the hands of the CBC, already the largest element in the country's news business, and the most powerful homogenizing influence in all the media, with its regional stations and national networks in both television and radio and in both official languages, and with its reach into every corner of the country. So much for diversity.

Recently, economics has encouraged more homogenization, with a consequent loss of individuality. The nineties have been a bad time for all the media—not to the point of closures, although there have been those too, but with loss figures showing up in annual reports, cuts in budgets, and layoffs of staff.

It is one of the paradoxes of the news business that news close to home is often more expensive than news from far away and of more dramatic and consequential happenings. Scenes, voices, written words from Bosnia—or Ottawa, for that matter—can be bought as needed from the world-wide and national news agencies, the supermarkets of news. On the other hand, covering the local city hall, police department, board of education, courts, chamber of commerce, labour unions and all the other "beats" requires staff with salaries, expenses and fringe benefits, fifty-two weeks a year. Therefore, when it becomes necessary to trim budgets, it tends to be the close-to-home news, which gives the local newspaper or radio station its individuality, that suffers first and most.

That cost-awareness fits in tidily with other, usually *ad hoc* arrangements with a homogenizing effect—joint polls, for example, which deliver the same research data to two large media corporations. Common data on public thinking can only lead the parties more surely to common conclusions. As polls are affordable only to the big entities in print and broadcasting, the results and what they make of them attract attention. Once in the public domain, the conclusions of the pollsters, and the conclusions of the clients of the polls, become, in the hands of all the smaller players in the game, conclusions on conclusions on conclusions—thus, very quickly, the conventional wisdom, or Media Truth. Another influence towards a more monolithic press is that of news-swapping arrangements between non-competing dailies—for example, *The Toronto Star*, which is dominant in Metropolitan Toronto, and the seventeen-paper Southam organization, which is dominant in most other middle-to-large centres from Vancouver to Montreal. Such alliances of convenience come on top of the Canadian Press and its broadcast arm, Broadcast News, the news business's very own co-operative, which takes from all to deliver to all, with a lot of its own reporting added. On top of all that, again, are the corporate chains and networks to which most of the country's news-gathering and news-delivering entities belong.

By far the greatest part of the news and commentary on all current affairs in Canada comes under half a dozen trade names—CTV and CBC, Canadian Press, Southam News, Thomson and *The Toronto Star*. The *Star* is not part of any daily chain, although it is itself the owner of a chain of community newspapers around Toronto. But it does have the largest circulation of any paper in the country, highly concentrated in Toronto. And Thomson, though known first for its dominance in the country's smaller cities and towns, usually without print competition, also owns *The Globe and Mail* and *The Winnipeg Free Press*.

Nor is that quite all. There is also the fact of various mutual interests such as, for instance, the law as it relates to the media. That interest has been particularly acute since the implantation in the 1982 constitution of a guarantee of freedom of the press—stated in section 2(b) of the Charter of Rights and Freedoms as "freedom of thought, belief, opinion and expression, including freedom of the press and other media of communication." All the constitution said was that freedom of the press could not be taken away; it did not say what that freedom was. That was left to be defined by the piling of decision upon decision in the courts.

Consequently, in the late eighties and nineties, lawyers for leading elements in broadcast and print journalism—usually in some combination of joint appellants—were in the courts in case after case, trying to ensure that the markers defining where freedom of the press begins and ends were set as broadly as possible. The Bernardo–Homolka multiple murders case in Ontario was a conspicuous example. Instant publication of evidence in the wife's trial—she was tried first, separately, and convicted of manslaughter—was forbidden by court order lest it prejudice a jury in the subsequent trial of the husband on various charges including murder and rape.

The court order, translated imprecisely in almost all reporting into a "ban", which suggests permanency, was made into a freedom-of-the-press issue that had all the detachment that might be expected of any totally self-interested lobby group fighting over some advantage to which it thought it was entitled. The arguments were made entirely from a media viewpoint, as "our right to serve the public right to know", and when and how the media thought this right ought to be exercised. Freedom of the press was to be defined as the right of a media oligopoly to prevail over the right of the individual—innocent until proven guilty—to the assurance of a trial before an unprejudiced jury.

Obviously there can be no quibbling about the right of the media, or any other body, to make the arguments they choose in appealing court orders they believe inhibit their constitutional freedoms. However, outside the courtroom, things are different. First of all, freedom-of-the-press issues usually set a press right against an individual right—in the law of libel, for example, where the right of the individual not to be publicly defamed clashes with the assumed right of the media to tell what they choose. Secondly, as controllers of the means of communication with the public, the media are in a uniquely privileged position: they can decide how much or how little of the other side will be heard in public. Those two considerations ought to impose a decent restraint against carrying over from the courtroom the fervent self-absorption of the litigant. Otherwise the media become mere propagandists, seeking to secure public opinion to one side of the argument—theirs.

There is more to be said on that. "But first," as they like to say on television, "this"—the media and the October 1993 election, beginning with television and politics as a twentieth-century spin-off from the Christians and the lions in the Roman Colosseum.

ONE
THE POLITICAL LABORATORY

AT ONE TIME IT WAS ASSUMED THAT PEOPLE READ THE news—and, when radio came along, listened to it—because they had a certain innate curiosity about what was going on in the world around them. Television has never been able to embrace that confident and generous outlook. Everything on television, news not excluded, has to have a little advance salesmanship; viewers need to be teased, their flaccid interest tweaked, lest they turn elsewhere, even to bed, which would be disastrous for the show's rating. Pamela Wallin, on CBC's "Prime Time News", was at it on October 18, 1993, one week to the day before the voting in the general election. "Voters say they are sending the message loud and clear—they are frustrated, angry and fed up with politics," she was saying, full of television authority. "But do the politicians get it? Do they understand why Canadians have lost faith in them? Are they willing to do anything about it?"

Thus the hype; then the message: "'Looking for Answers'—later on CBC 'Prime Time Election Town Hall'."

It is a small eccentricity of mine—I have larger—that I frequently talk back to the television screen, often enough aloud, but more often in internal rebuttals: "If Canadians are frustrated, angry and fed up with politics, is it not probable that this is attributable in part to people like thee and me, Pamela? In one medium or another, we supply Canadians with much of the raw material of the opinions they form about politics and politicians, and much else. Therefore, do *you* get it, Pamela? If there has been a loss of faith in government as a whole in this country, it will be necessary for more than just the politicians to understand that dreadful reality and be willing to do something about it. Which is to say, Pamela, *we* must. Us."

These repressed soliloquies of mine tend to be, in addition to unusually articulate, discursive.

Wallin was followed just before the break by her "Prime Time" partner, Peter Mansbridge. He was saying, in the prescribed hortatory manner of the medium, "Don't go away. This is a special extended edition of 'Prime Time News'. Pamela is next with 'Prime Time Election Town Hall': How politicians can restore the public's faith in government." Peter patently didn't get it either.

Four things were already to be observed here. One, that the premise from which the "Town Hall" would proceed was that the presence of rampant cynicism and distrust in the country was not in question; that was the established fact from which all else would follow.

Two, that the politicians were entirely and solely responsible for that malignant condition.

Three, that in this CBC-contrived forum, representatives of those politicians would be placed in the dock and made accountable to a jury selected by "Prime Time News", according to its own criteria, to say what they proposed to do about this blight they had brought upon the national spirit.

And four, they would be led through the accounting by the lady who, moments before, had declared them guilty of the charges as read. With that, they would be free to say what made them think they should be considered trustworthy.

All this amounted to a proceeding beside which the supposed Wild West method of dealing with suspected miscreants—"We're gonna give yuh a fair trial, then we're gonna hang yuh"—would constitute a model of enlightened justice.

As it turned out, Pamela was not quite next. First, to help set the tone, four of the program's tokens of voter frustration, anger and other aroused feelings were invited to say why they were there, which they did in the following genial one-liners:

"I am looking ahead to have an opportunity to make my voice heard."

"I want to hear that the politicians can be trusted."

"I think the politicians seem to believe that all they need Canadians for is one day, one day every four years."

"For God's sake, listen to us. We want to be heard."

Finally, Pamela again, from Glendon College in Toronto: "Tonight, we will tackle one of *the* critical issues of this election campaign—faith in our government and faith in the political process. Given the mood of the Canadian people these days, will they be satisfied with *any* government they elect, or will the cynicism, the frustration and the anger still be with us on, and even long after, election day? We have with us tonight politicians and voters, and together we will see if we can find some answers. The voters have come from right across the country. Most of them are undecided. The politicians we have with us are representative of six different parties. Jean Charest is the Conservative. Mel Hurtig is leader of the National Party. From the Liberals, Sheila Copps. The Bloc Québécois representative is Gilles Duceppe. John Rodriguez is from the NDP and Preston Manning is the leader of the Reform Party. So we begin. We go right to our first question from our audience, and we'll speak with the woman with the blue microphone. Go ahead."

Go ahead? She was poised to jump. "Yes," she said, "after decades of political corruption and scandal, it's hard to believe that any self-respecting individual would willingly enter that fray of federal politics. And, ironically, a certain elitism has entered into federal politics. You refer to us ordinary Canadians and commend yourself when you willingly do look at the public will. I think it's fair to say that we have lost confidence." (Speaking to the politicians:) "I would like each one of you to give me just one way in which your party will turn this perception around so it looks to Canadians as if you are serving our interests and not simply your own." That wasn't so much a question as an indictment; she didn't even lift her tone at the end as a gesture to the conventions of the spoken language.

What is most wrong with the "Town Hall" gimmick—not always, but when used as in this case—is precisely that it is a gimmick. It is not journalism but entertainment, about as much designed to inform Canadians on the substance of a national election campaign as the gladiatorial games in ancient Rome were designed to inform Romans on the feeding habits of Nubian lions. Rather, in both cases, the prime purpose was to deliver frissons of excitement to the spectators watching to see how well or how long the sacrificial offerings could withstand the teeth and claws. Wallin's suggestion that the six politicians and the fifty-odd voter-figures had been brought together "to see if we can work out some answers" was baloney—and as the saying goes, no matter how thin you slice it, it's still baloney. Consider some of the words spoken at this pretended let-us-counsel-together between the "Town Hall's" supposed representatives of The People and the politicians:

"There are two classes in this country who are not paying taxes, the unemployed and the rich. The Tories have given the rich all reductions in the top income rates, generous RRSP reductions, capital gains exemptions, to name only a few. . . ." "I am fed up to here with the debt load of this country and the demands on my paycheque to pay for the incompetence of the people we've elected over the past twenty years. . . ." "I want promises from politicians that are realistic and attainable, not a whole bunch more of the same. . . ." "I would like to tell the politicians that, once elected, they should stick to their promises. . . ." "Convince us that you have a vision of what this country means to all of us and convince us that you understand where we are and where we want to go in the twenty-first century. . . ." "I wish the politicians would quit their evil campaigning and trust Canadians to make a rational decision and quit their electoral rhetorics. . . ." "How can you run the country; you can't even run your own government. . . ."

The lugubrious recital continued:

"I come from a province where our way of life has disappeared and since 1949 we have not heard the truth. We are a passionate, hardworking people in Newfoundland and we want some politician, I don't care who it is, to tell what they are going to do with our fisheries. It is our way of life. For God's sake, tell us some truth." (Loud applause.) "I'd like to say that I feel Canadians vote out of fear. They don't vote for someone who is offering them a real constructive solution. They are voting out of who they feel will do the least damage to them and the country. For nine years, the Mulroney Conservatives excluded the voters from the decision-making process and made decisions in rather paternalistic fashion. . . ." "Well, I just want someone to tell us the truth. We've heard all this before."

There were more moderate words spoken, but these examples reflect the tenor of the "Town Hall" as a whole. Mainly, the participants—the prosecutors—asserted rather than asked; they knew rather than wanted to know. Some of what was said had a distinctly nasty tone, full of prejudice. None overflowed with a spirit of understanding and accommodation conducive to Wallin's "working out some answers", or with anyone—including the politicians—learning "how politicians can restore the public's faith in government." If the program had any effect at all on public faith in government, it would probably be to reduce it.

What was most spectacularly missing from the arguments of the Town Hallers, people presented to viewers as a cross-section of a public full of strong feelings, was evidence of any corresponding sense of involvement, far less of personal responsibility, in the affairs of the country. For example, consider the reference, not the only one of its sort, to the "incompetence of the people we've elected over the past twenty years."

People are elected to Parliament by people, having been nominated by people in the first place. That is the democratic idea. The response, then, to this complaint should be: "But if those elected were as incompetent as you say, in so many governments, over so long a time, how on earth did *you* come to elect them, more often than not with substantial majorities? Did *you* not try to ascertain that the people *you* were sending to Ottawa were competent? Did *you* not read anything, or listen to anything, about them?"

The same attitude of voters standing aloof, as judges rather than participants in the national life, appeared in complaints about not being heard by government. What that meant and how the exclusion manifested itself was not explained—but then, television is not good at explanation; it takes up too much time. One participant who did manage in a small way to state a case—the one who wanted to be convinced that politicians understood "where we are and where we want to go in the twenty-first century"—was less than compelling. To ask Canadians where they wanted to go in the twenty-first century was precisely the rationale for the Canadian Citizens' Forum on Canada's Future in 1990. At considerable expense, but having failed to stimulate more than a languid response from ordinary Canadians, extraordinary Canadians or any other stratum of Canadians, the Forum had reported just two years earlier. It seems our recollection of events is less acute than our awareness of our dissatisfactions.

As all this unfolded, Pamela Wallin stalked her show-ring, ensuring with repeated little flicks of her whip that her charges on both sides,

People and Politicians, did not dawdle at their tasks. "We just have to move on here," she said, and "Briefly to Sheila and Jean," and "All right, let's move on to the gentleman with the purple microphone," and "Brief and to the point, please," and "Could we get a yes or no on that?" and "Quickly, quickly, we want to get in as many questions as we can."

Getting in the greatest number of purported questions and quickly-quickly answers has nothing to do with rational discussion of "one of *the* critical issues of the election". It does not allow for considered explanations, which critical issues surely deserve. What it has everything to do with is creating drama and tension, putting some snap, crackle and pop into a show in hopes of keeping the folks in their armchairs, and away from their zappers. In this instance, the program was doubly hokum—as audience manipulation and as public-affairs reporting. It amounted to little more than a playback and probable reinforcement of all the reasons, real and imagined, that anyone could think of to be frustrated, angry, fed up, cynical or distrustful. (It's worth noting that CBC-TV news itself had had some recent loss of faith, but had not empanelled half a hundred taxpayers to say on camera what they blamed it for and what they expected the corporation to do about it.)

There was another problem with this program: whether by misconception or by design, its effect was not to elicit ideas on anything that might be changed, but to reinforce prejudice, to produce a performance rather than a discussion and to entertain more than inform—three of television's besetting weaknesses as a medium of political reportage.

Elections are queer things. They have aspects of a laboratory in which miniaturized working models of the whole politics of the country are concocted, all parts and functions brought into closer focus, intensified, speeded up, and the public is left to judge the performance—not, however, in quiet contemplation. Distractions are constant, and episodes of inspired irrelevance are created by both the direct participants and (see above) those who report on the process. Those two ostensibly separate entities, the participants and the reporters, become harder and harder to distinguish by function as the press move from being disinterested observers to being players, as campaigns go on. This was a big election, perhaps destined to be the most consequential of our time, yet it was reported very much in terms of trivialities—sometimes outrageously contrived ones.

It was Prime Minister Kim Campbell's misfortune, although not a great surprise, given the general ABC—Anything But Conservative—predisposition of the press corps, that she was selected, even before the campaign proper began, as the leader with the greatest gift of the gaffe. On September 2, six weeks and a few days before the voting, *The Globe and Mail* ran a page-one story by staff reporter Kirk Makin under the heading "Loose lips sink potential leaderships." It began: "The most unforgiving season is here again, when any chance blunder by a federal party leader may explode without warning into a campaign-crippling gaffe." That pretty well amounted to a statement of media intentions—"We're gonna getcha if you don't watch out."

The Makin story continued: "As the campaign develops, leaders and their entourages will spare no effort to guard against the gaffe. Political handlers will run drills, stage-manage public appearances, and chase away reporters who become too pesky. But . . . it will take a combination of impeccable savvy, good luck and media inattention, to carry each leader through unscathed." And then: "Prime Minister Kim Campbell—whose ironic humor and acid tongue make her a prime candidate for gaffes—has already tasted the lash this year."

Not only did Makin's comments constitute an exhibition of remarkable media arrogance and self-importance, but they went well beyond. For one thing, they made it difficult for anyone, with the worst will in the world, to produce a stronger condemnation of the standard of journalism being brought to the 1993 general election. Brian Mulroney, who arrived at the prime-ministership as very much a media nut, later took to talking about "gotcha journalism" to describe a form of reporting which, to his mind, was designed to produce a "furore" in the newspapers and on television by a species of verbal entrapment.

The early paragraphs of Makin's story could stand as its definition.

But is it the mission of political journalism to see that politicians get "a taste of the lash", or to turn chance blunders, which on closer examination may prove not to be blunders at all, into somehow consequential "gaffes"? If so, according to what mandate, to serve what purpose, and in whose behalf? What, in other words, is the point? Are the media in the business of communicating reliable information to readers, viewers and listeners, or of electing or defeating governments, and if the latter, ought they not to file public statements declaring their interests—as politicians are required to do where they may have conflicting interests?

On top of that, surely gaffe-hunting is trivializing? A gaffe, in dictionary terms—in both official languages—is a social error, a *faux pas*, an indiscreet act or remark, a breach of sensibility or good taste, a blunder, a boob. It comes, with remarkable appropriateness to Canada, politics and reporting in the 1990s, from the French *gaffer*, "to hook"—for which, of course, see also "gotcha" (U.S., *circa* 1980). In all circumstances it implies a misstep, embarrassing perhaps to the misstepper, but of no consequence.

Do we elect or defeat governments on the basis of inconsequential misstatements? If so, it imputes to Canadians—although perhaps, by a more generous interpretation, only to Canadian political journalists—an extraordinarily shallow national mind.

There is also a small matter of the rules of proper gaffeology, as seen in Campbell's alleged deficit-reduction-and-enemies-of-Canada gaffe. It is hard to see how, in the face of an election, it could be a gaffe for a politician committed to a line of fiscal policy generally accepted across the country to say that persons who outright opposed it were enemies of the country. A bit overstated, perhaps, but a legitimate opinion. It is hard even to see who could be offended by it. Certainly not the media, as constant and passionate upholders of freedom of expression, of which freedom of the press is a subcategory. Freedom of expression, as any editor rushes to say whenever the issue arises, is not limited to saying innocuous things.

Other politicians, then? The federal New Democrats in the 1993 election—as always—put deficit reduction rather lower on their list of priorities than other parties, but they did not disown it. They scarcely could, with three of the ten premiers being New Democrats, and all striving mightily to reduce spending. Jean Chrétien and the Liberals cleverly softened their position, coupling deficit reduction with a short-term job creation program and a borrowing from Bill Clinton, who had set out with just that prescription in mind but had been thwarted by Congress. The Reform Party? Hardly—its main theme was budget-cutting. Not Lucien Bouchard of the Bloc Québécois; in the English-language TV debate he had accused Campbell of withholding the latest deficit figures for fear they would show it rising even faster than she acknowledged. The implication was that she should have been stronger on deficit reduction, or perhaps that she should shut up about it.

The public, then? Jim Meek, an editorial writer and columnist at the Halifax *Chronicle-Herald* and a confessed non-specialist in public finance, succinctly presented a cogent lay viewpoint: "When you see every government, of whatever stripe, cutting programs from British Columbia to Newfoundland, you start to get the idea: politicians aren't doing what they want to do; they're doing what they have to do."

From all of that, anyone might conclude—still a little waspishly but with better reason—that, if anything, Campbell was guilty of posturing as the one true defender of fiscal responsibility against a vaporous lot of uncaring spendthrifts. But was this a political *gaffe*? Was she creating a furore, except perhaps in the overheated imaginations of a few reporters?

What was even more remarkable in our 1993 election campaign than the sudden rise of gaffeology to equivalence (or better) with substance was the fact that a clear, significant turning-point in the campaign occurred on the very day it began. That day, on the grounds of Rideau Hall, where Governor General Ray Hnatyshyn had just signed the election writ, Campbell held a press conference. Edison Stewart of *The Toronto Star*, a specialist at gotcha-ing, asked a dangerously simple question: "I wonder if you can tell us realistically, how long do you think they [the jobless] will have to wait before the unemployment rate is below 10 per cent?"

Given that the Statistics Canada figure for unemployment in October 1993 was 10.2 per cent, and that a drop of two tenths of a percentage point wasn't going to make a significant dent in an estimated 1.6 million unemployed, the only evident purpose was to toss a net in the water to bring in whatever might be passing—by preference, a fine, fat, firm-fleshed gaffe.

The prime minister did not answer the question well—if, in fact, there is a way a politician can answer an opinion question well, knowing that whatever opinion is given in reply will be treated as a firm promise against which performance will be measured forevermore. If the answer was a little stilted and wandered a bit, what was done with it by her interviewers was worse. Their interpretations of it ran through the whole campaign and beyond; it was still being cited in the post-mortems as an illustration of when and how the wheels came off for the Conservatives.

As the episode has been enshrined in the mythology of the 1993 election campaign, the relevant portion of the text is given here fairly well whole, edited only to smooth out one or two bumps of the sort that occur in almost all speech. After repeating the question for the benefit of reporters on the fringe who might not have heard, she began: "One of the frustrating things going through the 1990s is that we have what is sometimes referred to as a jobless recovery. We have structural unemployment that reflects more than simply the ups and downs of the general economy, in terms of demand, for example, and reflects the fact that the economy itself is changing in its nature and that our labour force and our way of doing business have not kept pace with that. So at the meeting of the G-7 countries (the United States, Britain, France, Germany, Italy, Japan and Canada) we shared our experiences of the industrialized countries facing this challenge of trying to move the labour force into conjunction with new economic circumstances."

Then, this crucial bit: "So I think, realistically, all the developed industrial countries are expecting what I would consider to be an unacceptable level of unemployment for the next two, three or four years. . . . But what we can do as a country. . . . We are a very huge country and we have some disadvantages in the sense of being a small population, but in other ways we have the capacity to respond to these new challenges. We have a parliamentary system that is able to act with real firmness and direction.

"I think of the American president [with] all the prestige and power of the presidency—he doesn't have the ability to deliver his policies in Congress. We are still a small enough country where we are able to articulate a sense of national vision, where we can work together with levels of government that share responsibility for areas of jurisdiction [and therefore] can work co-operatively together. I think if we tapped the resources we have in this country, of talent, standard of living, of possibility of education and all the things that are important to success, and tapped as well our capacity to govern with real effect when we use the political instruments well, then I think we can adjust to the changing world economy in a way that will get that unemployment rate down."

And then the second crucial bit: "I would like to see, certainly, by the turn of the century, a country where unemployment is way down, and where we're paying down our national debt, and there's a whole new vision of the future opening up for Canadians."

Boom! Kerpow! Crash! A veritable capital-G Gaffe. A senior Ottawa correspondent, plainly undismayed by this turn of events, was overheard to say as Campbell came to the end of that passage, "There's the election . . .," meaning "There it goes; she's blown it, right there." By that analysis, it hadn't taken much.

Campbell's remarks did not bring about the defeat of the Conservatives, which may have been foreordained, anyway, and their plunge to the depth of having just two seats in Parliament. However, the construction put upon those remarks unquestionably helped. Once the media interpretation of her answer had been sufficiently circulated —it did not take long—something existed in the lore of the campaign that could be brought out as needed in subsequent stories, to illustrate her purported personality, philosophy of government and political sensitivity, on all of which she was given flunking marks.

"It was a sign of her callousness," said Frances Bula in a column in the September 11 *Vancouver Sun*. "Her arrogance. Her cerebral, out-of-touch-with-reality approach." But Bula, one of whose assignments at the *Sun* is to write on media—a rare field in Canadian daily journalism—was not offering her own opinions. These were comments she had read or heard broadcast. Her column went on: "She [Campbell] was lecturing, as at least two headline writers put it, she was pessimistic. That's what journalists said about Kim Campbell's campaign launch, in the first round of 'gotcha' between reporters and politicians. . . . It wasn't Campbell's carefully prepared and delivered speech, full of talk of 'common sense' and 'renewal of social programs', and even 'hope', that prompted those judgments in talk shows and analysis pieces across the country. It was a quick answer to a post-speech question that got everyone into a frenzy. . . ."

With daily newspapers publishing morning and afternoon editions, and radio and television pumping out news all the time, and given, further, the tendency of modern media to want to be all the same, it is risky to say who originated what became the accepted analysis of Campbell's remarks. However, as *The Globe and Mail* is published across the country and there can't be an Ottawa journalist who does not read it, the *Globe* is the likeliest candidate for the role of Typhoid Mary.

Certainly Hugh Winsor, the *Globe*'s senior political writer, was out early and aggressively with a version strongly resembling what shortly became gospel.

"Progressive Conservative leader Kim Campbell may pay a political price for responding to the highly charged unemployment issue as if she were a professor of international economics rather than a candidate who needs to push the hope button," he said in his lead.

Then: "Instead of responding with empathy or compassion for the 1.6 million Canadians who are looking for work, Ms. Campbell responded with a lecture about the differences between structural and cyclical unemployment, noting that this was a problem being discussed by the governments of the leading industrialized countries." And again, "She left the clear impression there wouldn't be any improvement in the overall situation until after the year 2000."

As rebuttal to the Conservative leader's "pessimistic predictions" he quoted two studies, one by the Department of Finance early in 1993 which predicted "a drop in unemployment to 7.5 per cent by 1998" and another by the Institute for Policy Analysis at the University of Toronto which said the unemployment rate would fall to 9.6 per cent in three years and to 7.4 per cent by the end of the century.

I have a friend—I have some coarse friends—who says that something that is grossly apparent "sticks out like dogs' balls". The contradiction between these figures and what Campbell had said did not do that. She had said that economists in the industrialized countries expected unemployment to remain for several years at what she considered an unacceptable level. The Department of Finance prediction of 7.5 per cent within five years might have been borderline acceptable within *three*. The Institute for Policy Analysis anticipated a clearly unacceptable 9.6 per cent in that time. And Cambell had only said that she looked forward to a country where unemployment was way down by the end of the century. She had not said there wouldn't be any improvement *until* the year 2000. (If this is nitpicking, it should be remembered that those are Winsor's nits that are being picked.)

Thomas Walkom, who writes a column in *The Toronto Star*, said, "Prime Minister Kim Campbell says there is no choice, that more than 1.6 million Canadians will remain out of work until the end of the decade, that there is nothing she or any government leader can do." Walkom writes a fine column—his usual field is the government of Ontario—but those opening words simply did not reflect what was said.

However imprecise it may be to say that unemployment will be "way down a few years hence", that does not translate into "will remain the same". Also, whether or not she *thought* there was nothing she or any government could do, she certainly hadn't said so. Julian Beltrame, who writes for the seventeen papers in the Southam Newspaper Group, began with a question, "Are Canadians ready for the politics of pain? Kim Campbell clearly thinks so judging from her first days on the campaign trail, where she dampened hopes for quick relief to Canada's 1.6 million jobless. . . . It's a peculiar way to win votes. . . ."

What ought to raise eyebrows about these comments—of Winsor, Walkom and Beltrame, and others of a similar nature in all the media—is the short shrift they gave to principle. Even in the 1990s climate of cynicism and distrust, politicians should be entitled to the assumption that they are speaking the truth as they know it, unless there is concrete evidence that they are not.

That should be particularly true of the media. That mythical figure, the ordinary Canadian, might plead, "Well, it looked like to me like she didn't care, but I didn't know." That excuse ought not to be available to journalists, who profess to be in the business of selling reliable information, not suspicions.

The analyses above nimbly leapt over the possibility that the lady was sincere. Certainly the two economic studies cited by Winsor could lead no one to believe that "quick relief", in Beltrame's words, was in prospect. The International Monetary Fund had said that getting unemployment down, not just in Canada but in the industrialized countries generally, would not be done easily or quickly. What constituted the "gaffe" in all these analyses was the fact that Campbell had not pushed the "hope buttons" that she needed to push to see the Tories back in office.

Well, yes, but. . . . But what about those people on the CBC's "Town Hall" who were demanding that politicians tell them the truth, level with them, be honest, give them no false promises? If the major media insist that it is a political blunder not to push the hope buttons, however hypocritically, they endorse the raising of false hopes—which they themselves will denounce, to the further depreciation of "the politicians", when and if the promises become demonstrably false. Cynicism? There's the recipe for it.

If cynicism and distrust of our political institutions are as broad and deep as has been reported, they have not developed spontaneously. These are contagious diseases of the spirit, and it would be foolish to believe that the purveyors of information, plainly infected themselves, are not a principal carrier. I myself find it difficult to explain, if what we write and broadcast has no effect at all on the public mind, why on earth we keep doing it; simply to provide stuffing to keep the ads apart hardly seems enough. Which returns us to the question Pamela Wallin provoked—"Do the media get it?"—to which the answer must be, no.

A few days after the first spate of analyses, *The Globe and Mail* followed with a remarkable editorial headed "A gaffe is when you tell the truth." Having said that most of the analyses acknowledged that what Campbell had said was probably true—true, but not smart—the editorial went on to make some curious observations, curious certainly for a newspaper, about political journalism. For instance, it said that "to journalists schooled in the traditions of campaign coverage, [her remarks] *sounded* like a gaffe. And gaffes above all are what political reporters think they are supposed to spot. You could almost hear the murmur of the media comparing notes, each one anxious not to be caught out of the pack consensus."

Some paragraphs on, having taken a whack in passing at Jean Chrétien's infrastructure scheme as no plan at all, the editorial said, "We suppose most reporters know this. Yet the thrust of the first week's coverage was that Mr. Chrétien had had the best of the exchange. Why? Because the media expects of politicians, above all, that they should *play the game*. Elections, in this view, are not about issues; they are about elections. The public are endlessly manipulable dupes, like the audience at a magic show; the press's job is to uncover the strategists' techniques. Their interests soon merge: the better the manipulation, the better for the press to prove their skills at dissecting it, and hence their necessity to the public. Perhaps she was just taking the game to another level, but Ms. Campbell's truthfulness plainly discomfited them. . . ."

Ye gods; I could have written that. The first remarkable thing is that the editorial's substance was not posted on bulletin boards in the *Globe* newsroom and its Ottawa bureau *before* the campaign began. The notice could have said something like this: "Accepting that readers are endlessly manipulable dupes, we, as a responsible newspaper, have a duty to protect them. Therefore, our reporters, wherever and however schooled, are asked for the duration to give up the idea that gaffes, above all, are what they are supposed to spot. Especially, it is advisable not to make gaffes of what we believe to be true. Dupes or not, readers might not understand if they were to twig to the fact that we were simply playing a political game with them. Discomfiting as it may be, all reporters assigned to the campaign will please refrain from dissecting what candidates have not said in order to prove their skill in doing so."

That politicians manipulate journalists, or try to, is a stock belief among journalists, not incorrectly; everybody manipulates somebody sometimes. However, not much is ever said by journalists about their own manipulative tricks.

For example, *The Toronto Star*, in the issue of October 30, 1993, printed one of those where-the-parties-stand tables, like shopping lists, under the heading "The People's Agenda". The first two lists were headed "Progressive Conservatives" and "Liberals". Each reeled off the party's policy priorities as selected by the *Star*. At the top of the Liberal list was "encourage economic growth and job creation through modest government spending", which unsurprisingly corresponded with the *Star*'s pro-Liberal editorial policy. In the Tory list, again courtesy of the *Star*, "job creation" came last, behind even "press ahead with Canada–U.S.–Mexico free trade", which the paper disliked almost as much as it had disliked the U.S.–Canada Free Trade Agreement.

Alongside that layout there was a story, datelined Washington, under this heading:

RECOVERY IS
CANADA'S PRIORITY,
IMF SAYS

That too turned out to be one of those yes-but creations.

The story it heralded was by David Crane, the newspaper's economics specialist, and began: "Canada needs to bring its public finances under control—but Ottawa should hold off until the economy is stronger before taking tougher action, says the head of the International

Monetary Fund." It went on to say: "Stronger measures can wait until 'the recovery gathers strength,' Michel Camdessus told finance ministers and central bankers from around the world at the opening of this year's annual meetings of the IMF and the World Bank."

And this: "The IMF managing director was careful not to urge an all-out attack on deficits now, when economies are still weak, because that would make unemployment even worse and the recovery slower. . . ." (To say that someone took care *not* to urge something opens up infinite possibilities. It could be said with equal truth that he was careful not to say quite a few things, such as that Canada should not undertake a space-program in competition with NASA, or extend its territorial waters out to the coast of Europe.)

The friend who brought the story to my attention had been surprised to find the managing director of the IMF singling out Canada for this lecture. So was I. Camdessus could not have missed the fact that (a) Canada was in the middle of a national election, (b) the relative values attached to job creation on the one hand, and deficit reduction on the other, were central to the debate, and (c) coming down on the side of one against the other, as he appeared in the *Star* to do, he would be striking an unusually partisan note as the chief officer of an international economic institution.

Neither job creation nor deficit reduction was exclusively the objective of either of the old parties, or, for that matter, of any of the six in the campaign. But their emphases differed. Jean Chrétien's shop window featured his infrastructure program, a scheme whereby Ottawa, the provinces and the municipalities would share in a program of improving such essentials as roads, waterworks, sewerage and telecommunications systems, to stimulate job creation. The Conservatives put their emphasis on increased efforts at getting the debt down, with the objective of taking a bite out of the debt charges that consume a large part of every year's revenues to no productive purpose.

The crux of the argument was whether the infusion of an extra $6 billion of public money into the economy could produce in short order a return in jobs to equal the drag it would impose on deficit reduction, which no one seriously argued could be long left untreated. Now the top man at the IMF was saying—by the *Star*'s account—that Canada should hold off getting its finances under control until the general state of the economy improved.

Jean Chrétien chose to see the story as an endorsement. But in truth everything the IMF official had said had been directed at every industrialized country in the world—not specifically at Canada, as the *Star*'s heading and the lead to the Crane story might cause the reader to believe.

In thirteen single-spaced pages of text, Camdessus referred to Canada by name only once, on page eight: "Plans recently adopted in the United States, Germany, Italy and Canada [under the Conservatives] to name a few countries, signify a commendable recognition of the problem, but still they do not go far enough to secure the fiscal solidification that is needed." Fiscal solidification is to be read here as "correction of insupportable debt". What Camdessus was advocating was caution against rushing headlong in either direction—fiscal stimulus or drastic deficit reduction. The advice to *any* government to hold off efforts at further deficit reduction until the economy was stronger was indirect to the point of being scarcely discernible. The *Star*'s fault was to put a slant on Camdessus's remarks in the direction of the *Star*'s editorial line—and the Liberals'—beside which the Tower of Pisa could be said to be rigorously perpendicular.

The 1993 election campaign began with the assumption that the two parties which had always been the leading players would be so again. That premise had become decidedly shaky before the end, and ultimately one of those leading players was devastated, and another, the New Democrats, grievously wounded, almost circumstantially.

Though the rise of the Reform Party had been recognized several years earlier, its support seemed to have fallen off before the campaign began. The Bloc Québécois, it was accepted, would gain in Quebec, but the consensus was that it would do so mainly at the expense of the Liberals, because polls indicated that Jean Chrétien was unpopular in his own province. Anyone willing early on to bet that the Bloc would win fifty-four seats and become the official opposition could have got hundred-to-one odds. In the end, the Liberals won without even working up a sweat.

All of this, again, is not to say that the heavy anti-Conservative slant to much of the campaign coverage solely accounted for the outcome. For a start, the PCs were under the liability of having been nearly nine years in office. Brian Mulroney was disliked. The party and the new leader both ran poor campaigns, or perhaps both ran the same poor campaign. In any event, neither ever seemed to get around to saying clearly what they were about. And there were undeniable gaffes, although not so many or so serious as reported.

One was in the handling of the helicopter issue. Fifty costly helicopters were on order for the navy and for air-sea rescue. The Liberals and New Democrats said the dissolution of the Soviet empire made the helicopters unnecessary. Kim Campbell, late in the day, reduced the order from fifty to forty-three. That was vaguely reminiscent of the fifties, when the Conservatives kept after the St. Laurent government about the miserliness of the old-age pension. Just before the 1957 election the Liberals triumphantly announced an increase—$6 a month. John Diefenbaker, about to become the first Conservative prime minister since 1935, then lampooned them as "the six-buck boys". Reducing the helicopter order by seven was much the same thing! —an admission that the other side had a point, to which only a derisory response was warranted.

The television commercial that focused on Chrétien's slight facial paralysis was a blunder, but not because it brought into the campaign something that had never been commented on before. The Liberals themselves, three weeks earlier, had run a television ad in Quebec intended to turn their leader's lopsided speaking style to advantage as an attention-getter. It incorporated the line "He may look funny, but listen to what he has to say." The Conservative commercial did very much the same in reverse; the first words, spoken meaningfully, were "Is this a prime minister?" But in the context of a campaign in which Campbell herself had disowned any thought of using personal attacks, it was mean, irrelevant, desperate-seeming—and dumb.

The extent of the Conservative defeat also owed something to the quirkiness of the election system. In the country as a whole, the PCs got more votes than the Bloc, and only slightly fewer—by 2.65 per cent—than Reform, which finished third, with fifty-two seats to the PCs' two.

Still, in two aspects—the contrived gaffes, and the weight of what the media like to call their "scrutiny"—the election coverage had scarcely a semblance of balance.

At one point, reporters were surprised to hear Jean Chrétien say, about Reform's severe ideas for deficit reduction, that a too sudden and too drastic attack on public spending could create such hardship, hence divisiveness, in Canada as to lead to a situation like that in Bosnia. In the two big constitutional debates, on Meech Lake and on the Charlottetown agreement and the subsequent referendum, suggestions that unwelcome consequences might flow from rejecting the proposed reforms had generally been labelled "scare tactics" or "fear-mongering", and denounced accordingly. Yet Chrétien's extravagant off-the-cuff—and off-the-wall—Bosnia comment passed almost without mention.

One reporter told me he had been at work on that day's story from the Chrétien tour when he was asked by another if he was doing anything with the Bosnia remark. To the answer "Yes, a bit, . . ." the other thought a moment and said, "I think I'll give him the benefit of the doubt." Notwithstanding the preoccupation with gaffes, that one got little play.

Jean Chrétien was reported as having given voters in his home constituency of St. Maurice a nudge-nudge, wink-wink promise of prime-ministerial patronage if the Liberals were elected. This became a one-day, or perhaps even a one-story, wonder. He was quoted by Martin Mittelstaedt and Susan Delacourt in *The Globe and Mail* as saying, "I have the impression that when files from St. Maurice cross the desk of a minister (pause) . . . I needn't say any more." In April 1994, it was revealed that $4 million of federal money was going into a theme park dedicated to the St. Maurice area's industrial beginnings. Presumably the matter had crossed some minister's desk.

Other stories conveying the hint that patronage might not be quite dead under Liberal dispensation also proved to have no shelf-life. For example, just a couple of days before the voting, the Montreal *Gazette* reported a Liberal senator, Pietro Rizzuto, the party's chief organizer in Quebec, as saying that as soon as the election was over, he would begin to find jobs in the upper echelons of either government or private enterprise for any defeated Liberals who wanted them. There was scarcely time for that gaffe to get the attention it deserved, but it is another indication that there were gaffes, even gaffes related to politically sensitive subjects that left little mark.

As the campaign approached the end, a rare question was raised: "Has Jean Chrétien been getting a free ride?" On his "Morningside" show on CBC Radio, Peter Gzowski asked a panel of three: "Has he been pushed as others have to put some meat on the bones of his policies?" Chrétien had proved difficult to bring into the studio to be interviewed.

Gzowski's panelists that day—Christopher Waddell, then about to become Ottawa bureau chief for CBC-TV news; Dale Eisler, editor of the Saskatchewan-based *Leader-Star* news service; and Jennifer Robinson, national editor at the Montreal *Gazette*—agreed, in different degrees and for different reasons, that Chrétien had received light treatment. The explanations included Chrétien's not having predicated much change from the way government had operated in the past few years; the fact that there was a sort of "comfort factor" in media-Liberal relations, and a view of the Liberals as "the natural governing party"; and Chrétien's cleverness in diverting attention from mistakes in his campaign.

Gzowski was not satisfied. "Well," he said, "I've had an opportunity to ask Ms. Campbell about specifics of her policies. She's been everywhere. Very accessible. Later on this morning, we'll talk with Preston Manning, who will be in our studio in Brandon. I can ask him to spell out some of the changes—about zero-in-three, for example [zero deficit in three years]. Very specific questions. Jean Chrétien . . . where are his answers, as, for example, with what he would replace the GST? On what his deficit would be? And so on and so on."

Part of the explanation of Jean Chrétien's success in evading questions is to be found in the famous Red Book—not in what it told the world, but in its existence. In substance it was as porous as a tennis net. The marvel of the Red Book is that it worked. It put a shield between the leader and his interrogators. Policy questions could always be turned aside with "It's all in our Red Book. Read it. It's all there."

But another explanation is that the media were simply less anxious to nail down Chrétien than they were Kim Campbell, Preston Manning and even Lucien Bouchard. Almost a year after the Red Book made its appearance, the media, and Canadians as a whole, knew no more about the sort of things Peter Gzowski was concerned about—the replacement for the GST, the steps to be taken to reduce the deficit, the reformation of social programs, including medicare—than they had in the beginning.

In the Ottawa *Citizen* of October 20, five days before the election, reporter Chris Cobb provided a telling, and rare, illustration of the difference in media coverage. His story was headed "Reporters' baffling kid-glove treatment of Chrétien won't last past election." In other words, the honeymoon would be over as soon as the marriage was consummated.

He put beside each other two quotations, the first from Campbell, the second from Chrétien. Campbell's was "This is the worst possible time to talk to Canadians about fundamental changes in social programs. This is not the time . . . to get involved in a debate on very serious issues. . . ." Chrétien's was "Let me win the election and, after that, you come and ask me question about how I run the government. I just say that the plan of the party is clear: that the social safety net we have in Canada will remain."

Cobb said of the pair, "Campbell got into trouble for being elitist, negative, and secretive. Media coverage of her statement was swift and totally damning. When analysis is done of this campaign, it will be judged one of the defining moments in her demise. . . . Chrétien on the other hand simply got away with it. Nobody criticized him very harshly, nobody called him arrogant, aloof, or secretive. Yet he said essentially the same thing albeit with a Santa Claus sugar-coating at the end."

In fact, even the supposed sugar-coating—the assurance that the social safety net would remain—was meaningless, given that no one in any known party was suggesting, far less advocating, its end.

But Cobb, or at least the author of the heading above his piece, was wrong in predicting that Jean Chrétien's tender treatment by the media would not outlast the campaign. If anything it became warmer, even well into the first session of the new Parliament, even past a budget that left untouched most of the big questions that had gone unasked during the campaign. Was that evidence of a badly needed change in the Ottawa press corps, away from the routine savaging of government, or merely the effect of a change of government from one to which most reporters were hostile, to another more congenial to their private consensual preference? It may take the lifetime of the 35th Parliament of Canada for that to become clear—if it does then. But certainly the attitude at the changeover was in sharp contrast to the previous time, in 1984.

TWO

A DOWN WITH NO UP

THE SUNDAY MORNING AFTER THE CONSERVATIVES chose Brian Mulroney as leader in June 1983, Michael Valpy, then *The Globe and Mail*'s national affairs columnist in Ottawa, announced from the doorway as he entered the bureau, "This is going to be the shortest honeymoon in history." None of the several people working on stories for the next day's paper had to ask what he meant. Nevertheless it was mildly puzzling. Political honeymoons usually are reserved for new prime ministers. New opposition leaders are left to accustom themselves to the job with no more than the languid attention the Ottawa press corps accords opposition leaders all the time. Also, the implication of the term "honeymoon" is that for an indefinite period, usually short, the media will lay off being picky. Here was Brian Mulroney, just chosen leader, not even in the House of Commons yet to give anyone cause to lay *on*, and the end of a grace period that hadn't begun was already being forecast.

As there are Conservatives who are called Red Tories because they are believed to incorporate some attitudes borrowed from the political left, Valpy may be described with reasonable accuracy as a Blue New Democrat, leftish but with speckles of small-c conservatism. Plainly undismayed as he was at the prospect of the quick cooling of an already lukewarm media ardour for Brian Mulroney, Valpy scarcely could have guessed how short this shortest honeymoon in history would be.

Brian Mulroney put foot in the House of Commons for the first time as a member on September 12, after the summer recess and a Nova Scotia by-election. Elmer MacKay had resigned his seat to allow the new leader to try for it with nearly assured success; MacKay would return after the 1984 election to a place in the Cabinet. Mulroney had been in place only two days as Leader of the Official Opposition when a story appeared on page one of *The Globe and Mail* under the byline of John Gray, then the *Globe*'s Ottawa bureau chief: "Just 24 hours after his arrival in Parliament, Conservative leader Brian Mulroney walked straight into a political trap large enough to catch your average elephant." In tone, the story was gleeful; in substance, it was dead wrong—and it was the tone that was more important. The reporter's obvious satisfaction at seeing the new opposition leader bagged at his first parliamentary encounter was indicative of what was to come.

The elephant trap suggested by Gray consisted of Prime Minister Pierre Trudeau's having invited the new boy to join him in sponsoring a resolution to express the support of the House of Commons for Manitoba's New Democratic government, which was struggling, unsuccessfully, as it turned out, to have bilingualism implanted in the constitution of the province. Mulroney—gotcha—had instantly agreed.

"In doing so," Gray wrote, "Mr. Mulroney put himself in what the Liberals believe will be an uncomfortable spot. He will have to make a choice between the Conservatives opposed to bilingualism, and the Quebeckers he had hoped to attract."

In fact, though Gray and Trudeau seem to have missed it, Mulroney had made the operative choice years earlier. He kept to it with no sign of embarrassment, and in the next year's general election campaign he even publicly questioned the good sense of members of his own party who resisted the reality of bilingualism in Canada. He suffered no ill consequences. In that 1984 election, the Conservatives won in Manitoba *and* in Quebec, and, of course, in the country as a whole. It was John Turner, Trudeau's successor, who experienced some slight difficulty with the issue, when he expressed himself more equivocally on the subject. The elephant trap had proved transferable.

No government, and especially no government suddenly in power after years in opposition, ever manages to get through the first years of a four-year or five-year term without committing blunders, or worse, that attract "bad press". Certainly the first Pearson government had its troubles on taking over from the John Diefenbaker Conservatives after only six years out of office, in 1963. In 1984, the Conservatives had been out of power for nineteen years, except for Joe Clark's eight months as prime minister in 1979–80. But no government, at least in the years since the

Second World War, had faced so heavy an onslaught, so soon and, in the beginning, over so little, as the government of Brian Mulroney.

Even more remarkable than the amount of bad press heaped on the Mulroney Conservatives was the sometimes niggling, sometimes wilfully ignorant and sometimes curiously vindictive quality of it, which seemed to reflect events less than simple resentment at the voters' having elected this government at all. Even in its worst moments, the first Pearson government was not reported upon with the same hostility.

The government of Lester B. Pearson is brought in here for comparison because it and the Mulroney governments had more in common than a tendency to attract flak. The Liberals in the 1960s made great changes in Canada's social system, but did it with the wind of public opinion at their backs, and in a time when the revenues necessary to sustain large new programs were more readily available. The Conservatives under Mulroney made considerable progress in reorienting the Canadian economy to a more competitive world—the centre-piece of their efforts was the free trade agreement with the United States, and later the North American Free Trade Agreement (NAFTA), including Mexico. The Conservatives also made two brave but unsuccessful attempts to work out a consensus on how to amend the constitution for a more harmonious future. Either of those would have made the prospect of that future look more likely than it did in 1994, with a Quebec provincial election in sight.

The Pearson and Mulroney governments were alike in having their scandals and their political blunders. In the latter category, there was the early embarrassment suffered by the Liberals when Finance minister Walter Gordon's first budget had to undergo a factory recall in response to criticism at home and abroad.

The blunder that did the Conservatives most harm came much later in their time in office, when they set out to replace a tax that 90 per cent of Canadians had never heard of with one that would be right there in their faces every time they spent a nickel—and did so without carefully explaining the rationale to the public. That was the GST.

As to scandals, there is no three-star system for grading them, such as the Michelin Guide has for European restaurants. The Pearson government had several all rolled up in one, like a sixteen-part television series, which was not good. The Mulroney government had several but all separate and distinct, so that the next one arrived while the memory of the last was still fresh, which was worse.

But one great difference was that, from virtually the moment of the swearing in, the attack on the Mulroney government was very much directed at the prime minister himself. One episode in the Pearson government's scandal series engulfed the prime minister—he forgot or suppressed too long an important piece of information that had been given him by one of his ministers—but when it was over, the incident left no lasting mark. The negative focus on Mulroney never really left him.

That can be attributed, in part, to the fact that by the eighties and nineties, although quick to denounce signs of presidential pretensions in the country's prime ministers, the media had come to cover them more and more as presidential figures. They had done so by concentrating their attention on the one office of prime minister—unfortunately not altogether without the assistance of the occupant. Since the time of John Diefenbaker, Cabinet ministers had been subsiding to the rank of supporting cast, but the elevation of the leaders became more pronounced with Trudeau and Mulroney.

The result was to produce a thoroughly White House style of reporting, which supposes a head of state/commander-in-chief over whom a press corps sits in surveillance, playing the part of the people's watchdog. In Canada this is presumptuous, considering that an official watchdog, the parliamentary opposition, sits every day in the House of Commons. The intensification of the scrutiny that came with this more American practice was aided by new Access to Information legislation, by the hard focus of television on the small part of the parliamentary day it covers and by broader acceptance of the idea, also imported, that the proper stance of the political journalist is to be fundamentally opposed. One by-product of all that was much more reporting of a titillating nature but nil substance, requiring almost no work, and with a high capability to instil prejudice.

An example of this sort of trivia is the complaining about the supposedly imperial style of prime-ministerial travel which became a staple of the early Mulroney years. Such stories (purposely?) overlooked a number of points. One, travel abroad on official visits is part of the job. Two, prime-ministerial travels entail some entourage, overdone no doubt at times, but unavoidable. Three, governments tend to have particular hotels which they favour over a long time, like the Plaza Athenée in Paris, a few doors from the chancellery of the Canadian embassy, and such hotels tend to be pricier than bed-and-breakfasts. The Plaza has been the Canadian government hotel in Paris since at least the time of Louis St. Laurent. Pierre Trudeau received snide comments implying delusions of grandeur when he went to Claridge's rather than the Dorchester, which had been Canada's hotel in London since the time of Mackenzie King. Four, they had not been proportionately less expensive in the fifties than in the eighties and nineties. And five, the reporters who wrote with anguish and disgust at the burden of such expenditure on the suffering Canadian taxpayer were not themselves staying in hostels and carrying sandwiches brought from home in brown paper bags.

A more fundamental point, although still tangential to actual governing, is that Mulroney came to office with some dislike ready-made among Ottawa journalists. It was traceable to the 1976 Conservative convention, which chose Joe Clark as leader and did not choose, among others, Brian Mulroney. I was out of the country for seven years surrounding that time and consequently was not among the journalists who covered that leadership campaign. But those who did made remarks like the following: Well, he was too cocky. Well, he had too much money behind him. Well, he had that too-florid speaking style. Well, he was too much the politician. Well, he didn't, you know, sound altogether sincere. Later came, Well, he was manipulative. . . . That one flowered at the time of the 1983 leadership race, in which Mulroney became leader, unseating Joe Clark. Some political writers continue to insist that Mulroney, who had been out of elective politics in the interval, maintained a pious front of being loyal to Clark, yet did his best to undermine him. The allegation is familiar; the documentation remains fragmentary. Moreover, the implied sympathy for Clark carries the taint of hypocrisy; the parliamentary press, both print and broadcast, were never kind to Clark. Throughout his leadership, in opposition and briefly as prime minister, some of his auditors all of the time, and all of them some of the time, portrayed him as inept, a nerd, a hard worker for whom nothing ever turned out right and, on top of all that, a guy who walked funny. This was most notoriously true of his famous round-the-world trip, which was reported, by a clique that formed among the accompanying media, as a catalogue of mishaps (some of them invented). Clark's treatment in the press never reached more than minimal fairness until he had ceased to be considered a prospective leader. Thus all this lump-in-the-throat talk of Joe Clark's betrayal by Brian Mulroney looks more like covert shots at the latter than genuine warmth for the former.

Whimsical though it may seem, another explanation for the immediate hostility towards Mulroney may be found in the fact that long before he entered elective politics—from his university days, he had always been *in* politics—he was something of a news nut, someone who generally liked and was liked by media people, understood what they did, read and listened to what they produced and was usually available with information when asked. Once, not altogether unseriously, I advanced to Anthony Westell—a fine journalist, and a rare one in having thought a lot about journalism—the proposition that journalists in general suffer from a masochistic tendency which causes them to respect, and even admire, only those politicians who actively despise them. The obvious example was Pierre Trudeau.

During the Suez Crisis of the 1950s, with which Canada became very much involved diplomatically, the Canadian high commissioner in London was Norman Robertson, a great figure in the Canadian public service. One day he was told by his press secretary that numerous journalists had questions to ask and that he should see them. His reply, as recalled by one of his associates of the time, was "Why should I? They wouldn't understand anyway." Pierre Trudeau never quite succeeded in suppressing the appearance, and no doubt the reality, of holding a similar opinion. However, the main effect was to instil in the audiences at his infrequent press conferences a measure of fearful respect. A supercilious manner coupled with occasional put-downs of his interrogators—on camera, to be seen in their home offices—regularly produced sycophantic titters from those who had come pre-programmed *not* to ask questions—and a cowed silence in some who had meant to. He earned their trembling respect by not hiding the fact that they did not enjoy his. Mulroney's mistake was in believing that the previously good relations he had had with journalists could continue in office. That they looked upon as a weakness.

Westell's response to the journalist-as-masochist proposition was "What about Pearson?" It made a good answer. As a senior official in the Department of External Affairs, later in the Cabinet as Secretary of State for External Affairs and eventually as prime minister, Pearson had good relations with numbers of journalists with whom he talked from time to time, individually or in small groups, for their background information only—in other words, so that they would know what they were talking about, without necessarily disclosing how and from whom. What is involved is mutual trust—the reporter trusting that the information received will be true, the supplier trusting that a confidence will not be broken.

But that had all been thirty and more years earlier, before a new doctrine of correctness caused political journalists who maintained mutually beneficial good relations with politicians to be looked upon in about the same way as collaborators were looked upon in occupied Europe during the Second World War. In recent times, the extreme view of what it takes (in theory) for a political journalist to remain morally sound has gone beyond mere foolishness to the point of outright irrationality.

For just one example, early in the Mulroney regime, two or three journalists who accepted invitations to dinner at 24 Sussex Drive—not intimate little dinners for a private chat, but big official dinners with no chat of consequence, certainly not with the host—were taken to task here and there in the media, most particularly by Stevie Cameron and Claire Hoy, both print journalists and known non-admirers of Brian Mulroney—perhaps retained, in part, for that latter credential—who were performing as commentators on CBC television in Ottawa. Implicit in their admonitions was the demeaning suggestion that people who cover politics are capable of being lured from the path of journalistic virtue by a lamb chop and a glass of wine.

This stern new doctrine of anti-politician political reporting, if taken seriously, raises a question: how are political journalists to inform themselves, so as to be able reliably to inform others, if they do not mingle with those who have information? If they conscientiously refuse to receive information that may not be immediately attributable but is useful to their understanding, are they not depriving their readers, viewers, listeners, of something? The argument against, of course, is that if journalists enter into understandings based on trust, they make themselves susceptible to manipulation. This is true; obviously there is a risk of being taken in, as in all information gathering and retailing. But what is supposed to stand in the way is the reporter's judgement.

The point that is regularly skipped over in all such arguments is that, in other fields of reporting, the making of contacts is very much part of the job. Medical reporters seek arrangements of mutual trust with the medical profession. Book-page editors cultivate relations with publishers. Writers on legal affairs must have informal as well as formal contacts with members of the judiciary and the legal profession. Labour reporters make themselves confidants of union leaders. Writers on theatre, sports, fashion and everything else mix with the professionals in their areas of interest and absorb some understanding of what they do and why, to pass it on to others. It is only in politics that the people written about are regarded as the enemy—not by all reporters, obviously, but by many.

An adversarial relationship between press and government has always been present in U.S. politics. Government is power; the press represents a check on power. Fine. But there is a great difference between being an observer and being viscerally hostile, and the latter has not been part of our tradition. The idea that all institutions are inherently rotten is a borrowing from the conventional (young, American) thinking of the sixties and seventies. (The more recent political-correctness nuttiness is another example of that slight national derangement which is responsible for the Canadian taste for second-rate ideas second-hand.)

It is not surprising that the idea of the media as the government's *real* opposition came to Canada. What is surprising is that, having reached Canada, it lasted—or still lasts, pending conclusive evidence to the contrary from the Chrétien period—and in such virulent form, after it has become acceptable again for the American press to report on government without adopting all the objectivity of an old-fashioned pamphleteer. The Mulroney government had the misfortune to arrive just in time to catch the phenomenon in full bloom.

The 1984 general election was on September 4. The new Cabinet was sworn in on September 17. On October 4, "The National", then the ten o'clock network news on CBC, carried an item by reporter Christopher Walmsley based on Statistics Canada figures for September. They showed a rise of 0.6 per cent in unemployment. The message was that the government had failed in the prime minister's promise of jobs, jobs, jobs. To make the message more explicit, a clip was dug from the files to show Mulroney saying, "You're going to see tens of thousands of jobs created . . . just as soon as a new government can be sworn in." And of course it *had* been sworn in—a full seventeen days before the date of the broadcast, although only thirteen days before the end of the period to which the figures related.

Mulroney's statement had been undeniably rash, a piece of campaign blarney, as must have been evident even to the crew that taped it. It would be uncharitable to suggest that the producers and editors of the news show were so dim as to expect a perceptible change in the economy in thirteen days. True, the statement had been made publicly, of the candidate's own volition, and was therefore legitimate news. But it would be no less legitimate for viewers to think the newspeople were treating them as boobs, and to wonder what—other than malice—could cause the largest news-gathering agency in the country to make even a small something of it.

The viewers would be even more skeptical if they knew there was another, less ebullient statement on the record, which a deeper search of the CBC's own files might have produced. In the Maritimes in early August, Mulroney had introduced an "important caveat" in the matter of campaign promises. (One imagines a horrified staff member going to him and saying, "Please have a thought for tomorrow and don't say things are going to happen the moment the new government is sworn in. They won't.") The caveat was to the effect that promises would be fulfilled within the *lifetime* of the government.

(It is not the performance of governments but the performance of the media that is the primary subject here. Still, it is a fair question to ask: "Well, how was the promise fulfilled?" According to Statistics Canada, employment in Canada over the calendar year 1984 was 10,932,000, and in 1992 was 12,240,000, or 1,308,000 more. However, in that time the number of Canadians went up as well. The employment-to-population ratio in 1984 was 57.5 per cent. In 1992, the figure was 58.1 per cent. But it had risen steadily to 62.0 per cent in 1990 and then, with the onset of recession, sagged back in the next two years. The trend turned hesitantly upward again in 1993. The answer, then? Not spectacularly well, but not worse than in most of the industrial world.)

The day the first Mulroney government was sworn in, *The Globe and Mail* carried a front-page story, again by its bureau chief, John Gray, under a four-column heading: "Diefenbaker failure haunts Mulroney's Tories"—scarcely a benediction. Three days later, the cry was raised that the new government was choking off information to which Canadians were entitled—although it might be asked how much information so new a government could have to communicate. Still, the sensitivity of the media to their own interests, usually stated as the interests of Canadians, is never to be underestimated. The heading, again on page one, said:

PM TRIES TO CURB
INFORMATION FLOW
ON CHANGEOVER

The Great Secrecy Scare ran for two months, kept alive (for an audience that may have been less than agog) by lavish use of such editorializing headings as "Tories secretive despite their promises", "Clark orders curb on ministry press leaks", "Tory gag order more sweeping than reported", "Civil servants' gag rules to be released on Friday", "Ottawa invokes secrecy rules on Cabinet ministers' flights", "Gag on public employees loosened/ PM says remarks must be on record" and "'Stick to channels in advising minister,' bureaucrats told", until finally . . .

UNMUZZLING MULRONEY
MOVES TO LOOSEN GATE
ON GOVERNMENT INFORMATION FLOW

It is a question whether any muzzling ever occurred other than in the minds of those who said in print and on the air that it did; the diminution of information was not evident to the naked eye. But it is possible. New governments generally like to have a minimum of babble going on—especially from unnamed public servants—while still sorting themselves out. On the other hand, the media are not above hollering before they are hurt in order to impress on a new government that they are not to be trifled with. Whichever the case, it was clear in early December that Ottawa life was back to normal when *The Globe and Mail* was able to report, via a purposeful leak from a disgruntled public service union, that

FEDERAL INSPECTORS
ALLOW MEAT IMPORTS
WITH DIRT AND HAIR

Regardless of scare stories about gag orders, secrecy rules and curbs against information flow, it was apparent that the gates were wide open and the leak was alive in the land. And so was the spirit of prejudice-building. The real attack on the new government came with Finance minister Michael Wilson's first financial statement, a mini-budget, in early November, when the Conservatives had been in office not quite two months. Here, as a sample shower of negativity, are just some headings, from just one newspaper, *The Globe and Mail*, in that month:

"Youth Training Plan Caught in PC Freeze."
"Defence Gains May Force Cutbacks Elsewhere."
"$18 billion in Subsidies for Companies Has Been Largely Immune from Cutting."
"UI [unemployment insurance] Slashed, but $1 billion Pledged for Jobs / PCs to Cut Spending by $4.2 billion."
"Deficit Numbers Belie Tory Claims."
"Up to $30 billion Cuts to Be Imposed by 1991."
"Federal Youth Job Scheme Called Band-aid Solution."
"Social Welfare Advocates Decry Cuts in UIC, Job Training Subsidies."
"Cutback Equated to Being Told 'to Walk on Water.'"
"Social Spending to Be Slashed/Programs Face Reassessment."
"Third World Aid Workers Fear PC Axe."
"Public is Loser in Park Cuts Biologists Say."
"Research on Toxic Substances Dies in Tory Cuts."
"Foreign Aid Project in Jeopardy."
"Cradle-to-Grave Security Up for Possible Overhaul."
"Tories Mum about Advisory Board on Spending Cuts."
"Wilson Won't Reveal Impact of Restraint Plan on Jobs."
"$45 million in Halifax Works Cut."

"Wilson Seen Just Nibbling at Problems."
"Wilson Unimpressed With Job-Loss Figures."
"Federal Cuts Hurt Environment Programs, Critics Say."
"OFL [Ontario Federation of Labour] Assails Mini-Budget as Attack on Unemployed."
"Wilson Says Tory Spending Cuts Won't Cripple Manitoba." (In fact, he didn't say that. The story itself said he had *scoffed* at someone's, possibly the reporter's, suggestion that the spending cuts would cost Manitoba up to four thousand jobs.)
"Social Program Advocates Fear PC Axe."
"Government Focuses on Deficit Reduction Not Jobs."

Some of those headings identify routine post-budget stories. Rather more—of slashes and cutbacks and fears of axes; of dubious information, indifference to jobs, lack of frankness—have a distinct anti-government slant. They belong to the oh-woe, oh-woe, oh-woe school of political reporting, designed to inspire more fear than confidence. They instil prejudice.

What is curious about this oh-woeing is that it sprang from the fulfilling of proclaimed intentions. In many cases, those intentions had been not just anticipated but endorsed by both media and public—in the 1984 election, which produced a majority government. The popular word during the campaign was that this election was about Change. When the election result came in, it was said with even greater assurance that Canadians had voted for Change. It was to be towards more frugal government, in hopes of extracting the country from an imprisoning load of debt. As it happened, the best the Conservatives were able to do, in two parliaments, was to slow the rate of *increase* in the yearly deficit. The combined value of increased tax revenues and decreased operating expenditures never came close to equalling the sum—running to $40 billion latterly—that was being added to the total bill every year in debt charges.

As proposals were introduced, one by one, to effect the envisioned change, the reporting assumed the viewpoint of every pressure group with a selfish interest to protect. If it was less than a success for government to make no more than a start towards its objective, the reporting that stood in the way can only be said to have been dead wrong, as the weight of the debt ten years later attests. By 1993, when Brian Mulroney and a good handful of his most senior ministers left government, every provincial government in the country, three of them New Democrat, had accepted that reducing debt was inescapable. Yet every step considered by Ottawa to reduce expenditure was received with outrage by interest groups which was sympathetically reflected in the reporting. It is only mildly to burlesque the reality to say that the Canadian dialogue on the subject in the middle eighties ran about like this:

Q. Might not some small saving be made by partially—just partially—de-indexing old-age pensions?

A. Unthinkable—to tackle the deficit on the backs of old folks? Never.

Q. Family allowances, then; what rationale is there for mailing out monthly cheques to everyone with kids?

A. Cut there and the principle of universality is shot. Never.

Q. Unemployment insurance? Surely it has grown a long way from what initially was intended and needs to be rethought?

A. Not just a program but a way of life. Never.

Q. All right, then, the post office; perhaps if it were reconfigured it would not only reduce the demand for public funds but become more efficient.

A. What, and sell stamps in convenience stores? Never.

Q. The CBC; could it not be made to get along with less munificent annual increases from a current base of $1 billion a year?

A. What, and undermine a national cultural treasure? Never.

Q. Via Rail, then; don't passenger trains cost a bundle to maintain, and aren't they used by fewer and fewer people?

A. What, no more the haunting wail of the lit-up train as it rushes through the prairie night? Never.

Q. Privatize Air Canada to get it off the government's books?

A. Consign part of the fabric of the nation to the realm of vulgar commerce? Never.

Q. On the other side of the ledger, then, enter a free trade agreement with the United States in hopes of enlarging the national economy?

A. What, and risk having those sly Americans push us to undo our universal health program? Never.

Q. All right, in the absence of any of those other remedies for our distress, what about something big on the revenue side, say a consumption tax, a Goods and Services Tax to replace a less productive manufacturers' tax?

A. (No response but a loud scream.)

Some of those ideas were acted upon, and the world continued to turn—really quite well in some cases; for example, trade with the United States hit a new top in the first quarter of 1994. Nothing became of some of them—of which some were lifted into Jean Chrétien's celebrated Red Book, which suggests the original objections, including those by Liberals, had been less firmly rooted in principle than they let on at the time.

It shows the inconstancy of editorialists that *The Globe and Mail*—very much a fan of fiscal responsibility, as it's called—spoke up just a month after that first budget for a fraternal interest of its own, the CBC. "All right," it said, "the CBC had to share the general financial pain. . . . But that should be the end of it [sounds here of harrumph, harrumph]. . . . There are many ways to kill an independent voice of national interest, and whittling away at its funding is only one of them." If the paper had arguments to support the implicit proposition that one part of the public sector should be immune to further "financial pain", it spared its readers the tedium of reading them. If it had evidence of any plot to "kill an independent voice of national interest", it did not choose to expose it. Nor did it say, if its media friend was to be protected, whence the compensating saving should come.

Strange, strange. But, once more, the general eccentricities of editorial pages and commentators are not the prime subject here; rather it is the accumulating effect on public perceptions of the drip-drip-drip of daily news reporting. Governments regularly complain that they catch hell in the media for what they don't do, or do badly, but get very little recognition for what they do and do well. Even the most inflamed journalism chauvinist would find the truth of that hard to deny. The Trudeau governments complained about the negativity they faced in the media, but it was neither so persistent nor so pervasive as the hounding experienced by their Conservative successors.

In addition, the negativity towards the Trudeau governments appeared less in the news columns than in the commentaries—to which

I acknowledge having contributed my bit. But it has to be remembered that in positively the worst episode of the Trudeau years—the so-called apprehended insurrection in Quebec in October 1970—public opinion polls showed that 80 per cent of Canadians supported the government. A connection is not hard to draw between that remarkable figure and the even more remarkable fact that at least 95 per cent (by my estimate) of the reporting in all media, print and broadcast alike, was on that same side of the issue.

There were, then, differences between the Trudeau and Mulroney reigns. Charles Lynch, who had been doing a national affairs column from Ottawa for more than thirty years, wrote in mid-1991 that "the idea that the prime minister is somebody to be 'got' started with the media in Pierre Trudeau's time." But he added that after Trudeau had ticked off reporters for delving into his private affairs—a casual date in London, when he was single, had blabbed about a fancied romance—there followed "a surly saw-off that lasted until Trudeau retired." Some years later, the earthy background to the departure of Trudeau's young wife, Margaret, from the prime-ministerial residence was handled by the Ottawa press corps with unusual delicacy.

No similar delicacy was observed in the treatment of Brian Mulroney in a family context. Consider just three examples. One was the story in John Sawatsky's *Mulroney: The Politics of Ambition* about a mysterious illness (a nudge here) suffered by Mulroney after a night out with the boys while he was a student at Dalhousie University. Sawatsky's otherwise competent record of a career in politics was debased by that innuendo, which was cheap, pointlessly hurtful because irrelevant, founded on thirty-year-old student gossip—and became the basis for much of the publicity on which the book sold. In pure gossip-monger style, the sources of the tale were as flimsy as "word had it" and "or so the story went". And as word had it and the story went, Mulroney landed in hospital. Sawatsky either failed to check medical opinion or chose not to quote it; while hospitalization for venereal disease could not be ruled out, it would be a rare thing and then only in an extreme case. Sawatsky used the word "virulent". Beyond its more common use to describe forms of infection, virulent also means "bitter, spiteful, or malicious"—a term no less applicable to some forms of journalism.

A second was the picking up from *Frank* magazine, a rag, of a pretended contest to find the man who would "deflower" the prime minister's teenage daughter, Caroline. More fraudulent than *Frank*'s invention—not much is expected of *Frank*—was the defence of the story as politically justified by at least two commentators in the major press, Rick Salutin in *The Globe and Mail* and Allan Fotheringham in *Maclean's*. It was justified, in their view, because the prime minister had made political use of his daughter, and therefore exposed her to such comment, by taking her to a Conservative function in Toronto. Thus, what would qualify as nothing more than proud-fatherism in most male parents—any number of columnists, including this one, have shown off their kids in print—becomes exploitation for political purposes in a politician.

A third was the spreading of rumours that Mulroney, despondent after the failure of the Meech Lake Accord, was drinking heavily, and that a liaison existed between Mila Mulroney and actor Christopher Plummer—and that the marriage was on the rocks. That unsubstantiated gossip remained unknown to most of the world outside Ottawa, where it had evidently been enlivening dinner parties, until *The Globe and Mail*, with nine or ten reporters of its own in the capital, retained a freelance writer to bring it to national attention.

The story contained no scrap of documentation to say that the gossip had or had not substance. The writer, Charlotte Gray, was content with "Who knows? Perhaps . . ." and "Who can resist the logic of 'Where there's smoke, there's fire . . .'?" She identified *Frank* as "a much-quoted source", although not the only one, and said of it that "besides being delicious and malicious, it has also been oblivious to trivialities such as solid evidence." Presumably the *Globe* turned to someone outside its own organization to separate itself just that tiny step from a malodorous story, which it nevertheless was content to publish.

It would be generous to say that the capital press corps was unaware that some reporting on the government and prime minister was looked upon as not just "delicious and malicious", to borrow Ms. Gray's phrase, but ungracious and mendacious. Some of its own senior members had said as much at one time or another—to sour comment from their colleagues. In 1988, in an address at the Atlantic Journalism Awards dinner in Halifax, Jeffrey Simpson, *The Globe and Mail*'s national affairs columnist, acknowledged a certain tension between journalists and politicians as both natural and healthy but went on to say this:

> But the assaults on politicians for losing their luggage, the ridicule directed at them for certain physical characteristics or mannerisms, the morbid interest in their financial affairs, the bidding up of moral standards so that mere mortals need not stand for office, the relentless imputation of crass motives, the prurient fascination with the size of prime-ministerial cupboards, the intense search for significance in what politicians ate for lunch or where they stayed while representing Canada abroad, the altogether too-common assumption that only political considerations drive decisions, the reduction of complex matters to fifteen-second clips followed by instant analyses from those who do not know that they should know better—these are signs of a press badly in need of a wider perspective and an extensive bout of soul-searching.

The late Hyman Solomon, bureau chief and columnist for *The Financial Post*, wrote a piece in 1987 on the Mulroney government, the various scandals it had incurred and a "barely controlled chaos" in the Prime Minister's Office, to which the government's low standing in the polls could be attributed—in part. But he also cited as factors "the savaging by the media and the cynical Opposition tactics—bemoaning Parliament's declining image while hurling hearsay and flimsy charges at the TV cameras."

About the scandals, the Canadian public heard and read a lot; about the savaging by the media as a factor in the government's low standing, little or nothing. About the opposition's tactics, mainly in Question Period, they did not need to hear, because the worst bits, picked for sensation value, were on television night after night, where they became part of the media savagery referred to. With that kind of talk, Solomon was inviting accusations of toadyism in a hypersensitive Ottawa media colony.

In early 1991, Marjorie Nichols wrote in the Ottawa *Citizen*: "What this country really needs is a psychiatrist to analyse the hate and verbal violence that now permeate national debate. . . . Prime Minister Brian Mulroney has been a lightning rod for this rising tide of incivility. But, clearly, Mulroney is a victim, not a perpetrator. . . ." That, along with other comments not unfavourable to the prime minister, earned for

Ms. Nichols—who was dying of lung cancer—the whispers of some members of the press corps that her illness and its treatments had unhinged her.

At a greater distance, Michael Valpy, having gone from national affairs columnist in Ottawa to much-praised correspondent in Africa, wrote from Zimbabwe in 1987 about a prime-ministerial visit. He recorded his shock at the hostility evident in the accompanying correspondents. "Not even in the days of Joe Clark's prime ministership," he said, "did the press make such savage jokes and express such contempt for a prime minister and his staff and advisers. What the relationship must be between the Prime Minister's Office and the press gallery is staggering to contemplate. . . ."

This comment, remember, was from a reporter of long experience in the parliamentary press gallery.

It's of more than incidental interest that Valpy leapt, for his worst-since comparison, over Pierre Trudeau's last turn at the wheel in 1980–84, and the John Turner interlude, to Joe Clark. Federal Conservatives have frequently accused the parliamentary press gallery of being anti-Tory. Members of the gallery who have deigned to reply have as frequently insisted that it's all in the Tories' head. The record says otherwise. Antagonism to the Conservatives was implicit in the early start, the savagery and the sustained nature of the attack on that first Tory government in almost nineteen years. After that long, the bitterness could scarcely be attributed to any carryover of corrosive memories from the last government of the same stripe.

The Conservatives, as Official Opposition before the 1984 election, had performed creditably. The election campaign had been effectively run. The conclusion is unavoidable that the hostility the Mulroney government encountered was composed, even making due allowance for its own errors, of an ingrained anti-Conservative attitude in the Ottawa media community, now justified as a natural adversarial relationship between political journalists and government.

There is much academic literature in the United States on journalism and journalists, including their political orientation—not necessarily by party, but as small-l liberals and small-c conservatives. Whether or not it can be said to constitute a consensus, the weight of the writing in the U.S. says journalists are predominantly liberal. The next question is whether that has a bearing on what and how they report. Various studies have concluded that it has—which is not to suggest that the news is deliberately distorted, but that emphases may be affected.

For example, conscious and unconscious tendencies may cause journalists to cover more of the activities of like-minded politicians, or to turn to the like-minded for reactions to events, or to elevate in their reporting issues that accord with their own thinking, to the relative neglect of others that do not.

In a study published in 1989, *The Media, the Polity, and Public Opinion*, Robert Lerner and Stanley Rothman set out various conclusions, their own and others', on the evolution of American journalism over the past thirty-odd years. One conclusion was that a "neutralist conception" dominated in the period prior to the 1960s which found its model in the professions. From there journalists swayed to such ideas as the journalist-as-advocate and the journalist-as-adversary in relation to established institutions, pre-eminently government. Among some young journalists at the time, they said, objectivity became a term of abuse.

In Canada, journalists, and particularly political journalists, are reticent about where they stand politically, as if they hope to be accepted as free of taint or leanings if they do not acknowledge the possibility they might have any. Whether that or simple incuriosity is the explanation, not much is to be found of academic writing on the political attachments of journalists. In 1982, Peter Snow—then a journalism professor at the Western Ontario Graduate School of Journalism in London, Ontario, now in television production—conducted a survey of 118 national affairs journalists which produced results similar to those found in American studies. Forty-three per cent said that they belonged plunk in the middle of the political spectrum, neither left nor right; 42 per cent said that they were left of centre and 4 per cent that they were right of centre. In party terms their sympathies lay 37 per cent with the New Democrats, 17 per cent with the Liberals and 11 per cent with the Conservatives.

Those figures say two things—one, that the respondents had some difficulty in defining where they thought the middle lay, and two, that wherever it was, they were not to the right of it.

A more comprehensive study, encompassing journalists in the fourteen largest newspapers across the country, was done by Robert Bergen, now a reporter at *The Calgary Herald* but in 1987 a graduate student completing a master's degree in communications at the University of Calgary. At the core of Bergen's study was a nineteen-page questionnaire which was sent to 947 newsroom people and completed by 388—40.9 per cent, a good return.

The Canadian big-city journalist at the time was, by Bergen's figures, between the ages of twenty-two and forty-five (nearly 80 per cent); of middle-class background; male (nearly 77 per cent, unquestionably reduced since); had completed university (50 per cent), college or some university (32.9 per cent); and had a substantial income (largest group, $40,000-$50,000, also undoubtedly raised since).

No fewer than 73.4 per cent of Bergen's respondents described their political ideology as "moderate left". But when they were asked to indicate the *party* of their choice, only 32.7 per cent said NDP. The next-largest group was the 27.9 per cent who said they had "*no federal political leanings*". The Liberals took third place, with the support of 25.3 per cent, and behind them came the Progressive Conservatives at 12.8 per cent and "other" at 1.4 per cent. Although the responses became vaguer as the categorization became more specific, what was clear was that they were not Tories.

There is no reason to believe that Bergen's figures, just a few years old now, and Snow's older ones, do not reflect accurately where in the spectrum journalists in general place themselves. There is no reason to believe, either, that a similar study in Ottawa today would not produce the same results, intensified.

THREE

THE MINSTREL GALLERY

IN FEBRUARY 1952, WHEN I BEGAN WHAT EVENTUALLY became three stints in the parliamentary press gallery, there were 64 members. Forty-one years later there were just over five times that many. The 1993 membership list showed a total of 334, about half print and half broadcast, the first representing more news entities, the second, larger bureaus. The largest single presence was television, and the largest within that the CBC; there had been no broadcast journalists accredited at all in 1952, television or radio. In addition to the 334 regulars in 1993, the gallery recognized another 104 as support staff, persons employed by the press corps but working away from The Hill and, among its other facilities, the invaluable Parliamentary Library. On top of all that, the press gallery each year issued roughly 2,000 temporary cards to reporters and others on short-term assignments.

The parliamentary press gallery is the handy name given the people who supply Canadians with most of their news about official Ottawa. The title is a bit of a misnomer. Parliament itself has become a minor interest of the members. It follows that the gallery from which the group takes its name, looking down from above the Speaker's chair at the north end of the House of Commons chamber, is more often empty than full. And certainly the members are not press in the original meaning of the word. As they are only marginally parliamentary, only marginally press and only occasionally occupying the seats of the gallery, the name is more historical than descriptive.

The extraordinary growth of the Ottawa press gallery over the years is not attributable solely to the arrival of radio journalists in 1959, nor even of television. Obviously, television has been in Ottawa and around Parliament from the fifties, doing standup interviews outside, then in the foyer, later in the basement in a makeshift studio created for the purpose. It became a full-force presence only in 1977, when fixed, remote-controlled cameras were installed in unobtrusive positions in the Commons chamber. But the electronic media only accelerated the growth of national political news. The number of persons reporting has increased enormously in proportion to the number of persons reported upon and reported to.

The population of Canada was just under 14.5 million in 1952. Forty years later it had not quite doubled, but was within sight of it, a considerable increase but small potatoes beside the fivefold increase in the news brigade in Ottawa. The number of parliamentarians in the House of Commons and the Senate had increased relatively little. There are more newspeople accredited to Parliament than there are MPs—334 to 289. Only with the addition of the 104 members of the Senate, who are rarely looked in on at all, do the parliamentarians constitute a majority over the self-styled watchdogs of Parliament.

Not long ago, commentators looking for examples of bloat in government used occasionally to point stern fingers at the Cabinet and how it had grown—too large to be efficient, too expensive to be borne, indicative of too many departments. But in roughly forty years the Cabinet had grown only from the twenty-four members Louis St. Laurent made do with in the 1950s to thirty-nine by the time Brian Mulroney left office—a minuscule increase compared to the growth of the press gallery. In her pre-election Cabinet in 1993, Kim Campbell cut the number to twenty-five. Jean Chrétien went her one better, going back to the St. Laurent figure, but quietly added several parliamentary secretaries as debutant ministers.

Another stock topic for tut-tutting about Big Government is the whole public-sector payroll. Yet, counting only the core, the regular, full-time workers who constitute the Public Service of Canada proper—as distinct from, for example, staffs of various agencies, the armed services and part-time workers—the number of persons employed at the end of 1952 was 131,167. At the end of 1992, the figure was 217,691. Again a big increase, but picayune beside the proliferation of watchdogs.

How about, then, the number of journalists assigned to keep watch on Ottawa as compared to the number who are assigned to keep watch on their provincial legislatures? By recent count, the total of accredited members of the parliamentary press gallery comes just fifteen short of the combined total of members of all sorts in all the press galleries of the ten provinces *and* the territory of the Yukon. The valuable yearly publication *Canadian Legislatures* counted 349 such legislature reporters in 1992. Assuming usual practice, many of those would be sessional only—there while the legislature was sitting, elsewhere when it was not. Also, no fewer than 105 of the legislature reporters were in one province—in the National Assembly in Quebec.

Those figures must mean something. In the estimation of the editors of newspapers and the news directors of broadcasting in English-speaking Canada, the government closest to the minds (if not necessarily the hearts) of Canadians must be the central government in Ottawa. Of course, the reverse can be assumed to apply to Quebec editors.

The question is whether many more reporters, attuned to the negative rather than the positive in their reporting, contribute more to an informed and understanding public or to a distrustful and querulous one. If execration prevails over explanation, is more better than less?

It's not just because of my own arrival that I use 1952 as a starting-point for comparisons. It was about then that the gallery began to grow, after having stayed more or less steady since the end of the Second World War. In addition to the press gallery's being a fraction then of its 1990s size, it was also different in makeup and psychology. Except for The Canadian Press, which had an office downtown, mainly for administration—it also had a parliamentary bureau on The Hill, as did the other news agency, United Press—the entire press corps, wholly composed of newspaper reporters, occupied not a square foot of its own space in Ottawa, either owned or rented, that it used for news purposes. The whole shebang was located off the back corridor—which it overflowed into—on the third floor of the Centre Block of the Parliament Buildings.

The reporter arrived in the morning to a reserved parking space (by permit only; free) behind the Centre Block, and went inside and up to a long, open room with a fine view northward to the Gatineau Hills. The view inside was of a crowded clutter of littered desks and ancient typewriters, the whole thing bearing a resemblance to some odd sort of sweatshop. The amenities for members included—in addition to the free desks, free typewriters, free notebooks, free typing paper, free pencils, free phones and free answering service—free bound copies of the *Hansard* records of Commons and Senate debates; free copies of "the blues", the instant, uncorrected stenographic transcriptions of debates, available within an hour, and free clerks to see that a free copy of the daily printed *Hansard* was put in each member's pigeonhole in the mail rack each morning. They could also get, on application, free passes for the railways.

A non-governmental amenity, but made possible only by the free government space and free staff, was Ottawa's largest, all-hours bootlegging establishment, not free, but reasonable. Also, off the other end of the sweatshop, there was a lounge like some down-at-heels men's club of another time, fitted out with spavined leather-clad lounge chairs, a chesterfield to match, tables for cribbage or occasional late-night poker, a bookcase filled with miscellany that no one read, and framed group photographs of old gallery members. There was also to be found somewhere a small oaken cask with a spigot, which any MP with a mind to generate an instant party could fill with the booze of his (and it was his) choice.

The press gallery, taking into account all that, lived on Parliament and *off* it. When Parliament was in session, the focus of the day's output was on the House of Commons just down the hall. Except perhaps for the occasional twinge of conscience over how well the free accommodation and the rest accorded with professions of total and unwavering media independence, there was no evident embarrassment—no more, in any case, than at the fire marshal's having condemned the place as a fire hazard.

To the extent that it was thought about at all, the apparent rationale in the home offices of the gallery members was that, if sports could provide press boxes and phones and perhaps free sandwiches and coffee for sports writers, the government of Canada scarcely could do less for the reporters who covered the game there.

The journalists on the 1952 press gallery list, in addition to being all newspaper reporters—even magazine writers could aspire only to associate membership—were, with two exceptions, male. The two women were Evelyn Tufts, who had been a member since before the Second World War as a correspondent for Halifax newspapers, and Ruth Campbell, reporter for *The St. John's News* of Newfoundland, who also served as a stringer for one or two other papers. Judith Robinson, a tough-minded columnist for the Toronto *Telegram*, shortly became the third. The first two worked almost entirely from their homes. Whether they did so because they had been made to feel unwelcome, or because of a higher female sensitivity to squalor, is, as the saying goes, lost in the mists of time. At last count, the early-nineties total of women members of the press gallery exceeded eighty, still a long step from equality but, considering that journalism not many years earlier was almost entirely a male trade, a considerable rise.

Today's popular version of journalism history in Canada, mainly oral, says that political journalism forty years ago was not "tough" enough, was too narrowly focused on the House of Commons, too cosy with the politicians, too understanding of moral and other lapses by government, opposition and MPs as individuals—in short, too much a part of "the system". Perhaps. It is true that some older members of the gallery remembered with pride Prime Minister Mackenzie King calling them, as the historian Thomas Babington Macaulay called the parliamentary reporters at Westminster a century earlier, "the fourth estate of the realm".

That was to say, the reporters in their gallery were there as The Press, as a fourth estate of the realm after the nobility and the hierarchy of the established Church of England, both represented in the House of Lords, and the rest of the population, represented by the Commons.

That was not, at the time I went to the press gallery, my idea of where Ottawa journalists stood in relation to Parliament. It now seems bizarre to think that anyone suggested it. The question is whether a relationship in which the reporters may have been too routinely well disposed, too clubby with the institution reported upon, produced a worse result for the reader than one which amounts to almost no association at all, and sees itself and government as natural adversaries. The reporting nowadays is mainly on a higher intellectual plane; whether it is fairer and more reliable is another question. I think not.

If the supposedly easygoing attitudes of the fifties caused the suppression by reporters of significant news, or the playing down of controversial issues out of respect for the sensibilities of the government, it is curious that historians who have written on the period have not made much of their discoveries. They have fleshed out and put in better order and better perspective the events that were the issues of the day, which is what historians do that journalism lacks the perspective and time to do. But of matters of consequence deliberately shoved out of sight there have been few revelations.

On the other hand, a state of non-association as existed in the Mulroney years, and such unimproving developments as gotcha journalism—issue-making by entrapment—have certainly contributed to the embitterment of the public that the polls and the media themselves proclaim as fact. That same touch of tolerance that is supposed to have made the political reporting of an earlier time soft is what has been most missing. What we have had instead is a predisposition to suppose persons in public life, and particularly those in positions of power, to be villains—and to insist at the same time that they maintain higher standards than the average citizen (such as, for example, a journalist). In other words, the pendulum has swung too far in the other direction.

Marking where a significant change in any group practice took place is an imprecise business, but the great Pipeline Debate of 1956 will do well to mark a watershed in our political journalism. That debate remains the most dramatic parliamentary event since the Second World War. Although the issue as a whole was not disposed of nearly so quickly, the debate proper lasted just three weeks. Along the way, a number of unusual parliamentary happenings occurred.

Before debate had even begun, the government gave notice of its intention to invoke closure—a limitation on debate—in *anticipation* of obstruction. The rule of closure had been used rarely in the Canadian Parliament, and has not been used in the same way since. But although the rule confined to days the time for debate, it could not guard against the parliamentary day being prolonged by determined opponents beyond the usual closing time of 10:00 p.m. One result was that the House, raucous enough by day, went on into the evening in tumult—once nearly to dawn.

The rulings of the Speaker of the House, hitherto the next thing to sacrosanct, were repeatedly and noisily challenged. Even more strangely, the Speaker reversed himself overnight, following a particularly tempestuous late-night session, and ordered the clock turned back—to the embattled government's advantage—to the time at which he thought (or had been told, or had been instructed) he had gone wrong. At that, the usually correct and gentlemanly M.J. Coldwell—leader of the CCF, the predecessor of the New Democrats—stormed onto the floor of the House, shaking his fist at the Speaker. The next morning, the row was fed by a reporter bringing to the gallery a story of seeing a Cabinet minister's car outside the door of the Speaker's home, a few doors down the street from his own.

Greatly compressed, the whole tempest was over approving the government's bill to authorize an $80-million loan of public money to assist in bringing a gas pipeline, first, from Alberta to Winnipeg. From there, a spur would carry gas for export south to the U.S. border. Shortly after that, the line would be extended through the difficult country of Northern Ontario to Toronto. To permit a start to be made in 1956—it was not irrelevant that a federal election was in sight and a large new project would look good on the government's list of accomplishments—the bill would need to be law by the first days of June.

But Canadian economic nationalism was just then stirring, and with it what has become its inseparable companion, anti-Americanism. Lending public money to American interests to rush Canadian gas to American industries did not strike a responsive chord in quite a few Canadians. There were as many others who thought that, if public money was going into the project—notwithstanding that it was a loan subject to penalty if not repaid on time—the pipeline should join the ranks of such publicly owned entities as Air Canada and the CNR. But larger than either of those discontents was the resentment at the government's choosing to impose closure on debate of each stage of the bill's passage through the House, to ensure that its own deadline was met.

The pipeline debate was important in Canadian political journalism in several ways. First of all, it caused some reporters—or encouraged or allowed them, or was seized upon by them as an opportunity—to take sides, not necessarily on a party basis, but as supportive of the government or not. Television was then a minor player in political reporting, but the debate was given tremendous coverage in the newspapers, predominantly on the side of the Conservative and CCF parties, which acted virtually as one, their tactics co-ordinated, employing the rules of the House to good effect against the government's use of closure.

It was not unusual, after a late-night session, for a reporter to have a drink with MPs of one party or the other—more often the Conservatives, because the CCFers were not much on drink—to discuss next-day tactics. By day the CCF, with Stanley Knowles as their parliamentary rules-master, were the better source. With two parties from opposite ends of the political spectrum joined in denouncing what they saw as a stifling of debate, the issue was readily seen as one of principle rather than policies, which simplified the reporting.

I myself at the time was a hybrid, part-time columnist, still with duties to the news side, and not scrupulous in drawing a line between the two roles. The doctrine of the time said reporters were observers; they saw, they heard, they made notes and they wrote. But this was an important and exciting game and there was a pleasurable sense of not just observing but being part of it. In addition, it was not always easy, writing a new lead at midnight with the House in an uproar, to keep the two jobs, news and comment, surgically separated.

The effect of the pipeline debate, then, was to legitimate the intrusion of the reporter's judgement into accounts of events. The extent of that intrusion was vastly increased as television grew to be a great popular influence in news delivery—ultimately to the point that news became virtually indistinguishable from commentary. However, that happened gradually, over nearly forty years.

The pipeline issue and the reporting of it, followed by the defeat of the Liberal government the next year, left an impression of "the power of the press" that was probably greater than warranted. The election result, considering that the Liberals had been in office for an unbroken run of twenty-two years, was hardly a landslide—105 Liberals (plus one Liberal-Labour who sat with the Liberals) to 112 Conservatives, the rest spread among CCF, Social Credit and independents. Nevertheless, the predominantly critical reporting and commentary in even traditionally Liberal newspapers undoubtedly played some part in the defeat.

Canadians at the time tended to think relatively well of their governments. Whether they actually *liked* them, they were usually prepared to accept that their intentions were not bad, that the motives of the people they elected were generally to work for the public good, and were not, for inexplicable reasons of the politicians' own, to undermine the best interests of the electors.

Nearly forty years later, the watchdog proposition has developed to excess, so that the story can be seen at times to have proceeded under no necessarily stringent scrutiny from a conclusion to the evidence rather than the reverse. Motives are freely ascribed for which no rationale is apparent, as if predictably unpopular actions were taken purposely to court unpopularity. Such public floggings are most often applied to the leader, because hatred is more effectively cultivated if concentrated on one symbolic figure rather than spread over a disparate group of ministers or, worse, a lot of anonymous MPs.

Throughout much of his time in office, Brian Mulroney was characterized as the most unpopular prime minister in Canada ever. That was in succession to Pierre Trudeau, whose ride in the polls had been more up and down, from the heights of Trudeaumania to some considerable depths in which he was reviled, and up again at the end on the strength of a woolly but feel-good world peace initiative.

Dividing the years since the end of the Second World War roughly in two, it is not evident the quality of government has been worse in the second, the years primarily of Trudeau and Mulroney, than in the first, the years of Louis St. Laurent, John Diefenbaker and Lester B. Pearson. What has changed more has been the media attention government receives, which is infinitely more abrasive.

True, St. Laurent held office at an unusual time in which it was almost impossible for government to put a foot wrong. Canada enjoyed an exaggerated standing in the world because of the larger-than-life part it had played in the war and the good economic conditions it enjoyed as a result of having suffered no destruction of productive capacity during those nearly six years. It was a time when the Minister of Finance was criticized for budget surpluses, a word no person born since has heard in a budget context. The minister, as the complaint went, took more money from the taxpayers than necessary because the government arrogantly assumed it knew better how to use it than the people themselves. A fairer explanation would have been that the war left behind a lot of debt which a responsible government could not ignore with a flourishing economy.

Canada took an honourable and publicly accepted part in the Korean War, 1950–53, under the banner of the United Nations, and contributed hugely to the successful diplomacy in the Suez Crisis, for which Pearson won the Nobel Peace Prize, another boost to national self-esteem. Business and industry thrived, unemployment was not a great problem, incomes increased, young people embarked on careers, homes and families. With abundant revenues, debt did not inhibit government when moved by compassion, or politics, to do well by doing good. And the country was not in evident danger of breaking up.

Canadians, even well into a second generation since, have never really recovered from that aberrant time and the unreal expectations it encouraged.

The St. Laurent government's late troubles were those of a government too long in power and grown careless in the use of it; they were not due to constant carping and allegations of wrongdoing based on chimerical evidence.

John Diefenbaker, St. Laurent's Conservative successor, encountered more hostility, but never uniformly across the country. He remained to the end generally popular with public and press alike in his native west. And again, it was an issue of substance that did him in.

After slipping into power at the head of a minority government, Diefenbaker leapt the next year to the largest-ever majority, narrowly survived a third election and was finished within six years. The last of those elections merely confirmed what had become predictable after a very visible shattering of the Cabinet from within. The discord resulted from the prime minister's dithering about putting nuclear warheads on the Bomarc defensive missiles already in the Canadian armoury—and pointless, in both senses of the word, without them. It was not any passionate demand from Canadians for nuclear weapons that caused Diefenbaker's downfall, but his indecision. But Diefenbaker was by no means finished by the defeat in 1963; he remained as Conservative leader in opposition, determined to regain the government, and was an enduring pain in the neck (and elsewhere) to his successor, Lester B. Pearson, whom he faced in the House of Commons as if again a defence counsel addressing a recalcitrant witness.

The Pearson government's troubles came early, in a rash of scandals which, with one exception, were of demonstrated gravity. They began, for example, with the revelation that efforts had been made by persons with close political connections to secure the release of a drug smuggler from jail. (The prisoner, to the further embarrassment of the government, eventually escaped.)

The exception was what became known as "the furniture scandal". A Quebec investigation into possible fraudulence in a number of bankruptcies had turned up, incidentally, the names of two Liberal Cabinet ministers who owed some thousands of dollars to a bankrupt dealer in expensive furniture. The word reached two reporters, George Brimmell, then of Southam News, and Paul Akehurst, then of the Toronto radio station CHUM. They followed up the lead and eventually had enough information to confront the ministers—first Secretary of State Maurice Lamontagne, and a day or so later Immigration minister René Tremblay. The ministers acknowledged that they had bought furniture from the company. Lamontagne had made no down payment and paid no instalments before the company went bankrupt, even though nearly two years had elapsed since the first lot was delivered. Tremblay had made no payments until he heard from the bankrupt company's main creditor, the Bank of Montreal, at which point he paid off the debt in full. But the lapse of time in his case was just three months from the purchase, and at a point at which the order remained incomplete. Further, he had received no bill.

Except that the ministers were from Quebec, where the substantial issues of perhaps fraudulent bankruptcies arose, no relationship between them, their furniture dealings and anything improper was ever shown. Neither was it shown that the matter in any way affected their public responsibilities. Without the climate of scandal that hung over Ottawa, this affair would have been treated as it deserved, as of no real significance. Perhaps there were signs of the pack phenomenon in a nascent phase in the pipeline debate, but at that time the term had not yet been invented. The so-called Furniture Scandal was an early example of real pack journalism, with the press gallery rushing off whole (or close to it) on a whiff of wrongdoing and negligible evidence.

I knew neither of the ministers at the time, having recently returned from four years in Washington following three years in London. But later I got to know Lamontagne, liked him and was convinced that the worst that could be said of him was that he perhaps was not very practical in looking after his private affairs (not a universal gift in journalists, either, this one included).

But I had already written an unctuous column unfavourably contrasting Pearson's handling of the affair to that of President Dwight D. Eisenhower, who had summarily dismissed his White House chief-of-staff, Sherman Adams, for accepting a vicuña coat as a gift from a businessman who had business at the White House. Later I became less sure the two occurrences were on the same footing. The critical difference, I eventually decided, was that the White House aide had done a positive something—accepted a gift. A debt, however, with no evident effort on the one side to pay it, or on the other to collect it, might arouse suspicion—but proved nothing.

Pearson's response to the furniture revelations, which had swept through the gallery like the latest in a season of gales, was to stay calm and do nothing. Then, with the Liberals safely returned after a close election and the issue stone-cold dead, he dropped the two from the Cabinet. That made the column, which I had come to think had been hasty, seem worse. Had it helped produce this unwarranted result? I decided then that when scandal comes through the door, the good sense of reporters tends to go out the window—and I have been wary of too-quick judgements since, to the point of believing that most of our scandals are bunk.

The economic good times did not run uninterrupted through the whole of those first three postwar prime-ministerships; they never do over so long a time as nearly a quarter-century. But none of those governments, in downswings in the economy, or their own worst moments of misjudgement, indecision or pure bad luck, experienced the same public cynicism, or the same prejudice bordering on hatred, as their successors. If the rancour in the country in the early nineties was less accurately attributed to the failings of government than to changed conditions, the media neither made sufficient allowance nor were much inclined to consider what their own part might have been in producing that unhealthful phenomenon. Neither was fair allowance made for the drain on the time and intellectual energy of governments resulting from necessary concentration on the problems inherent in keeping the country together. Rather, there was evident relish in reporting the drama of the national disarray—all of which overlapped with a change in news marketing reflected in the growth of the parliamentary press gallery. Call it the Milwaukee Apples Manifestation, or the Rise of Supermarket Journalism.

When Theodore H. White, one of America's great reporters, was writing the first and best of his *Making of the President* books—one on the Kennedy–Nixon presidential race of 1960—he had in front of him material from the most recent census, which showed a population growth of 28 million since the previous census. What was more exciting than that, White said, was "the changing pattern of growth". In the big cities and in the countryside, population had actually declined. The growth was in the new suburbs. People in suburbs needed cars—for a start, to get to the jobs they had left behind in the cities. With cars, they didn't need the corner store. Mobile shoppers made supermarkets possible.

Twenty years earlier, White said, apple fanciers in Milwaukee had had a choice of thirty varieties—not all in one shop, obviously, but between this shop and that one. Now the commercially available types were down to four. The supermarkets had done that. They liked to deal directly with large producers, from whom they could buy fresh produce in giant lots. They had no room in their bins—or their marketing philosophy—for small quantities of varieties that appealed to only a few.

The first broad-scale marketer of news in Canada was The Canadian Press (CP), founded in 1917 by publishers of daily newspapers as a non-profit co-operative. CBC national radio is another early example, although, up to the Second World War, when it sent its own reporters abroad to cover the fighting, it took most of its news, domestic as well as foreign, from print news services.

More recently, *The Globe and Mail* translated its boast of being Canada's National Newspaper into a same-day reality by printing and delivering the paper from regional plants. The *Globe* had long been influential, but more distantly. It had influenced Ottawa—government and press alike—which influenced the news; now it could influence news readers, nation-wide, directly. Other broad marketers are the Southam and Thomson chains of newspapers, and the news services, of which CP's Broadcast News is only one, that supply broadcasters. But far exceeding all of those in both reach and influence is national television news, primarily CTV and CBC. Recent audience studies say CTV has significantly more viewers for its news, but, from observation, CBC continues to have more weight with journalists, for reasons more nationalist than rationalist. Canadian journalists tend to be nationalists and CBC has had more Canadian content, although never as much more as it has liked to suggest.

Television is the dominating element in Canadian news supermarketing. It offers items carefully selected, like White's four species of apple, to appeal to a common denominator of public taste and interest over the broadest geographical sweep. Also likę the supermarkets, it pays a lot of attention to packaging and presentation. Ask a network executive about such matters and the first answer may be, "Focus groups tell us the viewers prefer our on-camera people"—which is packaging, and has roughly the same relationship to the news as the box has to Krunchie Happy Hour Snax. The biggest difference between network television news and the supermarket may be that TV does home deliveries.

Since they themselves are national in their marketing, the brand of news the supermarkets favour is national, from which it follows that the big apple-grower is Ottawa. It regularly has product ready, in volume, on demand. More important, it has something of the character of a name brand: everyone across the country knows Ottawa, and is touched by it one way or another, most notably in the pocketbook. The same is not true of any provincial capital. A story arising from the government of Manitoba may sell well to a Manitoba audience, but it will need to be consequential to more than just Manitobans to sell in British Columbia or Newfoundland. A Prince Edward Island story needs to be a whopper to make it to the national news because it is so much less cost-effective off the island than almost anything datelined Ottawa. If the wife of the retiring premier of P.E.I. offers some household furnishings for sale to the province, the response of the viewer or reader in Salmon Arm, B.C., will be "So what?" The same story coming from Ottawa will be on the national television news, probably for several nights, and on every radio talk show, and on page one of every daily.

The troubles Premier Bob Rae of Ontario had with his public service unions and the federal NDP in mid-year 1993 were reported country-wide not just because of the province's large built-in audience, but because of probable ramifications elsewhere. What was happening in Ontario permitted conjecture, prime stuff of national political stories, about the effect Rae's departure from NDP economic orthodoxy would have upon the federal New Democrats in the general election that was in sight.

A secondary effect of the concentration on national-brand news has been a homogenization of the news. Once, city newspapers paid close, and even neurotic, attention to what the opposition down the street was doing, but little to what the paper a hundred miles away was up to, because out-of-town began far short of a hundred miles, and out-of-town was nowhere. In town, a story of local consequence in *The Daily World*'s first edition demanded a matcher or a sharp knocking-down in the next edition of *The Daily Universe*. (Even editions have disappeared in most places.) Today, the *World* or the *Universe* has gone under or been absorbed as the hind end of the nameplate, as *The Daily World-Universe*. Therefore, there is no one and nothing within the confines of the town to match or to refute; that bit of diversity has gone. The hole is filled with national news.

The weightier replacement from outside does not threaten the survival of *The Daily World-Universe*—not at least for the time being—but it does to a degree pre-empt the local paper's editorial decision-making. Outside news organizations, like *The Globe and Mail* and network news, do that by bringing their own product directly onto the local turf. If the local paper doesn't cover a local-interest story that the outsider carries, it is made to look remiss.

Even *The Edmonton Journal*, no small local paper, was chagrined to have *The Globe and Mail* bring into town an exposé series on Donald Getty, then Premier of Alberta—not that the *Journal* accepted uncritically all the interloper said, but like the mountain-climber's mountain, it was there. The *Journal* couldn't *not* have the story.

It is not for nothing that The Canadian Press puts out to clients advisories on what others are doing at main points where CP has bureaus. Thus the managing editor at the Regina *Leader-Post* can know what is on page one of the Montreal *Gazette* that morning, and the managing editor at the Halifax *Chronicle-Herald* learns what is big in the *Vancouver Sun*. But the news sources that get the most attention, because they come right into town, are the top few in the rarefied circle called, mainly by the members, the National Media.

The two networks carry great weight as the agenda-setters in other people's newsrooms because they reach just about everybody in every crossroads in the country, and people then expect to see more on the same stories in their local news outlets. CP has the same sort of reach, but one that is less apparent because it occurs within the newsrooms. It would be hard to find any newspaper in the country that did not carry a CP slug somewhere; in some papers, on some days, it is hard to find very much else. On top of that, CP has a status of its own as an institution in news delivery—and the remnants of a reputation, severely eroded recently, of objectivity, and resistance to slants, in its coverage. (CP had a shakeup in its Ottawa bureau in the late eighties when a few reporters developed a taste for anti-governmentalism that did not accord with CP's long-established balance. Signs began to show in the early nineties that the effect had begun to wear off again.) *The Globe and Mail*'s influence exists in the fact that it is right there, palpable, in however few copies, in the corner-box and drugstore counter downtown, where everyone can be counted upon to see it, perhaps buy it—and comment if it carries a big story of direct local interest that the local paper does not have, an oversight the local paper will quickly move to correct.

In all this, the CBC and *The Globe and Mail* hang together like a pair of testicles, the seminal influences, as they like to think of it, in national political journalism in Canada. More than any other two media entities they, singly and more certainly together, are capable of making the Big Story. Every reporter more than six months beyond his or her probationary period knows a Big Story on sight, but no one ever says what the qualities are that characterize it. The prime characteristic is that other media instantly pick the story up, elaborate on it, help make it the subject of angry exchanges in the House of Commons. That is why investigative stories and other candidates for Big Story status nowadays are written with an eye to other media as much as to the reader.

The essential of the Big Story, then, is that it immediately attracts attention. When that clearly has been attained—which television in particular is able to do, by repeating the substance of the original story in subsequent news programming—there is no time left for others to do much more than see if the party most affected by the story has anything to say in rebuttal—not so much to decide whether the story should run or not, but to ensure that a denial will be incorporated if it does.

If the decision is taken that the story cannot be ignored—it has to run—its main facts are then assumed, and the pack is unleashed in full howl.

FOUR

TAINTED TUNA, TAINTED SCANDAL

THE FIRST BIG SCANDAL OF THE MULRONEY REGIME broke on the night of September 17, 1985, with an item on the CBC-TV program "the fifth estate". It began with the words "Good evening. I'm Eric Malling with a story about cans of tuna fish, public confidence and politics. The tuna fish was tainted and unfit for human consumption, according to experts at the Canadian Fisheries Service. Their boss—federal Fisheries minister John Fraser—wasn't convinced."

The story, much condensed, went like this: for a couple of years Fisheries inspectors had been rejecting lot after lot of canned tuna at the plant of Star-Kist, a Heinz subsidiary at Bayside, New Brunswick, just along the shore from fashionable St. Andrews. Now nearly a million cans were said to be in storage, effectively impounded. The company had appealed, questioning the inspectors' criteria, methods and judgement. Richard Hatfield, the Conservative premier of New Brunswick, joined in to make the point that four hundred jobs in a poor corner of the province might be at risk in a disagreement about product quality involving a reputable company. The minister accepted one outside report and then ordered a second, and, having satisfied himself that no risk to health existed, ordered the tuna released to market.

After Malling's introductory reference to the tuna being "unfit for human consumption", the phrase came up six more times in the item, which, in transcript, runs to just over nine uncrowded pages. On the same night's CBC television news, Claude Adams reported in outline what the "the fifth estate" had said just a short time before—that the tuna had been rejected as rancid, "unfit for human consumption". Every day for more than a week, the Tainted Tuna Scandal dominated Question Period in the House of Commons. In nearly every reference, there and in print and on television, the product was said to have been rejected as "unfit for human consumption".

Significantly, the only Fisheries inspector interviewed by Malling on the show—Bruce Jackson, from the department's establishment at Blacks Harbour, New Brunswick—did not use that term. He went no further than to agree with Malling, and then only at some urging, that the tuna was "off". No one from the company—management, fish-cutter, canning-line worker or other—was there to say it was off, on or anything else.

Without hesitation, other media picked up the story. The Canadian Press delivered to its clients a story that said the Fisheries minister had overruled his department's inspectors and allowed distribution of "one million cans of tuna which earlier had been declared unfit for human consumption". Most newspapers take the CP service. The larger of them usually prefer their own stories, if they have them, as a point of pride. In this case it didn't make much difference, as they were all taking their facts from the CBC. Canadian Press and *The Globe and Mail*, among others, were able to have stories ready the next morning because they had been given previews and copies of the CBC transcript to help them prepare their material. *The Globe and Mail* got the obligatory "unfit for human consumption" into one of the few paragraphs in its page-one story. The *Globe*'s reporter, Paul Taylor, asked the Star-Kist general manager, Jerry Clay, if the firm had distributed such tuna and was told "that term was incorrect". The term *was* incorrect, as it turned out—not that Clay's saying so generated any traceable effort by other media to find with what justification he said so.

For the second day after the broadcast, the Montreal *Gazette* produced a patchwork story put together in its own newsroom from various sources, which said Fraser had "cleared the way for Star-Kist . . . to market one million cans of tuna that Fisheries department inspectors had twice declared rancid, decomposing and unfit for human consumption." The most likely (and perhaps the only) inference any half-awake reader could take from the phrase "cleared the way" would be that the Fisheries minister had done the company the favour of letting it market a product known to be bad.

In the west, *The Calgary Herald* said in an editorial that the Fisheries minister was solely to blame and should resign for "allowing almost one million cans of tuna . . . declared unfit for human consumption to be distributed to supermarkets." And on the east coast, the Halifax *Chronicle-Herald*, in a staff story from Ottawa, reported that Fraser "stood firm" in the House of Commons, in the face of cries for his resignation for having overruled his officials and approved "the distribution of one million cans of New Brunswick tuna earlier declared unfit for human consumption".

At the same time it was being said in Parliament, and duly reported, that the minister had "put politics before health in this country", that he had "overruled his own experts in a matter of health". Those examples came from, respectively, John Turner, the leader of the Liberal opposition, and George Henderson, the Liberal critic in Fisheries matters. Ed Broadbent, the New Democratic leader, asked, "Is the prime minister prepared to accept the judgement of the minister [who] was prepared to gamble with the health of Canadians?" Ray Skelly, another New Democrat, demanded passionately to know why "senior citizens in homes for the elderly, people in hospitals and ordinary Canadians should be subjected to this product . . . that, in the minds of many Canadians today, poses a problem for their health and safety."

That insistence on a risk to health and even life was not just in the face of repeated denials by the minister. It was also in the face of what the program itself had said. The message had not been trumpeted to viewers, but faint words of reassurance had appeared in the transcript: "After two hours in [Star-Kist's] pressure cookers, it's safe, nothing poisonous." Despite this affirmation that the tuna was not harmful, even two months later, at a Liberal party conference in Halifax, John Turner was still accusing the government of having trifled with the health of Canadians.

The worst fury in the House of Commons—and the media—had subsided by the end of the first week in October, two weeks after the CBC broke the story. However, that was not the end. The Great Tuna Scandal was still popping up in Question Period a year later, and it had a brief revival at the time of Brian Mulroney's resignation in early 1993.

Within the first week of the scandal, John Fraser had resigned from Cabinet. The same day he resigned, George Henderson, the Liberal Fisheries critic, who had been demanding his resignation, moved smoothly from saying he had done "the honourable thing by resigning" to asking, "is the prime minister attempting to use the Minister of Fisheries as his scapegoat for his own negligence." Goodbye, John; hello, Brian.

Before that ploy was exhausted, insinuations of cover-up had driven the prime minister to the extreme of saying that if any member wished to accuse him of having known earlier about the tuna and done nothing about it, that MP should stake his or her seat on it. The stake-your-seat challenge is the Commons' equivalent of the duel with pistols at twenty paces. There were no takers.

However, a smear had been left—and a name. Since Watergate in Washington, reporters had been attaching the suffix "gate" to anything in which a cover-up was alleged. The tuna affair became, with stunning unoriginality, Tunagate.

Leap ahead now six years. On May 12, 1991, in a lengthy interview with John Emberley, director general of the inspection service of the Department of Fisheries and Oceans, I asked: "What does 'unfit for human consumption' mean in terms of the Department of Fisheries?"

A. "We don't use the term. There is nothing in regulations that talks about 'unfit for human consumption'."

(Here, on the tape, the puzzled sound of an interviewer saying, "Huh?")

Q. "Well, that term was used throughout. . . ."

A. "It was used extensively."

Q. "It was said in flat terms, 'Officials pronounced this product unfit for human consumption. . . .'"

A. "Our terminology is, and continues to be, that it 'fails to meet acceptable minimum standards because of decomposition, taint or unwholesomeness'. . . ."

The difference between "unfit for human consumption" and "unacceptable because of decomposition, taint or unwholesomeness" is superficially slight. Neither is attractive. But the first purports to state a settled fact whereas the second is subject to interpretation. It was the subjective interpretation by the inspectors of those several broad terms that was at the root of the dispute.

Tainted in what respect—colour, taste, odour? Different species of tuna differ in all three. Rancid—meaning what? Butter, coffee, bacon and cooking oil become rancid, rarely harmfully. And decomposed, the most unpleasantly evocative of all? How decomposed, and with what effect? From the moment it is gathered, dug or killed, everything we eat—or drink, if we include milk and wine—is decomposing. Beef is deliberately aged because a period of hanging breaks down the tissue, making the beef more tender and improving the flavour. Blue cheeses are prized for the pungent taste of decomposition. A 1972 bulletin of the Japanese Society of Scientific Fisheries shows Japanese and American tuna specialists discussing decomposition not as a synonym for rotting but as a natural phenomenon in which only the degree matters.

On the other hand, the meaning of "unfit for human consumption" is starkly clear. If after a month of tuna stories an adult Canadian existed who did not believe political hanky-panky had caused every supermarket and corner grocery to be stocked with cans of rotten fish—a term actually used by John Turner in the House of Commons, in "get that rotten fish off the shelves"—that person must have been working an Arctic trapline somewhere in the wilderness. The real scandal of that September was that the scandal itself was more tainted than the fish.

The Tainted Tuna Scandal makes a textbook example of "pack journalism" and "media feeding frenzy", although a better term might be "induced predator psychosis". In current political journalism there is a latent predator tendency, ready to be induced at a level of psychosis at the sight of scandal. At that point, the rules that journalism professes to itself—rumours are only rumours until confirmed; fairness demands that both sides in a dispute be heard; conclusions come after investigation, not before—all those go straight out the window.

Even before "the fifth estate" went to air, stories were already in the works for the next day's newspapers. Virtually no independent research could be done, because there was no time. A day later there would be no need, because, what the hell, if everybody's saying it, it must be true. Follow-up stories sometimes take care that the initiator is given credit—or perhaps fingered in case the story turns out a dud—as in *The Globe and Mail*'s next-morning heading:

MINISTER APPROVED SELLING SUSPECT TUNA
CBC PROGRAM SAYS

However, the risk of the story-bubble bursting is minimized by the fact that (a) the story will have been established firmly within twenty-four hours as a media truth, and (b) since everyone helped push the story along, there is no great impetus to go back to re-examine the facts.

In the tuna affair, parliamentarians as well as media were prepped to respond. While reporters such as Paul Taylor were writing their next-day stories, transcripts of the show were on the way to Ottawa by courier, to the likeliest participants in the next day's Question Period. By the time the reporting on that Question Period was done, the facts were frozen in place. A scandal had been declared, with a posse of villains, including Star-Kist, the Minister of Fisheries, a sinister influence, the Premier of New Brunswick—and of course a corporate hero, the vigilantes of "the fifth estate".

The difference between news on paper and news on television does not begin and end with the fact that in one the consumer receives words with supplementary pictures (and usually not many of those), and in the other, pictures with supplementary words (and no more of those than will fit a tight and inflexible format). Glimmering wetly under studio lights, a can of gloopy-looking unidentifiable something doesn't need many words beyond "unfit for human consumption" to make the viewer's stomach heave.

There are other, less evident differences between print and television, one of which is a difference of overall purpose. Television is an entertainment medium with an information appendage; print is an information medium with an entertainment appendage. True to the medium's entertainment heritage, television news is performed with much more of an eye to dramatic values.

The other half of informational television, called "public affairs", is even more theatrical. The real news reports of world-wide happenings, as supplied to news addicts in all media, are an everyday thing. Most public affairs programs are *made* news—longer and more story-like stories, conceived, researched, written and performed by special-purpose units—and they usually run in seasons, like cop shows and sitcoms. "the fifth estate", no disparagement intended, is one of those.

At the time it received the tip that John Fraser had released a large quantity of tuna his inspectors had condemned, the program was three weeks from the opening of a new season, its eleventh. No one in a seasonal program can be unaware that, if the ratings go down, so, between seasons, may the program, right off the listings. That knowledge contributes to a keen awareness of the value of being talked about—in the case of any news-related show, being talked about as "controversial", "challenging", "hard-hitting", all macho terms that look good in press releases and better in the television critics' reviews. For an investigative show to be tipped to a story certain to be leapt upon by other media and to set off a row in Parliament makes a great start to a new season, the very point in the year when the critics are most grovellingly susceptible.

"the fifth estate"'s executive producer, Ron Haggart, says they became aware only as they went along that the opposition, CTV, had also received a tuna tip. However, CTV had yielded to an understandable caution. Not long before that, the network had been hit with the largest award of damages for defamation levied to that time against a Canadian media company. Consequently, instead of plunging ahead, CTV opted to try for backup material from Fisheries department files, via Access to Information.

The snag CTV ran into was that when information from government files relates to some outside party, that party must assent to its release. If it does not, a court is left to decide where the line runs between individual privacy and the public interest. On August 13, 1985, Star-Kist filed notice of motion in the Federal Court of Canada against the release. The company was following a least-said-soonest-mended line—a mistake, as it turned out, and not just for the company itself.

The chance victim of the snag was the Fisheries minister. Had he been able to table documents in the Commons as he was willing to do, his defence of his actions would have been easier and stronger. On top of that, whatever story was made of the issue on television—with two networks sniffing around, he could be sure one was coming—it would have to take into account additional information that would contribute to a clearer understanding of the process he had followed. (Star-Kist discontinued its motion on October 4, 1985. By then, Fraser had resigned, though the row in the Commons went on. No one noticed that files with important additional information were now accessible. No one cared.)

By the time his enquiries were suspended by head office, Robert Hurst, then in CTV's Ottawa bureau, had already interviewed the minister on camera. Fraser had agreed to the interview readily enough, as he did again when "the fifth estate" came along; he believed then, and subsequently, that he had nothing to hide. He knew what the inspectors had said. He knew they had reaffirmed their judgement on reinspection. He knew the company had complained of what it considered unreasonable severity in the application of wholly subjective analysis. He accepted the right of a company to appeal to the minister to adjudicate if it felt it had been unfairly dealt with. He was also conscious of the fact that, in a system of responsible government, he, not the bureaucrats, was ultimately responsible for whatever the department did or did not do. He had secured expert outside advice which had assured him that there was no risk to health. He was inclined to believe that, so long as the product was safe, quality was something the market could judge—and undoubtedly would, by buying or not buying. Also, he was aware that the St. Andrews plant processed about 40 per cent of all the canned tuna sold in Canada, which did not suggest a poor-quality product.

Taking those various considerations into account, he found it difficult to think what he could say to anyone, himself included, if the plant shut down and three or four hundred jobs disappeared.

The transcript of the CTV interview with Fraser reveals a work in progress. The CBC transcript is the finished product. Whether or not because of that, there is a marked difference in style. Hurst was more the conventional interviewer, looking for answers. His first feeling-out question—the questions became more hard-edged as the interview went on—was "I have talked with both sides in the dispute and I . . . really don't understand what lies behind the dispute. Can you fill me in?" Malling, not by nature lacking in self-assurance, came to the subject in the manner of a prosecutor with the facts of the case already in hand, needing only to be put to the jury. In a script of 276 lines, Fraser, as the accused, got a total of 52, including "That's right," and "I can't." Malling and two witnesses for the prosecution got the rest.

In an interview a couple of weeks after the show ran, Ron Haggart recalled how the story had begun for "the fifth estate". "It was obviously a tip," he said. "I am not going to say what it was, but obviously it was a phone call, or a brown envelope, or it was some information." (A "brown envelope" is shorthand for a leaked document received anonymously.) "We started to research . . . through the normal sources—the Department itself, the office of the minister, the Star-Kist plant, the Department of Fisheries lab. . . ."

It was only after the interview with Fraser, on the Thursday before the Tuesday show-date, that they decided they had a usable story. Even then there were loose ends, some new from the interview itself. A standby show was available, but the tuna scandal was much preferable as a season opener; the standby was on Gander airport, where asylum-seekers from Eastern Europe had been defecting in droves.

The telephone research was still being done on the Monday before the story was to run. As Haggart told it, the interview confirmed what "the fifth estate"'s researchers had found already—for example, that the minister had given the company the benefit of the doubt. (He had already said that to Hurst, and said it again later in the House; it was not a confession dragged from a shamefaced minister.) One of the new loose ends related to Fraser's own independent review committee of four food experts, which, in Haggart's words, "said that the fish could be sold anywhere in the world . . . but not in Canada. . . ."

Haggart went on: "Well, as so often happens, while the words of the minister were technically correct, they did not in our view mean exactly what he implied they meant. So we had to find 'those people'. . . ." What in particular made it necessary to find "those people"—the members of Fraser's committee—was the following passage from Malling's interview with Fraser.

> Fraser: "Well, what do you want me to do . . . seriously take the position that if it's good enough for Americans, or Englishmen, or Dutchmen, or Africans to eat, it's not good enough for Canadians to eat?"
> Malling: "Or decide it's not good enough for anyone to eat."
> Fraser: "Well, that's not what the panel said. The panel said it is good enough for most of the people of the world to eat. If twenty-five million Canadians ought not to have it sold to them . . . and it never went so far as to say that it *shouldn't* be sold to Canadians . . . it said we would recommend it be sold outside Canada."
> Malling [here addressing the viewers]: "Well, that's not quite what Fraser's committee members had in mind. If Star-Kist could get the fish past foreign inspectors and sell it somewhere else, go ahead and try, but only with the cautionary label to show it was not approved in Canada."

If that is what the independent review committee had in mind, it forgot to put the latter bit in either its executive summary of recommendations, or the elaboration of its reasons that followed. There was no mention of a label to say the product was not approved in Canada. Certainly a reference to the export being "subject to the importing country's government approval" was there, but not an explanation of what it was supposed to mean, given that every country has a right to rule on what food products it will admit, and most countries exercise it. Canada, for example, inspects, among other products, imported tuna.

First among the highlights of "the fifth estate"'s indictment, all of which were greedily taken up in the ensuing feeding frenzy, was the point that the minister had overruled his trained inspectors—Malling equated them with experienced wine tasters—and ignored the advice of his own review panel. According to Malling, Fraser had four different reports in his hands, in which "two levels of experts in his own department, plus his own blue-ribbon review committee . . . said 'unfit for human consumption'. But the agency hired by New Brunswick (the province's Research and Productivity Council) went the other way, saying most of the fish was OK. And what did John Fraser do? . . . John Fraser exercised his power and Richard Hatfield was among the first to know."

(In other words, by implication, the Conservative Minister of Fisheries was doing a favour for the Conservative Premier of New Brunswick.)

That passage had a high rubbish content. First, there were not two levels of inspectors. Certainly some of the tuna had undergone two *inspections*—that was the practice when first assessments were questioned—but most often the reinspection was done by the same person who had done the first one. Of that practice, the review panel cited by Malling said, wordily but with understatement, "Using the original inspector on a reinspection . . . introduces a possible bias. . . . His/ her prior knowledge that the lot has already been rejected, most likely by him or her, leads to a stricter interpretation of the standard to ensure that the original decision is upheld."

The review committee had *not* said the product was unfit for human consumption; it could not very well do so, having recommended clearing it for export, which would mean to humans. The closest the committee came to saying the tuna was unfit for human consumption was when it reported a sampling by its own members. Three cans—*three*—were picked at random from each of seven lots, any of which may have run to thousands of cans. Some of those lots the previous fisheries inspection had rejected, some it had approved. The report said, "Despite the limited number of cans sampled, the committee evaluation was consistent with that of the departmental inspectors." Three cans from seven lots—twenty-one cans from among perhaps ten thousand, some previously rejected, some approved—could not be called definitive of anything.

A second heavy piece of evidence produced by "the fifth estate" and snapped up by the quick-following pack was introduced in the context of the early build-up of "detained" tuna, the gentler term sometimes substituted for "rejected".

"So there it was," Malling told the viewers, "four hundred jobs at stake and Star-Kist president Albert Cropley complaining that his warehouse bulged with more than half a million dollars' worth of rejected tuna. Some went into cat food, but the bulk of it was offered to Ethiopia." Then: "Canada's famine relief co-ordinator, David MacDonald, turned it down, telling Star-Kist, 'It is wrong to offer others food that we have condemned as unfit for human consumption. . . .' " When the narrative reached the point of Fraser's decision to release the tuna generally, Malling announced: "So the trucks moved out. Six to eight hundred thousand dollars' worth of tuna, about a million cans that had been declared unfit for Ethiopia because of taint and decomposition, were on their way to stores in Canada."

When I talked with him in 1993, MacDonald, who after his time as food co-ordinator became ambassador to Ethiopia, remembered many offers of food, not all of which were accepted. For instance, New Brunswick potatoes were refused for two reasons—because of doubt that they would survive the voyage, and because they were not a food familiar to people in that part of Africa. He could not be sure the questioned quality of the tuna was the whole explanation, or the right one, for it being refused. Various canned goods were being turned down for various reasons: canned goods contain a large proportion of water and consequently are heavy for air shipment; they are bulky because round tins in square boxes leave a lot of waste space; they are difficult to make use of because the intended recipients often have neither can-openers nor containers into which to apportion the contents.

A third item in "the fifth estate"'s bill of particulars was introduced when the minister told Malling he had met some of the inspectors after deciding to release the tuna, and had told them there was nothing to be upset about in his having sought outside advice. He advised them to "go back and keep up the good work". Malling's response was to say, "Some of the big customers *rely* on that good work. For soldiers, lobster is a real treat, but they go through a lot of tuna. The Defence department bought $100,000 of it from Star-Kist, the cooks opened it and ordered the cans out of the kitchen. They reported a strong smell, tuna oozing out of the cans, fish that was not recognizable as tuna. It was quarantined and sent to the Fisheries department, which declared it unfit for human consumption."

If "quarantined", which sounds both ominous and significant, meant anything more than the cooks putting the remaining cans back in the carton to await someone's deciding what was to be done with them, it was not explained. Neither was any bacteria identified that would cause tuna to ooze from the can, considering that the high-heat cooking of the fish in the can would have rendered it sterile.

Two other points were missed in the excitement of the chase. First, the Department of Supply and Services, which buys for the government, had a standing directive in effect which said: "Each shipment [of fisheries products] shall be accompanied by an appropriate Department of Fisheries and Oceans inspection report form, or, alternatively, a certificate from the contractor [the shipper] that the shipment is *from stock originally inspected* by [the department]. These inspection reports must indicate that the goods supplied are to the grade specified. . . ." In other words, the product had to have been positively certified as inspected and *approved.*

Consequently, if the supposedly oozing, unrecognizable tuna was "off", the fault lay with the inspection service, not the minister.

Secondly, a Defence department document confirms, as stated in the show, that the tuna was sent back for reinspection. However, what it also shows is that the date was April 16, or one day short of two weeks before Fraser's order. Therefore, the tuna the military complained about couldn't have come from the impounded stock. Also, the reinspection that followed the rejection by the military was not quite as reported. Cans from that shipment were examined not just by the Fisheries department but by the Department of Health and Welfare, each using its own methods, and with quite different results. At Health and Welfare

Canada, where a case of the alleged-to-be-unrecognizable tuna was put to scientific examination as well as organoleptic (sight, taste and smell) examination, the scientific evaluator reported: "We have examined a carton and have found the appearance is normal, the odour is normal, and the microscopic examination is normal." The brief report also said that the microbiological content presented no risk to human health.

The report of the other reinspection, by a section of the Fisheries department concerned with "facilities and process inspection", said: "The three cans supplied . . . have been evaluated and have been found unfit for human consumption. Please note that we are not saying the lot is unacceptable as we have only evaluated three cans. . . . However, the fact that your ultimate clients [the cooks] have complained about the taste . . . should be enough basis for you, as a buyer, to deal directly with your supplier to tell him that the product is not acceptable."

It is odd that "the fifth estate"'s source passed on only the first few lines of the Fisheries department's equivocal report and nothing of Health and Welfare's more authoritative—and positive—one, unless it was with malicious intent. The unmentioned latter part of the report indicated a distinctly loose interpretation of the term "unfit for human consumption", in equating having a displeasing taste with being, by official designation, not to be eaten, which implies a danger. There are various species of tuna, ranging in colour from white to brown, with correspondingly stronger tastes; Canadians are less familiar with the darkest and strongest species, which is highly regarded in the sophisticated tuna market of Japan. The Canadian inspectors seem to have been among those unfamiliar with it; subsequent examination of their test scores showed a greater tendency to reject the darker, stronger-tasting variety.

A fourth important point in "the fifth estate" 's indictment, and the reinforcing indictments of the media pack, related to Fraser using the Research and Productivity Council of New Brunswick for a second opinion about what was to be done with the mountain of impounded tuna. "RPC," said Malling, "was hired to be impartial, but. . . ." His prime "but" was that the RPC was a creature of the province, of which the premier, Richard Hatfield—like the Fisheries minister—was a Tory. . . .

The RPC tested batches of the impounded tuna at random, as the

Fisheries inspectors had done. It also visited a Star-Kist plant in Costa Rica to make comparisons, and talked with management at Star-Kist, and with inspectors, to hear their different opinions about inspecting. But it also set up a non-expert consumer tasting panel composed of thirty employees in its offices and laboratories. They were given undifferentiated samples from batches the Fisheries inspectors had accepted and rejected, and asked to grade them on a scale running from 7 ("like extremely") down to 1 ("dislike extremely"). The scores—a mean of 5.3 versus a mean of 4.9—showed a slight preference for the rejected tuna.

But even the dispute, a problem for a Solomon, was not all that was wrong at St. Andrews. There was a bad feeling between militant and less militant workers within the plant. In the summer of 1985, that came to a head in two wildcat strikes over matters as trivial as whether the company was within its rights to hire several non-union outsiders to repair some stonework at a corner of the building, and over the quality of paper towels in the washroom—bleached white or unbleached beige.

Workers who did not join the walkout received threatening phone calls, windows in homes were broken, pets were attacked and eggs were thrown at persons entering and leaving the plant. Hubert McFee, the plant's procurement manager, was proud of a new car he had just bought. On the first day of the June strike, he was about to drive the few kilometres home to St. Andrews for lunch, as he usually did, "when some idiot who couldn't sing 'Solidarity Forever' without it in front of him yells out, 'No lunch today, Mr. McFee.' So I sat there for a couple of minutes and this rock came out of the background, bounced off my hood and hit the windscreen. . . ."

One product of the strikes was an application by the less militant workers to the Industrial Relations Board in Fredericton for the decertification of the union; it did not succeed. But the hearings, which occurred while the row in Ottawa was still warm, provided an opportunity for reporters to hear lurid stories about bad fish from the militants—"The workers knew the fish was off," "We know bad fish was canned, . . ." "the women all complained about [bad fish]. It was mush. Some of it was green." Other workers, who resented those stories as both false and reflecting on them, were not similarly interviewed.

A remarkable illustration of what happens to media standards when a feeding frenzy is on is to be found in a story, from which others followed, played by *The Globe and Mail* under a three-column heading on page one:

TUNA CANS SWITCHED BEFORE TESTS
FORMER STAR-KIST TECHNICIAN SAYS

The story said plant workers were sometimes told to substitute good samples for ones the inspectors had said no to. As the testing was all done by random sampling, if the inspectors somehow could be tricked into tasting substituted good samples on a second try, they would pass the large batch from which they supposedly came. The company was also said to have failed to test for high levels of mercury. These allegations were ascribed to Michael Dugas, "senior lab technician in the plant between January, 1982, and July, 1984".

The same day, Dugas, now described as a "quality control officer", was referred to in the Commons in connection with the *Globe*'s story, by the NDP Fisheries critic, Ray Skelly. Would the prime minister undertake to launch an investigation into these serious new allegations?

According to his boss at Star-Kist, Reg Sharkey, Michael Dugas—later known as Michael Dugas Georgeson—was something less than a quality control officer or a senior lab technician; he was on the quality control staff, but "he didn't have anything like a big job; they had three or four [people] on days and one or two on nights, and they were under the supervisor who was myself," Sharkey told me. This quality control staff had such chores as to check the fish for salt content, check the records of the retort in which the filled cans were cooked, check the cans for weight as they came off the line, and check for general cleanliness.

Q: "Relatively routine jobs?"

A. "Exactly."

Before Star-Kist, Dugas had worked for about a year at the Marathon Inn on Grand Manan Island, New Brunswick, where he was not remembered fondly, and for a shorter time at the Shiretown Inn in St. Andrews. After Star-Kist, he worked briefly at the nearby Wandlyn Inn in St. Stephen. When the president of Star-Kist Canada, Al Cropley, flatly denied Dugas's charges and said the company had never misled Fisheries inspectors—as, for instance, by switching cans—the newspaper replied editorially: "We would like to believe so, but the disputed statements cry out for an independent investigation. . . ." Yet nowhere did the *Globe* indicate what, if anything, it had done to corroborate its informant's allegations or to enquire into his credentials.

On the other hand, earlier at the CBC, Robin Christmas, a producer for the since-defunct "Journal", had interviewed Dugas face to face, off camera, and had been unimpressed. "A lot of what he said," Christmas related, "appeared to be just his opinion, substantiated by nothing." He also said Dugas had "a bunch of documents but what they meant was hard to see." When eventually I found Dugas by phone, he told me, as evidently he had not told the *Globe*, that he had detected cancerous tissue in fish at the plant. I asked Christmas if he had been told the same. He said he was not sure, "but it was the kind of thing he would say."

It remained for a study by experts, long after the excitement had passed, to put the whole issue in a saner light. Erik Nielsen had come and gone as temporary minister following Fraser. The plant was still shut down as a result of the post-scandal slump when Thomas Siddon was appointed minister. He soon set up a panel formally called the Tuna Standards and Inspection Committee. Its members were three food experts—Dr. A.B. Morrison, chairman of the Department of Food Science at the University of Guelph, Ontario; Professor Dr. R. Gravani, Department of Food Science, Cornell University, Ithaca, New York; and Dr. A. Anzengruber, associate director, Food Production and Inspection Branch, in the federal Department of Agriculture.

Among its terms of reference the committee was asked to consider and report on chemical diagnostic methods to evaluate quality by spectographic analysis of liquid and vapour. The committee said that sensory testing would continue to be important for the foreseeable future but that Canada "should move as quickly as possible to the use of objective chemical indices of quality", at least as an adjunct. That is what Star-Kist had been arguing from the beginning—that total reliance on sensory testing was too subjective, hence variable.

The report as a whole was of exemplary even-handedness. For example, "We were impressed with the professionalism, dedication and integrity exhibited by officers of the Fish Inspection Branch . . ." but also "Star-Kist is a company dedicated to the production and sale of good quality products world-wide. It is not company policy to produce shoddy, second-rate goods." Faults were also found on both sides: that

"Star-Kist did not always operate under conditions of good manufacturing practice," and, on the other side, that selecting a few samples at random from much larger batches selected at random was too loose an inspection method.

(An anomaly in the tuna exposé was that it focused entirely on the minister allowing fish to be marketed which had failed to satisfy the inspectors' standards, when the largest part of the total output regularly went to market in huge lots from which not even random samples had been taken.)

The report produced by the Tuna Standards and Inspection Committee was primarily directed at informing the Department of Fisheries and Oceans and the fish-packing industry, but it served little purpose to a tuna-packing industry that ceased to exist in Canada when Star-Kist shut down for good. Three important points in the report related to consumer concerns the media coverage had played upon heavily in the scandal:

"There is no evidence the product was unsafe for human consumption. The issue is *not* [italics original] one of safety; it is one of quality." That was very much what John Fraser had said—and been pilloried for saying—in both the House of Commons and the media.

"Providing they do not represent a hazard to health, foods of reduced quality may still provide valuable nutrients and be useful components of diet, particularly for persons who cannot afford top-quality products."

"It must be pointed out that Canadian inspectors would reject skipjack [a species of tuna] . . . as 'rancid' and 'decomposed' which Japanese inspectors strongly insist is neither." Skipjack is not an inferior variety, but one that is darker in colour and stronger in taste and smell. A parallel evaluation by Japanese and Canadian inspectors of eighteen samples showed that they differed on eight—of which the Canadians rejected seven and the Japanese one. What the Japanese liked and the Canadians would reject, or call "unfit for human consumption", were all but one skipjack.

What, then, was the scandal? If scandal means, as the dictionary says, a "disgraceful or discreditable action; an offence caused by a fault or misdeed", there was no scandal. In 1993, the day after he retired from the Department of Agriculture and a career spent mainly in food inspection (although not fish), I talked with Dr. Anzengruber, the only public servant on the Morrison committee. He said of John Fraser, "He made the right decision; the decision to release [the impounded tuna] was not wrong." He made it clear that he was not judging the minister's reasons, which perhaps had included a political component, but simply saying the decision was not wrong.

An intriguing question remains: did the tip to the tuna story just leak out, as often happens when enough people are privy to a toothsome piece of information, or was it planted to get the minister? That it was received by first one of the country's two main television networks and then, when it failed to take root, by the other, suggests greater determination than a random leaker might have.

Strained relations between the minister and his inspectors were not the only unusual things going on in the department at the time. For example, papers were lifted from the minister's correspondence files. Arthur May, then deputy minister, later president of Memorial University in St. John's, Newfoundland, recognized in one of two packages of papers that turned up a memorandum he himself had written to the minister. His reaction was to say to himself, as he recalled much later, "Good God, somebody in the minister's office did this to him."

A telex stamped at the recipient end "Cabinet du Ministre/Office of the Minister" and "Section de la Correspondance de Ministre" became the identifiable basis of a question in the Commons about whether the minister had released the disputed tuna before the New Brunswick Research and Productivity Council had completed its testing.

One person in a position to have firsthand knowledge told me that the tip about the minister overriding his inspectors had come from within the Fisheries inspection service. That remains unproved, but it's worth noting that the inspectors are members of the environment branch of the Public Service Alliance of Canada, and that one of their concerns was the minister's perhaps buying Star-Kist's argument that inspection should not rely solely on sensory methods, but on chemical testing as well, which likely would mean fewer jobs. That was what Fraser's attempt to reassure them had been about when he made his decision.

The disgruntled union members referred to in Chapter Two, who leaked a story about meat imports contaminated with dirt and hair being admitted against their judgement, were identified in *The Globe and Mail* as belonging to the agriculture division of the Public Service Alliance of Canada . . . fighting reductions in the number of inspections. They too were concerned about jobs.

The first of the consequences of the Tainted Tuna Scandal was the loss of John Fraser to the Cabinet. Brian Mulroney's defence of his minister had been tentative and timid. Ironically, that rebounded when the attackers turned to groundless charges of an attempted cover-up in Mulroney's own office, which undoubtedly contributed to the making of the term Lyin' Brian, the worst epithet applied to a Canadian prime minister ever. Eric Malling, a good investigative reporter, won a Gemini Award for documentary reporting for a story that was a long way from his best effort, and one about which he later seemed defensive. The Star-Kist workers at St. Andrews lost their jobs—although they probably would have done so sooner or later, anyway.

The Tainted Tuna Scandal was a great story *as* a story, but by the time it died down the public had lost a substantial measure of confidence in the government, a real enough effect. A similar, or greater, loss of public confidence could have occurred to the media but for the fact that it is the prime characteristic of pack journalism that it gives the public only one set of conclusions to consider—its own. This was a scandal that wasn't.

FIVE

NEGATIVELY WE ROLL ALONG

THE TIP "THE FIFTH ESTATE" RESPONDED TO IN THE Tainted Tuna Scandal was one no newsroom could ignore. It was an alert to something of genuine public interest—a food product, widely sold across the country, that the tipster said or implied should not be on the market. The fault to be found was not in the motive, but in CBC's too-ready acceptance of what the tip said or implied, and the determinedly eyes-closed followership of the rest of the media. No "other side" was ever seriously looked into, even to consider whether the tipster was innocently performing a good deed, or indulging in a sophisticated form of revenge.

Two questions that are still occasionally asked of journalists, although perhaps only by older and less cynical readers are, first, whether bias, personal, corporate or other, enters into our political reporting—to which the only conceivable answer is "Of course, did something lead you to think otherwise?"—and "They couldn't print (or broadcast) that if it weren't true, could they?" The latter, which unthinkingly embraces the proposition that anything published must have met some sort of advance test, would make the very reverse of what is implied by freedom of the press.

Among the biases that are always present is the universal media bias in favour of getting the Good Story, as against not getting it or playing it down. Then there is the bias (which is not confined to journalists) in favour of bad news over good; good is boring. Consider this: there are two old friends and neighbours, one of whom has moved 150 miles away. The other calls to say, "Remember the big old Smith house that we used to say was haunted when we were kids? Well, it burned down last night." If the story instead was that the old house had been sold for the umpteenth time, the latest owner having just finished seeing it expensively restored, and that it looked great—that could wait to go in a note with the next Christmas card. Bad news is urgent; good news can wait.

In political reporting there is also a settled anti-governmentalism which might be expressed—if a reporter's feet were held to the fire—as "Why are we here if it isn't to say what government is doing wrong? If government does something right, it is just doing its duty. If it wants praise, the prime minister can make a speech saying how great it is, which we either will not cover because no one wants to read that kind of crap, or will criticize as self-praise."

This inbred anti-governmentalism, like the media-as-adversary doctrine of the past thirty to thirty-five years which it resembles, is applied at different intensities to different governments. The adversary role is in turn related to personal, or group, partisan bias. While the doctrine of the media as adversary has not been disavowed in any discernible way recently, the treatment of the Chrétien government early in its first mandate has been much more benign than that given its predecessor throughout. It remains to be seen whether that will last.

Finally—for the moment—there is the media-pro-media (the don't-tell-no-lies-about-us-and-we-won't-tell-the truth-about-you) bias, which means in practice that one medium never, or almost never, publicly attacks another for its misdeeds or foolishness. But if the media are influential in shaping public thinking—which is the premise here—ought they not to keep watch on one another's performance, as they do with the government? Government, it is said, is at the consent of the governed, which may become more or less difficult to obtain depending on what the governed hear and read. Therefore, ought not the informants to argue a little, denounce each other's mistakes, point out fallacies and distortions and demonstrably insupportable conclusions? It would be at least enlivening, and perhaps might help stimulate thinking more than the strings of unilateral declarations on little-read editorial pages.

One way and another, all those biases were present in the affair of the tainted tuna—the determination in the pursuit of the Good Story at the cost of journalism's professed benign skepticism, which is supposed to act as a self-levelling influence; the ingrained anti-governmentalism, with more than a touch of anti-Toryism for seasoning; and the media-pro-media bias which is part of pack journalism and feeding frenzies. It can't be said that the original tip was trivial or constituted insufficient motivation. What the finished product nevertheless proclaimed was that, in journalism, the story follows the predilection. Bias does not always need to be invoked, although it often is. The rest of the time, it simply *is*, by nature.

What follow are three illustrations—call them Vignettes on the Theme of Bias—of prior influences at work in the reporting of quite unsensational stories on quite different happenings.

In mid-November 1990, before the Citizens' Forum on Canada's Future really began its work—its twelve members had been appointed only days earlier—Keith Spicer, the chairman, took a trip into the western Arctic. He talked with small groups of people in Inuvik and Tuktoyaktuk, trying out what he hoped the Forum would be able to do across the country—namely, get at what Canadians were thinking and, moreover, feeling, about their country. Robert Matas, a reporter for *The Globe and Mail*, was along, and wrote about an interview with Spicer in an airplane somewhere over the tundra of the Northwest Territories. Spicer, he said, had "elaborated on his views about the Canadian spirit" and called it "rudderless". Spicer, Matas went on, also "cautioned that the Citizens' Forum was not for cynics."

If that story and another by the same reporter a day earlier were not intended more to reinforce the cynicism of cynics than to convert them to generous open-mindedness—the *Globe*'s editors were inspired to head the story "Spicer seeks unity in poetry / 'We will re-centre the soul of Canada' "—the result was an effortless triumph. Rudderless the Canadian spirit might be, but Spicer, condescendingly described by Matas as dashing "from meeting to meeting, leaving behind a trail of metaphors and old-fashioned romanticism about the rugged life of the Far North", was scarcely depicted as a likely person to send looking for it, or anything else.

The day before, Matas had reported that, after listening to the views of plain folk over a weekend, Spicer had returned at once to "the regular crowd of Ottawa experts for advice on the mood of the nation", words richly suggestive of sham—a quick trip to the boondocks for show, a quick trip back to the Establishment to know. Certainly that remark was not designed to ward off cynicism.

Matas also said that Spicer, motivated by criticism of "his ties to the Conservative party", had sworn that he and other members of the Forum would stay clear of politics and politicians. What that was intended to imply, it would be hard to say. If Spicer had Conservative ties, I for one had missed them. True, Brian Mulroney had appointed him chairman of the Canadian Radio-television and Telecommunications Commission, from which he was on leave to conduct the Forum, if that could be said to constitute a "tie". But Spicer had come to prominence first as Canada's Commissioner of Official Languages, appointed by Pierre Trudeau, whose interest in official languages was infinitely more passionate than Brian Mulroney's in the CRTC. Again, the remark was hardly a boost—or whatever one does for the condition of being without a rudder—for the rudderless Canadian spirit.

That reporting by Matas fairly reflects how things started out for the Forum, which is to say, with a wary and even dismissive press. But, as is widely known (especially among reporters), if there is one thing reporters are not, it is closed-minded. Still, Spicer's idea of the Citizens' Forum remained elusive—that it was not intended to be simply another royal commission of three or four men and women receiving leaden briefs, leadenly delivered, by representatives of pressure groups in high school auditoriums. Not all participants, or even reporters, ever did manage to grasp the difference. And when some intending brief-readers turned up, dissertations in hand, and were told, "No; no briefs. We want you to sit down and, with other people in small groups, address yourselves to questions about your country and its future," there began to be complaints. Some sort of fix was said to be in; only agreeable views were wanted—although agreeable to whom, and for what, was not said. There were complaints as well that the whole exercise was no more than a grotesquely expensive public opinion poll.

That ignored Spicer's proposition that the Forum, an admitted experiment, might get people to open up, as no poll tries to do—to speak their minds, argue with one another. It was to try to find out not just how Canadians felt about their country—not in the yes-no-undecided way of the polls—but why, and against what background, and with what hopes. Gradually, led by a few more thoughtful and open-minded observers—such as Michael Valpy of *The Globe and Mail*, Roy MacGregor of the Ottawa *Citizen* and Bill Cameron of the

CBC's late "The Journal"—the reporting became less querulous and more constructive. But not all of it, not by a long shot.

On June 27, 1991, the Forum produced its findings in 168 pages of text. Keith Spicer wrote a personal foreword. In eight months, by the calculations of the staff, the Forum had heard from 300,000 Canadians, directly in discussion groups, by letter or by telephone over the free lines provided. The morning after the report came out, the Halifax *Chronicle-Herald*'s lead story, from the Ottawa bureau of the Canadian Press, ran stripped in one column down the left-hand side of page one. It brought the morning's readers their first printed words on the results of the great experiment, under this heading:

SPICER REPORT HAS "NO GUTS"

For those last two words, the heading writer had dug down to paragraph eight. They proved to represent the qualified opinion of one of the twelve conductors of the Forum. The story as a whole was negative enough, but not that negative. It said, along with much else, that the Forum "found people cynical and angry over the country's politics and politicians", which was scarcely news. However, if there was not enough in the front-page story to lead the reader to a thumbs-down conclusion, there was more inside. On page three, the main story, under a four-column heading—"Ordinary citizen unimpressed by report"—was about an ordinary citizen who was unimpressed. A third story, just below, was headed:

COMMISSION'S WORK BLASTED
FROM WITHIN

The dissenter again.

The top right-hand corner of the page contained a box headed, "Spicer report quotes". It contained seven quotes, five of them distinctly negative and two of a more philosophical nature, which could be described, according to taste, as neutral, meaningless or both.

So much for Vignette One. Small things, sure enough—but then, so are blackflies, and stories abound of hunters lost in the bush and driven nearly mad by clouds of them. The Spicer Forum was cynically treated in some reporting as a show staged by a government anxious to display an (insincere) desire for public opinion before a new round of constitutional negotiations. These were the same media which, in the the first round, repeatedly criticized the same government for having been insufficiently concerned to bring the public into consideration of the Meech Lake effort. Thus, heads, you lose; tails, you lose.

The Matas stories and others before, and the cool response after, as exemplified by the Halifax paper, could only be characterized as manifestations of genetic media negativity.

On to the second example of media predisposition to the negative. Ottawa's Parliament Hill is not much, as hills go—hardly a slope at all, up to the point where the visitor making for the main doors of the Parliament Buildings must climb a flight of concrete steps to a terrace under the Peace Tower. This forecourt attracts demonstrators because it puts them close enough to be seen and heard by the politicians coming and going, and, even more important, by the television cameras without which any protest is an artistic and strategic failure. It was there, in the early 1970s, that Pierre Trudeau delivered his pungent answer to a bunch of strikers shouting insults at him—"*Mangez de la merde*." In the late 1980s, Glen Kealey, an Ottawa-area small businessman with a very large beef against the government, took up station there as a one-man protest movement, with a message for the Mulroney government that was similar in feeling to Trudeau's for the strikers, but not so succinctly expressed.

Kealey was there for part of most days for three years. The greatest concentration of news bureaus in Ottawa, electronic and print, is in the National Press Building on Wellington Street, just across the street from the West Block of the Parliament Buildings and perhaps three hundred metres from the main doors of the Centre Block. Close or not, parliamentary reporters no longer flock to The Hill as a matter of course, but there is enough traffic to ensure that a protester of Kealey's persistence and volume won't be overlooked. To make that surer, he would occasionally go to the reporters in their offices, to keep them up to date. In Kealey's account, it all began with an attempt by Roch La Salle, an early Public Works minister in the Mulroney government, to extract money from him as the price of getting a government contract. From that, his complaints broadened to embrace other Cabinet ministers and Conservative party functionaries, and eventually the commissioner, the deputy commissioner and a previous deputy commissioner of the RCMP—sixteen men in all.

The alleged sin of the police was to have investigated numbers of politicians and laid no charges. That, to Kealey, smacked of corruption. But if any of his press friends ever undertook to follow up his allegations with investigations of their own, à la *The Washington Post*'s Woodward and Bernstein of Watergate fame, either they were defeated by the complexity of what they encountered, or they came up empty because there was nothing there.

Mostly, Kealey was quietly dismissed as a guy with a bee in his bonnet whose sense of grievance far outran the sum of his facts. Whether that impression actually changed, or was simply made to *appear* to have changed, Kealey was transformed overnight, in mid-July 1991, into a bona fide, fully certified, to-be-taken-seriously anti-corruption crusader. That occurred when an Ontario justice of the peace, Lynn Coulter, decided that Kealey could in effect become the prosecutor—a role ordinarily reserved for the Crown. In just the two days following the report of the justice of the peace, a sampling of six large daily newspapers—*The Vancouver Sun*, *The Calgary Herald*, *The Winnipeg Free Press*, *The Toronto Star*, *The Globe and Mail* and *The* Halifax *Chronicle-Herald*—produced thirty-two stories directly on Kealey and his now much-elevated charges. One story suggested a connection between this scandal everyone had discounted for three years and a sudden drop in the value of the Canadian dollar.

Just eight weeks later, the director of criminal prosecutions for the Ontario attorney-general's office threw out the charges against all of the sixteen except Roch La Salle, whose case was left for further consideration. With the report of the director of prosecutions went a tart comment about failure to differentiate between firm evidence and opinion, unsubstantiated suspicion and theories. At the expiration of the one-year statutory limit within which the decision had to be taken to prosecute or not to prosecute La Salle, the attorney-general's office let that one drop, too.

As this was at a time of intense distrust in the country, it may be justifiable to underline the obvious—that the decisions that caused this supposed scandal to fizzle were taken by the prosecutorial authorities of the New Democratic government of Ontario. On the other hand, all the politicos involved were associated with the Progressive Conservative government in Ottawa. Nothing in the shared time of those governments in office had shown either of them to be so accommodating of the other as to support even the worst cynic's suspicion that the result had been brought about by collusion. There simply was no evidence, or none that would stand up in court, to support Kealey's beliefs.

That leaves a number of questions. What caused so many Ottawa reporters to crank out so many stories, in all media, making solid scandal of what for so long they had been highly skeptical about? All that was new was the report of a justice of the peace and, not to depreciate them, the judgments of JPs are not at the level of those of the Supreme Court. Did that one report provide a tincture of legal authority sufficient to overcome all previous journalistic doubts? Or was the media response an expression of sympathy with the man who had been parading so long in front of the Parliament Buildings, in the wind, rain and snow—coupled perhaps with an expression of guilt for not having taken him more seriously? Or was it simply a matter of seizing "any stick to beat a dog"—the dog in all such instances being the closest government? Or was every news bureau thinking, "Everybody else is going to be playing this JP–Kealey story big, so we'd better get on it, too"?

The best answer? All the above, with special emphasis on the latter two.

Our third vignette begins with a heading on page one of *The Globe and Mail* on September 12, 1986. It says:

JUNEAU SOUNDS ALARM
ON CBC AUTONOMY
HINTS AT PRESSURE

Every reporter in Ottawa, in whatever medium, is in some degree a reporter on politics, but most write on politics incidentally to something else—economics, the law, social affairs, foreign affairs, defence. However, some are specifically assigned to keep watch on politics *as* politics, the interplay between parties, what goes on within the parties and what the polls are saying about the parties and especially their leaders. Hugh Winsor, the writer of the Juneau-sounds-alarm story, is one such, and the *Globe*'s most senior.

Pierre Juneau had been president of the CBC for four years. The story arose from a speech he made at an international conference in Edinburgh; Winsor had distilled the story from a CBC text. Part of what Juneau told his audience was that he felt government hovering close and was apprehensive. Some politicians had been asking questions such as "Why don't you stick to cultural production, to doing things which the private sector won't do?" and "Why should we be financing our own critics?" All of which was to say that veiled hints were being dropped that the CBC, which its detractors believed to have a leftist inclination, should get out of the news business. There was nothing new in that. The CBC had been moaning about such perceived threats since the days before television, and the Conservatives had been moaning for at least as long that the CBC was out to do them in. (The NDP had no reason to moan at all, being comfortably situated on the other side of the Liberals and never having held power in Ottawa.)

Winsor's story said, "He [Juneau] did not refer specifically to Brian Mulroney's Progressive Conservative government, but said that support for the arm's-length principle of an independent news and public affairs organization has been diminishing for 15 years. He also said he had witnessed no attempts to interfere directly with information programs, but suggested that the tightening of the network's purse strings could be linked to politicians' irritation with unfavorable publicity."

Arm's-length principle? Attempts to interfere in programming? In any list of public persons *not* entitled to complain about government failing to maintain a clear separation between itself and the public institutions, Pierre Juneau's name would need to come at or near the top. The most blatant flouting of the arm's-length principle, before or since, occurred in his own appointment as president of the CBC in 1982. He, Pierre Trudeau and Gérard Pelletier—Pelletier served in Trudeau's first two cabinets and then went as ambassador to France—were all charter members of the circle of young Montreal intellectuals from which *Cité Libre* sprang, in the late forties, as a small but influential journal of political opinion. Juneau's association with Trudeau, therefore, was old and close.

His stops on the way to the throne room at the public broadcaster included the National Film Board and the Board of Broadcast Governors (predecessor to the CRTC as broadcasting's regulatory body), of which he was vice-chairman and then chairman. Nothing wrong with those, in the curriculum vitae of a future candidate for the top job at CBC. But then there was the further brief stop at the Cabinet table as Minister of Communications in the Trudeau government. The brevity of his term as minister, one month, is explained by a political accident. Along with Pelletier's place in the Cabinet, it was intended that Juneau should also inherit Pelletier's safe Liberal constituency of Hochelaga.

Seats in Parliament are not transferable—not without the assent of the voters. When Juneau ran in a by-election, the people of Hochelaga unexpectedly said no. Juneau resigned. In a few days he was back as special adviser in Trudeau's own office. Subsequently, he became chairman of the National Capital Commission, also a Trudeau appointment; undersecretary of state, also a Trudeau appointment, and Deputy Minister of Communications, the same. Then, after a lapse of two years which encompassed the Joe Clark interregnum, Pierre Trudeau, once more in power, appointed Juneau president of the CBC and chairman of the board.

As to the exercise of government influence within the CBC, Juneau, of all people, could not have forgotten the row that occurred in the first year of his tenure over the setting aside for the prime minister, on request, not one, not two, but three prime-time slots in as many nights in which Trudeau would instruct Canadians in a proper understanding of the depressed state of the Canadian economy—which was to say, his. Paul Hellyer, a politician of long and varied experience, was doing a column in *The Toronto Sun* at the time. He called the talks "sermonettes" and said the corporation, by its unheard-of open-handedness with network time, had allowed itself to be transmuted into PropCan—"a propaganda arm of the government of Canada".

Nor does it seem likely that Juneau, as a former chairman of the CRTC, would have heard no word of the unusual happening when the CBC went before the commission in 1978 to request the renewal of its network licences, something all licensees must seek at intervals. The unusual happening was that the anchor of the CBC's own national television news appeared as an intervener with some points to make about things he thought needed correcting. That was Peter Kent, who subsequently—not unwillingly, but uncommonly quickly—became correspondent in Africa. Only some of his criticisms to the CRTC related to political matters, but they were meaty—like, for example, his saying that confusion had been created in editorial decisions by influences from the Prime Minister's Office (PMO).

He had some instances. In April 1977, the news department had decided that a speech by Pierre Trudeau to the Canadian Association of Broadcasters in Winnipeg would not be broadcast live. The next day, after representations from the PMO, it was decided that it would be. In early 1977, it was decided by the news department that a speech to the Economic Club of New York by René Lévesque, still new as premier of Quebec, would not be broadcast live, and the decision stood. Almost exactly a year later, the same decision was taken apropos of Pierre Trudeau; after a call from the PMO, the decision was reversed. In February 1978, it was decided that the network would broadcast live the opening morning and the closing afternoon of a three-day meeting between Ottawa and the provinces on the state of the economy; the in-between portion would not be broadcast. A late-morning call on the opening day brought word that the prime minister would address the meeting again in the afternoon and that it should be covered; it was.

None of what Kent complained about had anything directly to do with Juneau, who had not been president of the CBC at the time, but Kent's intervention before the CRTC caused an undeniable stir; if at the time of his Edinburgh speech Juneau felt the hand of government hovering close, he cannot have believed he was suffering a unique experience.

Above all there was the memory, shared by everyone in the Ottawa journalistic community at the time, of the ready-aye-ready performance of the CBC in the supposed crisis in Quebec in October 1970. Ten years later, by which time he was anchor of Global's nightly news, Peter Trueman recalled the briefing given him as executive producer of CBC's national news on the rules that would apply to news-handling in the misapprehended (as it turned out) "apprehended insurrection". "We were to avoid commentary and speculation of all kinds," he recalled in his book, *Smoke & Mirrors* (McClelland and Stewart, 1980). "We were not to use man-on-the-street interviews or shoot film of any public demonstration. We were to air no panel discussions on the Quebec Crisis and were to avoid reporting speculation, particularly speculation about what the government was doing.

"I was told, still in hushed tones, that the policy had been adopted by the highest levels within the corporation. In effect, I clicked my heels, saluted, and returned to duty."

The "highest level" referred to was George Davidson, the CBC president, a former senior civil servant of many years' standing. Not withstanding that his own background in news was nil, Davidson undertook, in an interview, to instruct the rest of the media, as well as the CBC's own people, on their responsibilities. Canadian Press reported: "He [Davidson] said the news media, *including* the CBC, have 'given far too much attention, particularly in the area of speculation,' to the kidnappings." As Trueman recalled, the cigarette-pack manifesto, as he called it, because it was there he had made his notes, was soon rescinded, as were more detailed instructions elaborating on the manifesto. But a "climate of timidity" had been created. So far as he knew, Trueman said, no story was actually killed, but "it would be a mistake to assume that no damage was done. It affected the CBC's coverage until the crisis was over." If no story had to be killed, the explanation may be the circumspection with which the stories were written, in light of the instruction that "special restraints be applied to all news and current affairs programs. . . ."

Clearly, the CBC and the government were not then at arm's length. In fact, through the life of the corporation their relationship has been a thing of variable interpretation, depending largely on the colour of the government in power. The idea has been assiduously cultivated, not least by the CBC and its friends in other media, that every sin that has ever been committed by government against the corporation has been committed by Conservatives. As the story goes (and goes, and goes), the Tories, deep, deep down, have always wanted the public broadcaster dead; but, hesitating at assassination, they have made do with meanness, denying it all the public money it would like, and exerting underhanded pressure on news and public affairs departments to produce programs more to their liking.

That theme of sheltering the CBC from partisan (i.e., Tory) attentions underlay the Juneau speech in Edinburgh in 1986. It underlay a public letter written within weeks of the Mulroney government's taking office in 1984, pleading with the Tories to spare Juneau. The seven signatories wrote of rumours that they said "reflected very partisan views relating to the future of Pierre Juneau as president of the CBC. . . ." And then: "We recognize he has been identified with the Liberal party, however we have the utmost respect for his impartiality. . . ." It was signed by Louis Applebaum, Pierre Berton, John Hirsch, Ran Ide, Gordon Pinsent, Walter Pitman and Sam Sniderman.

It also underlay the cries in 1992 against a Senate subcommittee that had the temerity to enquire into the historical reliability of the film series *The Valour and the Horror*. The subcommittee, with its majority of Conservatives, was said to be acting as a surrogate for the government and harassing the CBC and the film-makers, not because many Second World War veterans were angered by what to them was a false rendering of parts of their history, but because the Tories were out to throttle the CBC. No substance for that accusation was ever produced by anyone.

Having known and read Hugh Winsor for thirty years helps me in making the assessment, with all the assurance possible in such matters, that engraved on his heart, in the box labelled "Politics", is the word "Liberal". He is also a staunch friend of the CBC. Given as well that he would know all the background cited here on the arm's-length relationship between government and the CBC, and the supposed deterioration in it, the story displayed a degree of wilful ignorance—a media phenomenon on which more will be said in the next chapter.

News reporting is and always has been susceptible to biases, prejudices, beliefs—pick your term—but the source of them, the nature of them and the force and effect of them have all changed, largely with the coming of television. At one time, newspapers of quality made more than a pretence of trying to separate news and comment. When they failed, it was in the direction of the editorial-page line, which had at least the merit of carrying a consistent thread. Television has erased the distinction; as there is no declared editorial line, there is nothing for pure news to be distinguished from. All news has become comment, and all comment news.

A newspaper's influence nowadays, particularly on public opinion about national politics, is where television's is—in the news department. There it is in the hands of reporters and (in print only) of headings writers, who constitute an influence of which readers may be less aware but which is nevertheless potent. (Headings are designed to draw the scanner into the story. They also must be terse. Therefore they tend to make strong, unqualified statements.) Behind those, in reverse order, come editorialists and columnists, the newspapers' declared commentators. Beside a sustained drumbeat of reporting and headlining critical of government, the most cogent of commentaries are puny.

One reason for that, apart from the greater prominence of the news, up front and seen first, is that reading or listening to the opinions of others has become very much a minority taste, faintly masochistic. Another factor is that reading habits have become more *looking* habits. Actually reading the newspaper, or any part of it, has been down-rated—even for some former devotees—to an occasional and casual thing to be fitted in between periods of voluntary illiteracy, otherwise known as watching television.

More often, the newspaper is *seen*, as in "I saw in the paper the other day . . ."—which may only mean that the newspaper was scanned in the bus on the way to work, between periods of gazing out the window, or was looked at during a small break in the day because the TV set was too heavy to carry to the bathroom. In either case, it will have been "seen" just long enough for the energized messages of three or four headings to be digested, and, with luck, a paragraph or two of text.

What works against commentaries, in competition with a more frenzied and judgemental page one, is that columns and editorials are written to be read whole. For the writer of commentary, the point of the exercise—assuming there is a point, as is always desirable—is not to tell the story in the lead paragraph and then work backwards through whatever documentation there may be room for, but to write a coherent small essay designed to be taken all of a piece. That faces the skimmer with the discouraging reality of all those words, probably 750 to 1,000 of them, to be lifted tediously off the paper, one by one, and absorbed—so unlike television. Television, at the touch of the right button, sluices all the news of the day (or the illusion of it) over the passive viewer, like a warm shower.

At one time, the essentials of reporting as laid down for young reporters were (a) answer the five Ws—who, what, when, where and why—and (b) keep yourself to hell out of it. To cite those rules is not to argue that they produced perfection; they were too restrictive. But political reporting in recent decades has gone beyond the point of balance, from being empty-pipe passive—the reporter acting as a simple conduit through which information is fed from source to consumer, virtually untouched—to being opinionated and judgemental, and often not disinterestedly so.

An adversarial relationship with all government in itself is a declaration of bias. That is a proposition which assumes that all government is inherently corrupt and is kept straight, to the extent it is kept straight at all, only by the vigilance of *us*, the media, acting as a permanent, all-seeing—and, it has to be added, self-appointed—scourge. It has led to what one editor has called the watchdog-turned-attack-dog phenomenon. Not to be overlooked, either, are the party preferences of the reporters—and, of course, groupthink, or the tendency to howl as one.

Of the vestigial distinction between news and commentary in television not much is to be said; since the earliest days, when the medium's news side moved out of the studio and into the live world, there has been scarcely a distinction at all. The facts have always been subject to being liberally dosed with the meanings extracted from them by the reporter. A large part of the explanation is that words (other than those of a reporter) are difficult for television to handle; as words are time, and people in the news cannot be counted on to speak to time, the reporter has to paraphrase the message, though a few words may be shown coming from the horse's mouth, for cosmetic effect. The message may or may not faithfully reproduce the meaning of what was said. Short of turning to *Hansard*, the viewer can never know. It was not so much the frequently loaded paraphrases of questions in the 1984–88 Parliament as the selections of them for television that brought about the low public respect for the House of Commons in the mid-1990s that the Spicer Forum subsequently found and reported upon.

In fairness, the same can be said, although in different degree, about quotation and paraphrase in print journalism, where the actual words spoken are increasingly used only to punctuate the reporter's dissertation. And of course all journalism, in whatever medium, is very much a matter of selection. Although print, with its more generous format, is able to accommodate many more items in a day, the stories used always constitute a minuscule proportion of those available. Similarly, selection applies to the facts that any story contains—this fact is important, it goes in; this one is marginal, it can be dropped. Where television has the advantage over print is in the impression it creates in the viewer's mind of actually having been there: "I *know* he/she said it; I saw it myself on television." That, most often, is an illusion. True, a person was seen speaking, but the words superimposed were the reporter's.

Some of this adapting to the style of television has undoubtedly done harm to print journalism, not just in the quality of the product but in readers' loyalty to it. In April 1992, the School of Journalism at the Ryerson Polytechnical Institute in Toronto organized what was called a brainstorming seminar on newspaper content. Michael Adams, president of the polling firm Environics Research Group, reported—under the heading "How Canadians Value Their Newspapers"—on two studies by his firm, five years apart, of the feelings of Canadians towards the media generally. The responses, he told the assembled newspaper managers, showed that readers considered their newspapers to be serious, informative, helpful, believable and honest; that was their opinion in 1986 and again in 1991. Great stuff. Unfortunately, the numbers who assigned such desirable characteristics to their newspapers had decreased in the meantime.

It is not difficult for even a confessed, irredeemable devotee of print to understand why more Canadians turn to television for their news than to print. Why stick with the less easily assimilated product if the two grow more alike? In fact, the growing more alike of news presentation as a whole may be the worst threat of all to newspapers, which already suffer under the handicaps of being awkward to handle, a problem to get rid of, and sometimes dirty, without the added handicap of having to get themselves read. What newspapers need most is to become more different, and less driven by television's subject-choices, which lead only to fad news.

In one of the great issues of the time, the free trade agreement, CBC Radio's "Sunday Morning" in 1988 found a difference between two newspapers a sufficiently newsworthy sidelight to the debate to be worth a mini-documentary. The subject was the different coverage of the issue by *The Toronto Star* and *The Globe and Mail.*

The difference in the end products was not as great as "Sunday Morning" may have thought, but certainly, as the program pointed out, there were two different philosophies of news presentation at work—one that most current journalists regard as a throwback to the reactionary past (bad), the other modern (good). It could be assumed from the moment free trade was raised as an issue in the 1980s that the *Star*, the established newspaper voice of economic nationalism, would oppose such an agreement, especially in the hands of a Conservative government. It was also assumable, because it would be no more than in keeping with the *Star*'s personality, that it would bring all guns to bear, in the news as well as in the editorials.

Even back when journalistic correctness dictated complete separation of church (editorial) and state (news), the *Star* was never an adherent. But what had been long apparent was put into words by Beland H. Honderich, who began at the *Star* as a stringer correspondent and became chairman of the board, in a convocation address at Carleton University in Ottawa in June 1989. Among other things, he said this:

> A newspaper's value system—what it thinks is important—originates with the owners and publishers, the kind of newspaper they want to publish and the audience they are trying to reach. These considerations determine editorial policy as reflected on the editorial page. And they establish the basic framework that guides reporters and editors in the handling of news. My concern is not that newspapers reflect opinion in their news pages; that is inevitable and certainly desirable if the public is to have access to different points of view. Rather, it is the mistaken importance that the public places on objectivity. . . . The distinction between what the public sees as "objective" or what it sees as "bias" is frequently some tenet of conventional wisdom. If what you publish confirms the conventional wisdom, you will be seen as objective. But if you cross the line and challenge public institutions and policies, you will frequently be accused of bias.
>
> [Later, turning specifically to the free trade issue, he said:] We thought the details of the agreement required critical examination and discussion, particularly as to how it might affect employment and social benefits and we set out to do just that. Over the course of the debate, we explored all aspects of the agreement and, in doing so, published more stories that were critical than supportive of the free trade agreement. This led, of course, to charges that we were biased, a complaint which, I am happy to say, was not sustained by the Ontario Press Council. We were able to demonstrate that while the over-all coverage was critical, we did not ignore arguments in support of free trade. Indeed, we went

out of our way to ensure that all pertinent speeches, statements and events in favour of the agreement were published in the paper.

The approaches of the *Star* and *The Globe and Mail* to free trade were not as different, in the end, as "Sunday Morning" may have thought. Neither was quite so absolutist as portrayed. The *Star*, as Honderich implied in his reference to the Ontario Press Council, did not suppress facts and arguments favourable to the other side. And *The Globe and Mail*'s news coverage, especially early in the campaign, certainly was not free of a negative slant; the editorial page was strongly pro, but the newspages were not.

In the *Star* newsroom, editors and reporters are aware that editorial policy "guides reporters and editors in the handling of news"; the ambitious young reporter—or, come to that, the old and housebroken one—would be only prudent to know what the paper's editorial policy was. Then, if the story in hand took on a contradictory slant, he or she would not be surprised if it failed to make page one and instead wound up, as the phrase used to be, back among the truss ads.

The opposite philosophy, which implies that the corporate personality of the newspaper will not intrude on the thinking of the news pages, does not guarantee objectivity in reporting; it merely transfers such influence as there may be from inside to outside. Consequently, the most effective influence in Canadian political reporting is towards conforming to the collective wisdom of the parliamentary press gallery. When the gallery is as plainly hostile to the government as it was in the Mulroney period, the Honderich approach becomes more attractive than I, for one, would have said thirty years ago. At least it puts behind the product a set of corporate values which remain fairly constant over long periods, are recognized within and knowable without, and are capable of being attacked by other media—or would be if only the informal mutual non-aggression pact that exists between media entities were abandoned. In the matter of biases, to my mind, better the devil we know than the devil we don't.

SIX

A MARRIAGE OF CONVENIENCE

THERE IS A PROFESSOR IN THE PHILOSOPHY DEPARTMENT at the University of Alberta in Edmonton—Ferrel M. Christensen by name—whose quintessentially 1990ish eccentricity is to believe that not all the beastliness in this world that is committed by one sex upon the other is committed by men upon women. By his own account, in February 1993 Professor Christensen sent out to every major newspaper in the country a small essay of the sort that newspapers use on their op-ed pages—the page facing the editorial page, where outside writers are invited to provide a leaven to the heavy intellectual dough of the paper's own ruminations. With the article went a note saying, "Please consider this article for publication. As it is time-sensitive, please let me know promptly if you intend to use it." Two months later he had received three replies in the classic rejection-notice form: "Thank you for your interest, but. . . ." From the rest, he heard nothing.

Certainly the article was timely; it represented another side to an issue that for at least a decade had been at or near the top of a list that has a place in every editor's mind—as Subjects That Really Matter. It was particularly timely at that moment because a new study of male-female relationships in Canadian universities had just received considerable publicity. Professor Christensen's response seemed to the lay eye to be well documented. And he observed the proprieties as to balance: in condemning the female bias of the study, which mainly left male respondents to write "yes" or "no" to a checklist of forms of beastliness they had inflicted on women in the preceding twelve months, the professor did not minimize the notable characteristic of male sexual abuse, namely that it is the more severe.

His point was that men may do more grievous harm, because they are larger and more physical, but according to the numbers, women in dating, cohabiting and marriage relationships are guilty of as many violent acts as men or more. "Women," he said, "commit at least half of the battering of children, and surveys of lesbian couples, with no males present at all, have found high levels of partner abuse. Within intimate relationships—in sharp contrast to the world outside them—women tend to be at least as abusive as men."

The study that generated his riposte had been described to its participating students as "the first national Canadian survey on problems in male-female dating relationships". Its authors were two Carleton University professors, Walter DeKeseredy and Katherine Kelly, under the sponsorship—$236,000 worth—of the federal Department of Health and Welfare. Unless The Canadian Press got it all wrong in its first report on the project in April 1992, the study was to be about "date rape among college and university students", and would also "end the debate about how violent women are in intimate relationships." The report issued in February 1993 proved not to be about date rape at all—perhaps there was none—and touched upon female violence wholly in the context of self-protection, retaliation or anticipation of attack; in other words, self-defence. It was the concentration on the seemingly one-sided victimization of women at the hands of men that caused Professor Christensen to say in his critique that the study as presented owed more to "the reigning ideology of the day" than to science.

On publication of the DeKeseredy–Kelly report, the media lunged immediately for the most attention-grabbing figures and conclusions. As exemplified here by *The Globe and Mail*, the first stories—there was some backing off later—stressed that "Women on Canadian campuses almost overwhelmingly say they have been victims of abuse in dating relationships" and "About 81 percent of the women questioned said they had been subjected to sexual, physical or psychological abuse by a dating partner."

Katherine Kelly, the co-author, quickly replied with an article expressing regret over the use of the global figure of 81 per cent. She explained: "The most controversial items in the 81 percent figure are those that relate to verbal/psychological abuse. Much has been made of the fact that three of the items included in this definition—insulting and swearing, putdowns in front of friends or family, and accusing a partner of flirting and having an affair—make up the common currency of most relationships. The answer to the question, 'Do these actions constitute abuse?' is quite simple: Sometimes they do; it depends on what is said, the importance attached to the opinion of the person making the statements, and how often negative opinions are expressed.

"If these items are not invariably abusive, why then were they included in the survey? For two specific analytical reasons. First, survivors of abuse repeatedly indicated that this form of abuse was often more damaging to them than were other forms. That included physical injury, because verbal attacks, in part, lowered their self-esteem. . . ."

The justifiable reply (male; mine), of course, comes as a question: "If verbal/psychological abuse often is more damaging than physical abuse because of what it does to self-esteem, ought not the scientific interest to be more evenly spread—assuming that the male psyche has a similar susceptibility to slights—to find the extent to which that form of abuse is used on the female side in the war between the sexes?"

But the subject here is media, not social studies, and what have the media to do with all this? The connection is in the fact that it is mainly in the unholy accord between media and interest groups—originally known more precisely as "*single*-interest groups", and more realistically as "pressure groups"—that the iconization of certain issues and interests has taken place. With the viewpoints of such groups raised to the level of sacred doctrine and certified correct, a certain disinclination has followed naturally in the media to question them, or to suggest that there might be another side worth hearing.

It is not just the feminist lobby that has been accorded this standing as a near-untouchable in our reporting. So have others of the loudest and most insistent. The most important—which is to say, the worst—effect of the close association of pressure groups and media is upon our politics. More and more the pressure groups, with media support, usurp the place that used to be filled by our elected politicians. Intended or not, the regular denigration of politicians by both ends of this media/interest-group alliance has the effect of elevating both of the latter in relation to the politicians. The more Canadians are led to distrust the people they elect to look after their interests *broadly*, the more they must be attracted to persons and organizations outside the political system who profess to be guardians of their interests *narrowly*. And with business, labour and professional lobbies pressing their private economic arguments at one end, and the whole gamut of supposed citizen lobbies pressing their select-group interests at the other, the ordinary Member of Parliament, who is elected precisely as a representative of the people, is squeezed into near irrelevance in the middle.

Is there some exaggeration in this rating of the relative influence in current politics of our elected politicians alongside unelected, unrepresentative, unresponsible (but not always publicly unfunded) citizen lobbyists? Perhaps a little. But it makes a good bet that, by the time she stepped down as stage manager for the National Action Committee on the Status of Women, Judy Rebick could have put together a book of press clippings—not to mention a list of television and radio appearances—better than anything any fifty backbench Members of Parliament could assemble collectively.

Certainly the feminist lobby, within which the National Action Committee (NAC for short) is by all odds the loudest component, warrants being selected as the number-one, prototypical 1990s Canadian interest group/politician-substitute/ideological preceptor to the media. But there are others.

The environmentalists are strong, earnest and still capable of striking fear into the hearts of people with warnings of dangers to their continued well-being, if not actual existence. Some of these dangers may even be real and present. But the environment is a large and diverse subject and the movement is very much fragmented, so that no one person speaks for all environmentalists in the way that the designated spokesperson for the NAC regularly does for all women, whether they want to be spoken for or not.

The unions, the only lobby with its own political party; the native people, who have learned with remarkable speed and effectiveness how to command attention and exert pressure via publicity; the economic nationalists (or anti-American lobby; either term serves), who have been present for more than thirty years as an organized force, as distinct from just a defining characteristic of the country—all of those constitute large, continuing, non-parliamentary influences in the governing of the country.

The nationalists, under their latest name, The Council of Canadians, remain strong (although less strong than in the 1960s and 1970s), earnest and full of, among other things, dread. The Council denounced the North American Free Trade Agreement, which brings in Mexico, unabashed at having proclaimed even more fervently a few years earlier that the U.S.-Canada free trade agreement would be the death of us—a thesis not notably supported by the fact that the rise in Canadian exports to the United States provided one of the first few bright spots in the struggle out of the lingering nineties recession. That is not to say that the free trade agreement was responsible for the rise; it is to say that the agreement did not prevent the rise by making industry withdraw from Canada, as Canadians were warned in dread-filled messages.

But nationalism does not rest upon threats to trade alone. So long as there is a CBC and a Friends of Canadian Broadcasting as its lobby, the media will not want for frissons of fear to pass on—fear for the survival of the distinct national identity which, in the eyes of the Friends, The Corp uniquely embodies. "The CBC is being destroyed by a callous government," said Pierre Berton in a typical Friends of Canadian Broadcasting fund-raising letter addressed to Dear Fellow Canadians, under a Friends of Canadian Broadcasting letterhead. Naturally, the government he was speaking about was the Mulroney one.

What is oddest of all about the ready acceptance of interest-group facts, figures and arguments by political journalists is that it is in such sharp contrast to their distrust of government. Government, it seems, is always out to manipulate them, plant untruths in innocent media minds, lead them into error. But not lobbies—except for business lobbies, which are different; they are manipulators, like politicians, laying traps for the unwary.

There is an explanation for the marvellous affinity which exists—or has existed—between certain large public interest groups and the media. (It is necessary to put it in that indefinite way because the relationship, founded upon shared anti-governmentalism, may be on the point of falling apart.) When the Conservatives were in power, the interest groups constituted a rich source of negative quotations—"This measure completely fails to meet the needs of the time", "Too little, too late", "Heads should roll over this latest abdication of responsibility" and the like—which reporters could get for the price of a phone call. On the media side, a ringing denunciation to put at the top of a story in print that television has run the night before serves very well as a freshener.

On the lobby side, the small task of being ever-ready with predictable negatives is more than rewarded by the pleasure—and, of course, the publicity value—of being quoted.

Reporters have never acknowledged their reason for turning more to interest groups than to, say, Members of Parliament, who are elected to have opinions on public business and the handling of it. By some unfathomable logic, interest groups have come to be seen by journalists as somehow more *of* the people than the people they have sent to Parliament—government, government supporters, opposition and all. Those are politicians or, even more dismissively, "*the* politicians", therefore suspect—a great and debilitating nonsense. It is nonsense because it says that experienced journalists, in their distrust of the partisan wiles of politicians, have lost sight of the fact that lobbies are, by definition, partisan—partisan to their own limited interest. To be biased is what they exist for; a lobby without a self-centred complaint is a lobby out of business. They are committed to the advancement of one cause, with no necessary concern for how it fits with the total needs or capabilities of the country. Therefore, to adopt the assumptions and facts of one or a handful of such special pleaders is to adopt one or a handful of narrow biases. That is not a prescription for realistic reporting.

Whether the relationship between political journalism and interest groups will continue under the new government should make a useful study for government-watchers of all sorts, including journalism and political science students. If the Ottawa press corps adopts a less adversarial attitude towards government, the need for a constant supply of predictable negatives will become less, thus the influence of the lobbies will decline. Perhaps the first body to feel the effect of a budding new tolerance in Ottawa has been the anti-smoking lobby, whose interest had been sacred for years. When the Chrétien government hit upon cutting the taxes on cigarettes as the way to stop smuggling, the main reporting accepted calmly the government's explanation that the tax cut was a matter of law and order. Health concerns, which had previously dominated all discussions of cigarette marketing, became secondary.

But the interest groups are numerous, tough, publicity-wise, manipulative, not altogether scrupulous in their methods, inexhaustible, inflexibly certain, and influential. They will not go away, nor is there a reason why they should be anything more than deflated—which could be done simply by the media applying to them the skepticism they have been so ready always to direct to the elected.

To the most effective lobby of all, the activists of what a British writer has called "tooth-and-claw American feminism"—the singling out of the American brand may be attributable to a too-narrow experience—all the adjectives above apply, with perhaps the addition of dogmatic, demagogic, egocentric, boring and humourless.

In late 1991, *Maclean's* magazine, which knows an icon when it sees one, ran a cover story titled "Women in Fear". Under that headline, on the cover, was this: "Abductions, sexual assaults and murders of women are causing growing alarm among Canadians. A campaign to end the reign of terror has begun." The story inside was under the same head, with the underline "Experts are searching for the key to men's reign of terror against women" as an added inducement for the reader's blood to run cold. The story itself contained such revelations as these: "Across the country, women are pointing to a torrent of assaults by men—and demanding that governments act," and "Feminists charge, and statisticians acknowledge, that men have always abused women. The number of women being killed . . . has grown in recent decades roughly in line with the population increase," and "A parliamentary subcommittee examining the issue deplored what it called 'men's war against women'."

Men's reign of terror against women? *Men's* war against women? Torrents of assaults by *men*? All meaty stuff. However, along with the acknowledgement that the murder rate for women had grown roughly in line with the population increase—surely an unintended admission that the phenomenon was less new and less dramatic than the language used would suggest—the magazine might have acknowledged the effect of its own statistics.

Those, represented in a graph on a later page, showed that the murder rates for women and men were relatively in step. The numbers were far apart—many more men are murdered than women—but the lines did not diverge. From 1980 through 1985 to 1990, evidently the "recent decades" mentioned in the text, they moved together. Not only that but, while the trend line was up over the decade, it was slightly down again for both sexes in the last five years. That, turning the thinking around, could be made to support the more positive conclusion that things are improving—but then again we trip over the old proposition that bad news is good news and good news is boring.

Maclean's, having opted for the good bad-news option, left some obviously unintended thoughts to be derived from its figures and its arguments:

1) If Canada has a problem with violence, it is not confined to one sex. Even if all the murders on both sides were the work of males, it would be imprecise to say they represented "men's war against women", given that men would have dispatched at the same time upwards of ten times as many of their own.

2) To apply such terms as "reign of terror" and "war" to one identified group in society would qualify in most contexts as hate literature.

3) If the job of the media is to nourish public understanding with reliable information, we don't do it very well by feeding them baloney. What is most wrong with the assertions of the all-men-are-vile faction of the feminist lobby, and of the reporting inspired by it, is that they can only implant the idea that a tendency towards violence is *wholly* a masculine characteristic. What does not get reported, because there is no lobby pounding on the doors of Parliament to express it, is the fact that there is a considerable literature, mainly American, which says that no form of person-to-person violence (rape perhaps aside) is exclusive to either sex. One point that emerges from several studies, by seemingly reasonable people at respectable universities, is that, while violence may be initiated by either partner—and is, in roughly equal proportions—male violence usually is more damaging. But that, of course, is a qualitative difference, not a quantitative one, which does not quite warrant the description "men's war against women".

But the issue also has its ludicrous side. The following statistics were compiled by no more methodical system than throwing clippings at random into a folder over a period of time. No claim of comprehensiveness is made.

One in four women is sexually abused before age seventeen. Between 80 and 90 per cent of working women have experienced sexual harassment during their working lives. One in eight women reported she had been sexually harassed at work. A third of female engineers at Ontario Hydro have experienced sexual harassment. One-third of female (American) journalists say they have been sexually harassed in their newsrooms. One in ten women has a relationship with her therapist. At least one woman in ten is attacked by her male partner. One in ten of Ontario physicians has been guilty of sexual misconduct. One in six—16 per cent—of female graduate students at the University of Manitoba say that they have altered study plans to avoid sexual harassment. In Canada, an act of male violence against a woman occurs every six minutes. Sexual assault will happen to one woman in four during her lifetime. Eight out of ten aboriginal women in Ontario are battered, threatened or sexually abused by a family member. Disabled women are twice as often sexually assaulted as able women. One in four university women in the United States is a victim of rape or attempted rape. Twelve per cent of females have been victims of childhood sexual abuse. Fifteen percent of murder victims are wives killed by their husbands. In Canada in 1988, 57.4 per cent of women murdered were murdered by someone with whom they shared a domestic relationship. Surveys indicate that 10 per cent of therapists, psychiatrists and psychoanalysts have sex with their patients. The number of sexual assaults reported in Canada increased by 87 per cent in the mid-1980s. Women are six times as much at risk of being sexually assaulted as men. About 1.2 million Canadian women (15 per cent) and 300,000 men (4 per cent) believe they have been sexually harassed—harassment being defined as leering and other gestures; verbal abuse; unwelcome remarks, jokes, innuendoes or taunting about a person's body, dress, age or marital status; unwelcome invitations or requests; condescension or paternalism which undermines self-respect; unnecessary physical conduct such as patting or pinching or physical assault. Oh yes, and 93 per cent of sexual abusers are men.

Whew! Can *all* those figures be true? Obviously such things happen, but are the numbers believable? Or do they illustrate careless acceptance of questionable data from sources with a propagandist interest? If so, why? Because they couldn't *not* be published, for fear of offending a large audience and perhaps inviting accusations of suppressing the facts of a social issue of topmost importance. But must they not ultimately do harm to credibility at both ends of the alliance—especially at the publishing-broadcasting end, which lives by selling credible information?

The same is true of treating with equal cluck-clucking seriousness and sympathy clearly manufactured stories of injustice. Two notable recent cases together made a howling absurdity. The subject was bare breasts—in one case on paper, in the other in the flesh.

First, a twenty-year-old student at the University of Guelph, Ontario, was arrested for walking bare-breasted on the street. It was argued in her defence that one bare chest is essentially the same as another; therefore, as a matter of equality under the Charter of Rights, she should be no more required to cover hers than any man. The judge said that anyone who thought the two were the same was not in touch with the real world, and fined her $75 for indecency. When other women demonstrated in sympathy and five more were tried—and acquitted—they enjoyed the backing of such as Judy Rebick, head of the National Action Committee on the Status of Women, and Phyllis Berck, national chairwoman of the Women's Legal Education and Action Fund—both pillars of the feminist lobby. "Why," asked Ms. Berck, "are women's bodies defined as obscene whereas men's bodies aren't?" Obscene? No more than men's are women's secondary sexual characteristics obscene. Obscenity wasn't the question, but whether chests are different—as women for at least three thousand years, in different societies and times, have demonstrated by variously hiding theirs, provocatively semi-draping them, decorating them with cosmetics, cantilevering them for better elevation, emphasizing them in tight sweaters or baring them outright.

Next, a complaint was taken to the Ontario Human Rights Commission seeking the removal of skin magazines from the racks of convenience stores, where, it was alleged, they create an uncomfortable atmosphere for women. "I feel I compromise my integrity when I go into a store," one of the complainants said. "That demeans me." Another woman, not one of the complainants, said on television that when men were poring over skin magazines, she felt as she walked past that the louts at the racks were measuring her with their eyes. Perhaps, perhaps not; peering into another person's mind was difficult even for Sigmund Freud.

But should it be considered material for anything but satire that at the same time equally sober claims, soberly treated in the news, defended the constitutional rights of women on the grounds that (a) *au naturelle*, a chest is a chest is a chest, and gender has nothing to do with it, and (b) the female chest, *en photo*, is capable of so arousing male lust as to warrant suppressing the publications that trade on it? To uphold both arguments, it would be necessary to take the view—decidedly demeaning to men—that the reality is unaffecting but the image is inflammatory. One might be tempted to say to editors, "Get serious"—except that they are so damned serious already, in matters they fear *not* to be serious about, because humour has come to be seen as hostility by the nut-brown fringe of feminism.

None of this would matter if the iconification—the creation of sacred subjects that may not be touched except with reverence—did not flow over into our political reporting. Sometimes it is easy to imagine, posted on bulletin boards of Ottawa news bureaus, lists headed Good and Bad. Political parties are Good anywhere left of centre and need not be so in any discernible way, so long as they make the proper sounds, e.g., the Chrétien Liberals. (In political journalism, a report on anything emanating from the Fraser Institute in Vancouver is routinely identified as from "a right-wing Vancouver think tank", so as to warn readers to expect a conservative slant which may not be instantly apparent to the lay eye. A report from, say, the Canadian Labour Congress, the CLC, will not be identified as "left", because left is Good, therefore no warning is warranted. Unions in themselves are inherently Good; business, whose interests the institute is said to reflect, is Bad.)

This sort of counterpoising of icons and bogeymen by class goes on instinctively and endlessly. Canadian peacekeepers are Good but the military (who are the same people but with guns) are Bad. Consider the soldiers in Bosnia and in the so-called standoff with Mohawk warriors at Oka in the summer of 1990. In the first they are Good, in the second—and in the most blatantly prejudiced reporting in recent memory—they, and the government that put them there, are the villains.

People who shoot other people are Bad, but if they are caught and imprisoned they are Good, because prisons are Bad. Immigrants are not Bad unless they take jobs from others who came earlier; however, if they entered the country as illegal refugees they are automatically Good, because they wouldn't be refugees if they had not been persecuted, which is Bad, therefore they are Good.

Cutting down trees is Bad, but selling lumber is Good because it creates jobs, which are Good because people at work pay taxes, which in themselves are Bad but become Good if they make the individual burden lighter, which is Good. Three goods to two bads make a Good.

Militant women, in addition to being Good on their own, are predominantly aligned with the political left, which in turn is the political arm of the unions, both of which, as we have seen, are Good in themselves. It is in that light that the political—and media—reactions to the respective sins against womanhood of John Crosbie (Conservative, non-union, male) and Daryl Bean (New Democrat, union leader, male) deserve to be looked at. Crosbie's sin came in the context of a debate on proposed changes in unemployment insurance which would pay no benefits to persons who quit a job without cause.

There immediately arose a howl that women who quit because they were sexually harassed would, or *might*, be excluded, although why that would not be considered just cause was unexplained.

If Crosbie's indiscretion is not well remembered, the reason cannot be that it was insufficiently publicized. But this is what he said, to laughter from a mixed audience in his home province of Newfoundland: "Apparently just about everybody who quits their job is being sexually harassed. We must have a hell of a lot of attractive people working. If this is the case, I have to admit to you that I have never been sexually harassed. If I were, I would certainly want to make it known that I had been so favoured." Unwise? Obviously, recognizing the risk of headlines such as "Crosbie sparks outcry with harassment remark/MPs castigate 'Crosbie-saurus'", and charges that his comments reflected "abject ignorance". But if Crosbie made sexually harassed women the butt of a bad joke—a dubious proposition—Daryl Bean, national president of the Public Service Alliance of Canada (PSAC), spoke directly and used strong words in letters to three women members of PSAC.

The women had written him to complain of intimidation and threats directed at them for having continued at their jobs when the union struck in 1991. Bean's reply began with an acknowledgement, and then: "First and foremost, I have no intention of entering into a correspondence exchange with a SCAB. Therefore I will ignore your comments and simply provide you with Jack London's views of a scab." Bean's passage from the American author ended with these lines: "A scab is a two-legged animal with a corkscrew soul, a water-logged brain, and a backbone of jelly and glue. Where others have hearts, he carries a tumor of rotten principles. No man has the right to scab as long as there is a pool of water to drown his carcass in, or a rope long enough to hang his body with."

Sexual harassment? Hardly—but, remembering the definition of harassment in our list of statistics, why not? The quotation from Jack London included at least verbal abuse, and no doubt unwelcome remarks. Had any minister written the same to any Canadian of either sex, demands in Parliament and the media for that minister's resignation would be assured. But compared to Crosbie's unwise joke, Bean's intemperate letter was passed over with little comment, none touching on anything like Beanosaurus or abject ignorance. There are several probable explanations for the difference.

First, a minister of government is accountable to the public (which means the media) for whatever he or she does in office. The leader of a large public service union, which exists to represent persons in the unelected side of government, is responsible to no one except the union.

Second, the complaints of the three women came to public notice via David Somerville, head of the National Citizens' Coalition (slogan: "For more freedom through less government"), undeniably Right, hence Bad.

Third, there is in media practice what may be called the Law of Predictable Returns. It says that in order to write a story slanted *against*—against what, doesn't matter—while appearing professionally disinterested, one must find persons to quote who will provide the right words.

The Canadian Press reported the day after the Crosbie indiscretion that "several female MPs and women's groups said he should be dumped from cabinet. . . ." Sheila Copps, the deputy Liberal leader, was the only one of the mentioned MPs who spoke in the House. CP sought out two others—Liberal Mary Clancy and New Democrat Dawn Black—both of whose comments were as predictable as Copps's. It seems scarcely necessary to say that those of Judy Rebick of the National Action Committee were the same. Mary Collins, the government minister responsible for the status of women, made as little as she could of what she wouldn't dare *not* say; she said her colleague's remarks were unfortunate.

There were no comparable words to be quoted *for* Crosbie's right of freedom of expression, nor, it can be counted upon, did CP go out of its way to find out if there were any to be had.

That brings us to a second Law of Predictable Returns, which says that, if the purpose is to play *down* a story, one doesn't go looking for quotes. More than a week after the Bean letter came to light, I called Nancy Riche, vice-president of the CLC (and of the NDP), to ask her what she had to say about the matter, given her own recent statement that violence against women was a major national and trade-union issue. She replied that she hadn't said anything, because nobody had asked. She added that she'd been happy no one had. Riche hadn't been asked—my guess—in case she said what she said to me: "We don't condone violence of any kind."

Q. And violence of language?

A. That's right.

Q. And that includes him—Bean?

A. Yes.

In all the instances cited here, the Good side in the issue, as represented in the reporting, was the side upheld by an aggressive interest group. For both media and interest groups, then, their relationship has been a marriage of convenience, guaranteeing on the one hand gratifying publicity for whatever cause, and on the other an assured supply of comment that will accord with the reporter's own thoughts, but will be delivered with a more persuasive appearance of disinterestedness by the use of quotations from surrogates.

And then there is another, quite different journalistic trick—highly effective in the production of negativity—called Wilful Ignorance.

SEVEN

DIVORCE FROM REALITY

WILFUL IGNORANCE IS WHAT A JOURNALIST COMMITS when he or she looks away from known or readily knowable facts because acknowledging them would leave a story so weak it could not survive the transition from idea to print or broadcast. Wilful ignorance is also one of the most potent forms of gotcha, because it is difficult to deny, the premise having been false to begin with.

For example, the reporting of Kim Campbell's number-one gaffe of the 1993 election campaign, referred to in Chapter One, was an exhibition of wilful ignorance on a grand scale, taking into account the variety and durability of the withering assessments that followed. The main fault alleged against her was that she spoke to Canadians on the delicate subject of jobs in a detached and academic way, like a professor of international economics; that she showed no trace of compassion, and that she would pay a price for it in votes, blah, blah, blah.

But what that ignored—which seems the charitable way to put it—is that this was not a speech to Canadians as a whole but to a press conference with journalists of some acquaintanceship with politics and economics. If it was delivered in an academic, even stuffy manner, it was their journalistic responsibility to unstuffy it while keeping the substance as little harmed in the process as possible. The same would be true (although it might be commented on as unusual) if the remarks had been delivered in pig Latin. Reporters deliver information, not what they think the consumers would or should think of the style. Or so I think the consumers might think if they thought as I think.

Wilful ignorance occurs not just in election campaigns but often in political journalism, in miscellaneous circumstances and in the reporting of stories of substance and stories amounting to scarcely more than fillers. The evident purpose in both is to create prejudice. Consider, beginning with the least and simplest example, a squib put out by The Canadian Press that began: "Canada has joined the ranks of Syria and Panama as a country that tolerates significant harassment of journalists." It said there had been fifteen assaults, harassments and other attacks on journalists or journalism in the previous year, most of them during that summer's (1990) struggle between police and the army on one side and Mohawk warriors on the other. What was not said, but was to be found in the annual report of the source agency, The Committee to Protect Journalists, in New York, was that three of the fifteen alleged occurrences—actually fourteen, because two had been made of the same incident—had been at the hands of the insurgent Mohawks. "Canada", which implies public authority, could not be accused of having caused or tolerated those.

One was related to a small U.S. magazine held up, then admitted, by Canadian Customs; it could not properly be called harassment, and certainly not assault. One referred to an action by a court, which is a process of law, not of politics or police. Two more referred to the "beating", by unspecified persons in undocumented circumstances, of two freelance photographers for Spanish-language publications at a soccer game—again questionably an offence either committed or tolerated by "Canada". Of the seven remaining, two which involved police confiscation of news agency videotapes may or may not have constituted harassment; a court might find the police had acted properly in the line of duty.

The rest were petty grievances from persons with inflated notions of journalists' rights—which are no different in law from anyone else's.

To say those incidents put Canada on a plane with Syria and Panama was wilfully ignorant—wilfully because The Canadian Press could not have failed to know that what it was saying was nonsense, and that the only effect could be to make Canadians have a little less regard for their country. To say so is to argue, not for only feel-good news in our media, but *against* the gratuitous addition of manufactured examples of the opposite.

Next up in this parade of wilful ignorance is a product of the media obsession with patronage, most notably in appointments to the Senate of Canada. Since 1867, there cannot have been a reporter covering

Canada's Parliament, this one included, who has not at some time written or broadcast a piece saying the prime minister—pick a name—had just filled X number of vacant seats with a matching number of assorted bagmen, time-expired Cabinet ministers, involuntarily retired provincial premiers, retainers in the party apparatus and just plain old pals and cronies—beneficiaries of patronage, hogs to the trough, all.

The crucial point such stories wilfully ignore is that, if patronage is evil, it is a constitutionally sanctioned evil. At least three thousand appointments of all sorts, from Chief Justice of the Supreme Court of Canada through deputy ministers and ambassadors down to part-time members of advisory boards most Canadians have never heard of, are assigned to the prime minister to make. All those are, in the strict sense of the term—"the power to make appointments to government"—patronage appointments.

Consequently, patronage itself is neither good nor bad. It is only when the persons appointed are demonstrably unfit, and owe their positions solely to party affiliation, that the appointments deserve to be called "patronage" in the bad sense. The rub is that the term is so freely used in that bad sense by persons—for which may be read "journalists"—who have not the foggiest notion if the appointees have the credentials for the jobs or not. In fact, few would be able to say what the essentials are. That makes an argument for having all nominees, at least for significant positions, publicly examined within Parliament on their qualifications before appointment. What it does not do is to justify the indiscriminate use of the term "patronage" as a virtual synonym for a species of graft.

Another point wilfully ignored is that the Senate is a political body, as it was with a vengeance—literally—in the Mulroney years. In circumstances of an overhanging majority of the other party in the Senate—the case through most of that time, during which the Liberal majority routinely harassed major initiatives of the elected government—what else would any prime minister do but appoint adherents of his own party, at least until a majority had been attained? Not to do so would be to go so far beyond noble restraint as to represent political lunacy. It does not follow, either, that in this rectification of a situation left behind by a previous regime, all the appointments made will be of plain boobs and superannuated hangers-on.

The provision that a Canadian prime minister might appoint extra senators to ensure the supremacy of the elected House of Commons over the unelected Senate was installed in the 1867 Constitution on the strong recommendation of the British government, which foresaw the danger of stalemate. When the Mulroney government chose to use the provision, there were even suggestions that the clause might somehow have gone bad from having been so long unused, as if constitutional clauses, like perishable foods, carried a best-before date. Considering that the constitution had never been out of the hands of experts in the previous thirty-odd years, and that the clause remained unchanged and alive, the argument about its shelf-life was not to be taken seriously—a magnificent example of wilful ignorance. Against whom did the argument create prejudice? The government of the day, of course. The criticisms of "patronage" in Senate appointments were never so shrill when Pierre Trudeau was creating the Liberal majority in the Senate as when Brian Mulroney was trying to outnumber it.

Obviously, so long as the Senate remains unelected, there are certain things that can be done to improve the way appointments are made—beginning with the old idea that the government should produce nominees, not just for Senate appointments but for various sorts of senior positions, which then would go to a parliamentary committee (or committees, by category) for approval. A refinement of that, where Senate appointments are concerned, might be to leave the government free to make appointments on its own, and, likely *of* its own, until the supporters in the Senate on the side of the party in power equalled the holdovers, at which point further appointments would need to be considered and approved in committee.

Still, the most effective prescription for taking some of the heat out of the issue of patronage would be for reporters to accept a self-denying ordinance against the use of fabricated evidence rooted in wilful ignorance.

The next example in this recital is an anomaly—perhaps not an instance of wilful ignorance, but tainted by tilt, uncertainty of interpretation, undue quickness of judgement and questionable knowledge of idioms. It was damaging to Brian Mulroney's standing as prime minister and may have affected the Meech Lake Accord, coming just as Clyde Wells of Newfoundland twitched over the decision to say yes or no.

The story was by Susan Delacourt of *The Globe and Mail*, from an interview she and Graham Fraser, chief of the newspaper's Ottawa bureau at the time, and Jeffrey Simpson, the national affairs columnist, had with the prime minister in the last days of the debate over the accord, which had spread over three years. The best account of what happened within the *Globe* bureau and in the Toronto newsroom after the interview is to be found in David Hayes's *Power and Influence* (Key Porter Books, 1992). Delacourt and Fraser differed over what was significant and they filed parallel stories from their different viewpoints. Toronto decided for Delacourt; her story was more dramatic. It led off with Mulroney having plotted in advance to bring the whole final negotiations to a pinch, at which time "we're going to roll the dice".

The roll-the-dice phrase was taken up in the subsequent commentary, and affected public opinion more than the revelation that Mulroney had worked according to a predetermined strategy, which many Canadians probably would think was no more than a conventional gambit in negotiating. Rolling the dice sounded trivializing, a gamble, flippant, a case of the prime minister being arrogantly ready to take a chance without sufficient thought for the greatness of the consequences that might follow. Given the influence this "more dramatic" story may have had on the premiers—which, at that point, meant primarily Clyde Wells—the interesting question for historians is, was it a reasonable interpretation of what was said and what was meant?

The irony of all is that the derivation of the "rolling the dice" phrase has the opposite of the frivolous meaning that this affair attached to it. Unable to think at once of where "the die is cast" originated, I looked it up. The encyclopaedia produced Julius Caesar, and that led to *Plutarch's Lives*, Dryden's translation, corrected from the Greek and revised by A.H. Clough, volume four, page 291. Caesar, back from years of triumphs in Gaul, was marching on Rome, bent on seizing control of the government. He knew that once past the Rubicon in northeastern Italy, there could be no turning back. Here, the narrative passes to Plutarch:

> When he came to the River Rubicon, which parts Gaul within the Alps from the rest of Italy, his thoughts began to work; now he was just entering upon danger and he wavered much in his mind when he considered

> the greatness of the enterprise into which he was throwing himself. He checked his course and ordered a halt, while he revolved [*sic*] with himself, and often changed his opinion one way and the other without speaking a word. This was when his purposes fluctuated most; presently he also discussed the matter with his friends who were about him (of which number Asinus Pollio was one), computing how many calamities his passing the river would bring upon mankind, and what a relation of it would be transmitted to posterity. At last, in a sort of passion, casting aside calculation, and abandoning himself to what might come, and using the proverb frequently in their mouths who enter upon dangerous and bold attempts, "The die is cast," with these words he took the river. Once over, he used all expedition possible, and before it was day reached Ariminum and took it.

A difficult, troubling decision? Enough so, according to Plutarch, to have given Caesar a bad night. "It is said," reported Plutarch—no mere surface-scratcher he—"that the night before he passed the river he had an impious dream that he was unnaturally familiar with his own mother."

Wilful ignorance pops up everywhere, with one constant characteristic—the deliberate avoidance of some fact necessary to a complete understanding of an event, so that the event is misrepresented. Here is an illustration from Mulroney's visit to Hong Kong and Tokyo in May 1991, a mission intended to stimulate trade and investment.

The Toronto Star said in an editorial on May 28, "At every stop, he persists in bashing Ontario's $9.7 billion budget deficit as an example of Canada's fiscal disarray. . . . 'I know what they [his hosts] think,' Mr. Mulroney assured reporters in Tokyo who wondered why he kept raising the subject himself. . . ." But the *Star*'s reporter, Edison Stewart, did not need to wonder why the prime minister "kept raising the subject" because he had been at the May 25 press conference in Hong Kong where it originated. He himself had asked the questions that led to it. The transcript shows Stewart prefacing a question with a reference to the objective of the visit—to reassure businessmen that Canada's unity problems would be overcome and the country would remain a good place in which to invest. This, remember, was at a time when Canada was in the round of constitutional agonies that led to the Charlottetown agreement and the unsuccessful referendum. Stewart asked:

Q. In your conversations with these [Hong Kong] business leaders, have you discovered that unity is indeed a concern, and is the uncertainty costing us in any way?
A. It is not an overwhelming concern, Ed. I believe that the general view is that Canadians have the maturity and the wisdom to resolve these challenges to our unity. They seem to be operating on that premise. And I've sensed some concern, but not alarm because they are clearly giving Canada the benefit of the doubt. And I think they're right in doing that. I think we will be able to resolve our difficulties and. . . . But as I've indicated to them in public statements, I can't give any guarantees, obviously.
Q. One of the businessmen we spoke to yesterday, after your speech to the chamber of commerce, said that a lot of the investment now is in Ontario and British Columbia anyway, and it's not so much in Quebec. Do you get any sense that businessmen, if they say that we're . . . that they're confident in investing, it's only to the extent that they're not going to invest in Quebec for the time being?
A. I didn't get that. I didn't get that feeling. They're aware that the problem has emerged in Quebec, and that is never good for investor confidence. But no one made a federal case of it. There were references to it, as there were to the quite astonishing—to quote one of my interlocutors—Ontario deficit rise. That has concerned them. And quite frankly I received more specific comments about the Ontario deficit number than I did about anything else. Which is not to say that they spoke about it morning, noon and night. But when it was raised, the Ontario deficit came up oftener than anything else.
Q. Is that hurting investment in Ontario?
A. Pardon?
Q. Is that hurting investment in Ontario?
A. Well, look what happened to the bond rating, look what happened to the Triple A rating; you know, when you lose your rating lead like that, I don't think it helps.

That in total, word for word, is all that was said on the subject, in a transcript that runs to twenty-seven pages.

Two days later, in Tokyo, the question of the Ontario deficit came up again, not in a formal press conference but in a scrum that produced one sheet of transcript. This is the relevant portion, again word for word:

> Q. Any concern over national unity or the Ontario budget?
> A. The question of . . . I addressed the question of unity simply because I was invited to speak and I probably pre-empted some questions by referring to it off the top and obviously the question of public finances is the single most important factor in any judgement the Japanese make.
> Q. Did they express to you any concerns about the Ontario budget and the effect . . . ?
> A. They don't have to. I know what they think. And I can assure you, if you just look at the deficit numbers in Japan and extrapolate them on a per capita basis, the Japanese figure out very quickly what's going on.

Period. Full stop. The end. Those were the grounds of the controversy.

Did all of that qualify for the *Star*'s criticism that the prime minister "persists in bashing Ontario's deficit", let alone bashing it as "a sample of Canada's fiscal disarray"? Or that he had kept "raising it himself" at every stop (of which there had been two)? The prime minister's error was not telling the reporters to get lost.

Much of the home-based comment that amplified the similar stories that every reporter on the tour filed, in true pack fashion, was to the effect that Mulroney had talked about *domestic affairs* (oh, the shame of it) in front of foreigners—like telling the neighbours about Auntie who regularly shoplifted from Woolworth's.

In a collection of items labelled "Bouquets & Brickbats", the Montreal *Gazette* awarded the prime minister a brick: "A more refined sense of tact would have prevented the chief representative of all Canada from resorting to partisanship and running down a major part of the country while touring abroad." Andrew Cohen in *The Financial Post* said, "Mulroney should not have raised a domestic dispute in a foreign country. No doubt his critics over-reacted, but we have come to expect this kind of indiscretion from the PM. He is Canada's lip of state." Christopher Young of Southam News, in a column headed in the Ottawa *Citizen* "Partisan PM takes arrogance on the road", said: "He breaks a well-understood tradition that our leaders . . . do not take internal quarrels to foreign audiences." Said Jeffrey Simpson in *The*

Globe and Mail: "Foreign trips are designed to boost a country's image, not denigrate it." And Peter O'Neil, in *The Vancouver Sun*'s Ottawa bureau asked plaintively, "Is Canada too fragile to withstand Mulroney's uncontrollable tendency to take partisan shots, to grind opponents' faces in broken glass?"

Yet it was not the PM who raised domestic affairs before a foreign audience, but journalists.

For another perspective on the rank phoniness of all this emotion over the damage supposedly done abroad, it is necessary to return to Edison Stewart. Having played his incidental part in setting the story off, he later wrote a retrospective in the *Star*. In that analysis, he said, "The controversy was ignored in Japan—for the simple reason that virtually no one knew about it. Mulroney's remarks about the Ontario budget were made to Canadian reporters, not Japanese, who probably wouldn't have cared about it anyway."

Eight months later, in January 1992, The Canadian Press reported, "An influential Japanese financial journal warned that a rising dollar and Ontario's pro-union stance could discourage foreign investment in Canada. . . ." In February 1993, *The Globe and Mail* reported from Tokyo that a top economist at the Japanese Centre for International Finance had said, "The increase of the debt by the provinces is something that we are watching carefully." Not long after that, the Ontario government turned sharply away from its former course and undertook a serious effort to get its expenditures down and its revenues up. And to think that the Japanese would never have caught on if the Canadian prime minister hadn't blabbed that the largest and richest province in the country had a dangerously deep deficit.

What is most wrong with stories of this kind is that they become the foundation of hokum controversies, and a form of journalism perhaps of some small sensation value in the business but of none as reliable information to the consumer. With that there goes an unnatural drive not to be left out of any excitement that may be going, genuine or manufactured. As excitements in political journalism almost always derive from something governmental and inevitably negative, the incidental effect is to feed the public cynicism and distrust that the same media otherwise piously deplore.

It is an old, old complaint to reporters from persons in public life that "You guys don't care what you write just so long as it sells newspapers." The complaint is somewhat misdirected. The depth of the indifference of most reporters to selling newspapers, or selling commercials on television, is scarcely capable of being estimated. Selling is a management function.

Obviously, at a time when pack journalism is in fashion, there is personal satisfaction in being the leader of the pack. There is also the plainer satisfaction of producing the story that takes the top spot on the night's newscast, or is run under a large head, above the fold, on page one. On a foreign assignment, it is better to get a phone call from the home office saying, "Your story today was a clean beat. Nice piece. You doing a follow-up for tomorrow?" than to get a call saying, "Where were you yesterday with the PM-boobs-again story? You're doing a follow-up, we hope. What's he saying about it? What's the reaction there? It's all over everything here."

It is from management that such accolades come, both spoken, and—in the placement of stories—implied. The reporter cannot be unaware of that fact, or the fact that in time such approval may even be shown in more concrete form, in better assignments and (in extreme cases) even pay increases. Reporters, then, cannot be absolved altogether of having an interest in selling newspapers and newscasts, however abstracted their interest may be. Still, the keeping of the corporate conscience resides primarily in the hands of management, and if management is content to publish or broadcast baloney, baloney the public will get.

EIGHT

PRESS FREEDOM: A ONE-WAY STREET

THE TELEVISION CRITICS LOVED THE SERIES *THE VALOUR and the Horror* when it first ran on CBC-TV in mid-January 1992—hated the subject, which was three episodes in the Second World War (ugh, nasty), but loved the treatment (mmm, villain-seeking; quintessentially Canadian). These are examples:

Douglas Sagi, *The Vancouver Sun*: "Do not . . . groan, 'Not another re-hash of the war' this Sunday at 8 pm. It is not a re-hash and it is not to be missed. . . . [The producers] argue Canadian soldiers and flyers were needlessly sacrificed, misled, lied to by their own and British leaders. War correspondents of the time—particularly the CBC's Matthew Halton—are accused of being military boosters, filing untruthful reports, perhaps because they relied too much on official sources."

Bob Blakey in *The Calgary Herald* concentrated on the first of the three films—on the doomed defence of Hong Kong against the Japanese. "The film contends that 2,000 untrained Canadian soldiers were offered up as lambs to the slaughter, assigned an unwinnable task to appease the British who didn't want to put their own soldiers in jeopardy on the Crown colony."

Tony Atherton was lyrical in the Ottawa *Citizen:*

> The Valour and the Horror, CBC's heart-rending, mind-numbing six-hour account of Canada's participation in the Second World War is not a documentary. It is impassioned testimony. . . . Director Brian McKenna and his brother, reporter-narrator, Terry, are providing a dramatically-lit stage upon which others can bear witness, the ordinary Canadian soldiers who were made to endure the unendurable, to embrace the unthinkable, to risk their lives in . . . battles that were

often futile, for staff-officers whose concern for them was sometimes obscured by ambition.

Curiously, Ted Shaw of *The Windsor Star* had that same phrase about the ordinary Canadian soldier being made to endure the unendurable, but in quotation marks, from a telephone interview with Brian McKenna. Interviews, face to face or by telephone, were part of the heavy advance promotion for the series, and resulted in not just quotable chance phrases but whole undigested chunks of film-maker thought being relayed to the public as the judgements of informed critics. An example that turned up more than once was the assertion that the true facts had been kept from Canadians until the moment the McKenna brothers courageously ripped aside the curtain and brought them to public attention.

From the beginning, the assertion of secrets finally revealed was passed on by reviewers and other commentators with complete trust: Canada's historians simply had not done their job. In all the coverage of *The Valour and the Horror*, which became a considerable issue over the rest of 1992 and beyond, there was almost no sign of that benign skepticism which is supposed to drive journalists to seek corroboration of what they have been told, especially by persons with vested interests.

That same Ted Shaw, for example, showed no trace of skepticism in reporting, "McKenna [in his war documentaries] has followed a simple creed: 'If you don't tell the whole truth, you are lying.'" It is indeed a simple creed. Even taking into account a generous allocation of six hours of television time, two hours to each of three episodes, it gives one pause to think that in the telling of two large, convoluted and immensely important military campaigns in Europe, one air, one ground and a smaller third in the Pacific, no fact essential to the whole truth was missed, and none was adjusted to fit someone's preconception of what the truth ought to be.

Mike Boone of the Montreal *Gazette* devoted most of his space to a glorification of Brian McKenna, based upon an interview with Brian McKenna. It had the incidental merit of identifying some of the biases upon which the series was founded—for example, that "war is appalling and monstrous", scarcely a new thought, and that "our historians have done an appalling job. . . . As journalists who make films, my brother and I felt very strongly we held a responsibility to tell the real stories."

Implicit in those words was the proposition that "Here, at last, is Truth." Prospective viewers were invited to believe that historians, squeamish about revealing what might be unwelcome facts, had turned their heads away. Now all was being put right; the villainy, the dark and dirty secrets, the savagery, the failures disguised as successes, the incompetence of leaders, the untrustworthiness of war correspondents, all finally were being exposed to public view.

Another bias, not stated but generously portrayed, was that our British allies were really rather rotten, to some extent politically, considerably in their military commanders and most particularly in the person of Air Marshal Arthur Harris, leader of RAF Bomber Command, in which one group—6 Group—was Canadian. (Not all Canadian aircrew in Britain were in 6 Group; many more flew in RAF squadrons.) The actor in the role of Harris, all supercilious eyebrows and sneer, most often was shown against a background of the Union Jack as a symbol of malignant influence.

Peter Trueman, in *The Toronto Star*, opened with this: "Next weekend . . . CBC is due to distinguish itself by beginning some long overdue programming on the obscene nature of war, the perfidy of politicians and military staffs, and the astonishing courage and decency of ordinary Canadians." The first and third parts of that could be called ritual moralistic embroidery, but the middle bit, about the perfidy of politicians and military leaders—where did that come from? Obviously from the film-makers.

The rave reviews of *The Valour and the Horror* were very much a case of the films being judged for their entertainment value—the pull on the emotions of sights or sounds, of searchlights pointing, shells exploding, buildings burning, aircraft crashing, engines thrumming, bodies falling—all this against a background of doomsday narrative and stirring music. The facts were either taken on faith or assumed to be irrelevant.

What ought to make us uncomfortable about all this is that the impact of television is so great. It is a speculation, but not an unlikely one, that those three films, shown twice nationally, will have been seen by more Canadians than will have been influenced by all our historians together. And recommended by whom as worthwhile our paying attention to? By susceptible critics of an essentially entertainment medium. Take some further account of how many more may have seen, or will see, just the companion book or the videos, and the reach of that one viewpoint on an important part of our history becomes immense. The videos, and perhaps the book, went into quite a few schools, obviously intended to be used in teaching. (Merely the best in a rich harvest of errors in the book was to translate Operation Overlord, the code name for the invasion of Europe—D-Day—into Operation Overload, as if the troops came from a company providing temporary office help.)

Another preview that helped the marketing of the series is from *The Globe and Mail* and its prime television watcher, John Haslett Cuff. He spoke, he said, as a member of "the first wave of baby-boomers", whose memories of the Second World War, necessarily derived mainly from parents, were "at odds with the patriotic twaddle in many history books". He did not identify any particular patriotic twaddle he had in mind.

He continued: "Brian and Terence McKenna's searingly emotional yet ruthlessly unsentimental probe into three major campaigns in that war combines the most insightful of personal reminiscences with investigative zeal; the result debunks much of the official history and reportage about these events." And again: "The McKennas have created an invaluable and engrossing series of quasi-historical documents. Fingers are pointed, the reputations of high-ranking individuals are besmirched, the heroism of young men and women is commemorated. . . ."

All of which was to say he loved the films. However, it was a waste of his time to say he belonged to the baby boomers, "those of us forty something". The whole tone of the piece, and the attitudes it revealed, proclaimed the fact—particularly his satisfaction at finding "the reputations of high-ranking individuals are besmirched". That was straight from the "make love not war", "power to the people", "trust no one over thirty" populist twaddle (to borrow a term) of the sixties.

Only one critic in my initial sampling of big-city commentary—and almost none in dozens of columns that I looked at later—raised even a question about fact. The exception was Bob Blakey in *The Calgary Herald*, and he did so diffidently. He found, he said, "one weak assertion". That was the first film's proposition that "the Brits conned Canada's Prime Minister Mackenzie King into committing ill-trained

Canadians [to Hong Kong]." That, he said, overlooked the possibility that "Churchill believed Hong Kong was relatively safe." What the record says is that Churchill *did* recognize the unlikelihood of Hong Kong surviving if Japan attacked. But Japan was not at war then, and he did not know danger was imminent—any more than Franklin Delano Roosevelt knew that Pearl Harbor was about to be attacked and a significant part of the U.S. Pacific Fleet sunk at dockside. But, Churchill or no Churchill, it was the government of Canada, sovereign then as now, which took the decision to send troops to Hong Kong. Canadian governments, at least since the Laurier government sent a contingent to South Africa and the Boer War in 1899, had been reserving that sort of decision to themselves. Tony Atherton at the Ottawa *Citizen* said it was Churchill's *decision* to sent Canadian soldiers to Hong Kong, which cast an odd light on a 1990s perception of where Canada stood in the world in the 1940s.

The story of the controversy over *The Valour and the Horror* is in two parts, of which the second received far more media attention because it involved an affront to the media, whereas the other affronted mainly a bunch of doddering veterans. The second—the great (and phony) freedom-of-expression, freedom-of-the-press scandal—we will come to, but first things first.

That includes what its makers said about it and what its critical critics said about it, as distinct from the TV critics with their near-unanimous rave reviews. Was the series a fair and reasonably balanced account, paying due respect to the context of a desperately fought war? Or was it a morality play, historical in background but with happenings and decisions selected and spliced together for dramatic effect, the better to convey the producers' own anti-war—and subsidiary anti-political, anti-military and anti-British—prejudices? And, if the latter, why was it not labelled for what it was?

Not surprisingly, no such questions were invited by the film-makers or the CBC at the time of release. A month before the first showing, a CBC publicity handout said, "According to social historian Paul Fussell, 'The real war will never get in the history books.' Fifty years after the fact, The Valour and the Horror . . . attempts to set the record straight. The CBC-TV Current Affairs special [combines] investigative journalism, documentary and drama to tell the unvarnished story of three

Second World War campaigns." A story, perhaps. But unvarnished? The reference to drama in the blurb was explained a few paragraphs later as meaning the use of actors to "quote the memoirs of survivors, or the letters of the dead" and the use of Canadian soldiers "to re-enact actual battles". Thus even the dramatic portions were asserted to be just another way of presenting hard truth.

At no time was Brian McKenna, as director, co-writer and principal flack for the films, less than 100 per cent immovably certain; the facts, he insisted from the start, were "bulletproof". Later, he allowed that there might be differences over interpretations, but the facts remained untouchable. In a letter to *The Toronto Star* in August 1992, he said: "We are quite prepared to defend the historical accuracy of the series in a legitimate public forum. Criticisms have consistently been based on nit-picking and outdated and incomplete research." In November of the same year, he told the Senate subcommittee on veterans' affairs, which did *not* come on his list of legitimate forums, "We do not say these films are perfect; we say they are accurate."

As late as January 1994, Terence McKenna was saying the same in a letter to the editor of *Maclean's* magazine, this time on the excuse that historian J.L. Granatstein, in a review of the CBC's new mini-series on the Dieppe débâcle, had taken some "gratuitous shots" at *The Valour and the Horror*—a bold stroke in light of brother Brian's condemnations of historians. The letter went on to say, "Granatstein and our other critics in the Senate and elsewhere have been trying for the past two years to find script errors in our. . .series. They have failed."

For just one whopping "script error", there was the story, read by Terence McKenna in his role of narrator and perhaps written by him as co-author, of Arthur Harris, Air Officer Commanding Bomber Command, and his differences with the Supreme Allied Command over plans for the invasion of Europe in June 1944. Harris objected to having his force diverted from its strategic bomber task to the more tactical work of bombing mainly transportation facilities in the invasion area. Harris believed Bomber Command was best employed continuing to strike at German industrial production. Then this: "Arthur Harris would have none of it. . . . In the end, Harris got his way."

Harris did not get his way. For just one illustration of the untruth of that, there is *Reap the Whirlwind*, published by McClelland and

Stewart in 1991 (before *The Valour and the Horror* ran), by Spencer Dunmore, novelist and expert in air operations, and William Carter, historian. They said, "His [Harris's] polemic failed. On March 4 [1944], he received his orders. Bomber Command was to mount a series of pre-invasion attacks on railway targets. . . . It called for widespread damage to the railways around the proposed landing area so the Germans would be unable to use them to bring up reinforcements."

Reap the Whirlwind is a detailed, unsensational and plain-spoken history of the role in the air war of Canada's 6 Group, from its operational beginning on January 1, 1943, to the end. An appendix lists all operations flown by 6 Group in those years, and how many crews took part in each and how they fared. In the period of March through July 1944, which encompassed D-Day (June 6), 6 Group squadrons—the rest of Bomber Command can be counted upon to have produced similar figures—attacked 13 targets in Germany and 154, mainly in France, but also on the launching sites of German unmanned flying bombs on the Channel coast, and at offshore locations, planting anti-shipping mines.

By early 1994, when the junior McKenna told *Maclean's* readers that all the critics had been unable to find an error in the films, he was sliding dexterously past the dissents of an impressive lot of historians—including professors David Bercuson of the history department at the University of Calgary, and Sidney Wise of the history department of Carleton University, Ottawa. They had been retained by William Morgan, the CBC ombudsman, to do independent studies of the episodes in the war on which *The Valour and the Horror* was built. They were not the only persons he consulted, but their analyses were important guides to his decision on whether the series came up to the CBC's published journalism standard. The ombudsman's answer to that, reduced to the essence, was no, it did not.

Those two reports still have not been made public as this is written, in mid-1994. They disappeared at once, slipped under the chairman's desk blotter, locked in the vault, put out in a blue box to be recycled; who knows? That in itself made a curious turn of events. Roughly similar sorts of documents on matters of the public business usually are obtainable from *government* via Access to Information, unless classifiable as Cabinet secrets. The same is not true of the CBC; it is exempt. More curious is that the CBC's brethren in the media showed no interest in pursuing the matter to see if the reports, clearly pertinent to a matter of public interest, could not be pried loose for publication. More curious again is that this lassitude should show up at a time when the media, including the CBC, were being increasingly aggressive in asserting the constitution's guarantee of freedom of the press to protest against any real or imagined restraint on publication—such as, for instance, any withholding order of the courts against immediate publication of evidence in trials.

Why not, then, the same concern for "the right of the people to know"—a media euphemism for "our self-interest"—when a member of their own clan plays the wicked suppressor of information essential to public understanding? However, sensitivity to double standards has never been a strong media characteristic.

Still, those unusual behaviours are not unexplainable. Within the CBC, release of the ombudsman's report, and management's acceptance of it, with an accompanying public apology from president Gérard Veilleux, had caused CBC production staff to cry out against a lack of corporate backbone. Management had no wish to risk making the internal problem worse by bringing out more—and more severe—criticisms.

The ombudsman's report not only had been edited to the bone, but was gentler than the consultants' reports. He gave more importance as a shortcoming to the extensive use of actors to mouth the asserted words of real persons, living and dead. That could be considered simply a mistake in judgement, detrimental only in that it might leave doubt in the viewer's mind about where reality ended and theatre began. The consultants' concerns were more embarrassingly concentrated on fundamentals—stretched interpretations, lack of context, lack of balance, predetermination of conclusions, non-factual facts—which, remember, were said to be bulletproof. (The statement here that the ombudsman's decision was less severe than the reports of the consultants is made confidently. I was able to read them. Comparison will become generally available in the fall of 1994, when McGill-Queen's University Press publishes a book by Bercuson and Wise based on their texts.)

The explanation of the lack of interest by other media in getting at the background to the ombudsman's report is that throughout the affair, and especially after it was transmuted into a media issue, the least attractive of the biases which afflict Canadian journalism was very much in play. That is the media-pro-media "All for one and one for all" bias, embracing the proposition "Stick together. If we are *all* right, we are *all* all right; if we are *all* wrong, nobody is wrong." The Corp, as a charter member of the gang, was entitled to its protection—if by nothing else than the others' silence. Here was Big Brother itself being held accountable, ye gods, for what it put on the public air. Appear for a moment to criticize, to show a lack of faith, even, and in no time everybody would be wanting *all* the media to be accountable, as a regular thing.

That solidarity became evident slowly, first as indifference. Some letters to the editor were published, but there was no rush by print-press editors to see if there might be more to the criticisms than simply the resentment of a few crotchety veterans at the intrusion of revisionists on their remembrances of past excitements. The CBC, having made the ritual response of all media in all such circumstances—"We stand by our reporters," i.e., the film-makers—sat back, complacent in the belief that the complainers needed only to be fobbed off with soft answers for a while for the whole tiresome fuss to go away.

When eventually some of that fobbing-off correspondence became available for me to read, a number of interesting letters turned up. One was a reply on CBC letterhead from D'Arcy O'Connor, identified as associate producer, *The Valour and the Horror*. That letter appeared to be the CBC replying; it was to the CBC, after all, that the viewer had written. And it is true D'Arcy O'Connor was an associate producer, and chief researcher, for the Bomber Command segment of the series. But not for the CBC. His part in the enterprise was through Galafilm Inc., the private company that had made the series—mainly with money from the CBC, the National Film Board and Telefilm Canada, all emanations of government. O'Connor usually used Galafilm letterhead. It makes a queer sort of accountability to the public for any media company, and particularly one twice responsible to the public—once for most of its income, and again for the quality of the information it supplies them—to farm out that accountability to an unrelated third party through a letter, or letters, of disguised origin.

Subsequently I learned from within the CBC that several persons with Galafilm connections had been enlisted to help with the corporation's mail load—whether as writers over their own names, or simply as providers of answers for others, I do not know. In either case, the circumstances clashed with the words of the CBC president, Gérard Veilleux, to another correspondent. "Please note," his letter said, near the end, "that The Valour and the Horror was produced by an independent production company, Galafilm Inc. . . . Messrs Brian McKenna and Arnie Gelbart [of Galafilm] are the program's producers; they are not spokesmen for the CBC." To which his correspondent would have been entitled to reply, "Oh?"

Trina McQueen, then vice-president for news, current affairs and "Newsworld", later vice-president for accountability and now in private broadcasting, replied to still another letter-writer, "The stories told in 'Death by Moonlight' were not in any way based on the opinion of the producers," which she questionably was in a position to vouch for, and which, in addition, was patronizing gibble-gabble; before work on *The Valour and the Horror* even got going, Brian McKenna had his opinions lined up. McQueen went on: "As well, the issues raised by the bombing campaign were validated clearly by the two Canadian pilots featured in the program, themselves members of the valiant air crews of Bomber Command." The two, Douglas Harvey and Ken Brown—both articulate, both with splendid operational records—obviously validated the Bomber Command film to a degree just by being in it, but they had next to nothing to do with how it was put together, its emphases, its viewpoints or—not to overlook them—its distortions.

In March 1992, as protests against the film on Bomber Command gained strength, Harvey replied to a letter from a friend. "As for The Valour and the Horror," he said, "what can I say? Everyone is on my back as though I had produced the fucking thing. Brown and I had no part in the production. We were not consultants and never knew what the producer had in mind at any time. . . . We had no control whatsoever and the producers would not sit down and discuss things. They were really as bloody-minded as Harris. Everything had to be spontaneous. We couldn't speak to or see the people we were to meet (until we met on camera, cold), like the women in Hamburg in the cemetery. After they left, Brown and I were asked to comment on camera and I made a little speech saying in effect, 'What the hell else could the Allies do?' We couldn't invade, so how to hit Germany? It was ignored like many other statements. Sure Harris was a bastard but it sometimes takes bastards to win wars and he wasn't all bad. . . ."

Something else Harvey said was this: "McKenna had a fixed agenda that he would not discuss. . . ."

That theme was repeated by Terry Copp, a historian at Wilfrid Laurier University, and author or co-author of several books on the Canadian army in Europe in the Second World War. He and Brian McKenna had discussed the projected series when it still existed only in outline. As Copp put it later, McKenna described how he was approaching the subject. "Later he asked if I would be the researcher for the Normandy episode. I have known Brian McKenna since he was a student at Loyola College in Montreal in the 1960s. . . . I have the utmost respect for [him] as a journalist. . . . But my response . . . was a flat, unequivocal, 'No.' It was clear from our. . .conversations that he had already decided what he wanted to say and the job as researcher was to provide material that could be used in developing his personal interpretation of the war."

Gilbert Drolet, whose field at Le Collège Militaire Royal de St-Jean was war literature, wrote a combined review of *The Valour and the Horror* films and the by-product book for the June 1992 issue of the *Canadian Defence Quarterly*. An introduction said, "The reader should know that some time after the showing of *The Killing Ground* [an earlier McKenna war film], Brian McKenna . . . approached the present writer as a potential consultant for the TV series now under discussion. This reviewer made 97 books available for research purposes but when he realized what direction the investigation was taking, and after pleading for an objective stance, he recalled the books. . . ."

His review, considering the mixed feelings with which he must have approached it, was fair but not without the occasional sharp comment. About Terence McKenna's words which introduced each of the three films—"This is a true story; there is no fiction"—Drolet said, "There is as much fiction as that which they pretend to eliminate." The pretensions of the book to tell "the untold story of Canadians in the Second World War" were dealt with succinctly: "It is not a fact that this combined CBC-NFB effort is the untold story of Canadians at war. In fact, the story has been told, and well told, repeatedly, in countless books . . . many of which were consulted by the McKennas to tell their 'untold' story."

The *other* side of the *Valour and the Horror* story, the side away from the ecstatic reviews, has a better claim to being the story that has never been told. In all the commentary on the films, very little time was wasted in examining the contents. The newspapers, in their early indifference, and their later virtual boycott of the issue, at no time used their vaunted investigative skills to find what the offended veterans were offended *about*.

Here it is necessary to declare an interest: in the second half of 1942, seven new Canadian bomber squadrons were formed. Bomber Command was preparing for a great 1943 offensive. I as pilot, Ev Brown as navigator, Andrew (Red) Wilson as bomb-aimer, Jim Miller as wireless operator and Bill Blue as rear gunner began flying with 424 Squadron soon after it was formed in October 1942. We did not finish the standard thirty-trip tour for raids over Western Europe, not through misadventure but because, precisely at mid-point in our tour, 424 Squadron and two others were detached to fly our outdated two-engined Wellingtons to a grass airfield (and tents in an olive grove) in Tunisia. Our purpose was to attack targets in preparation for the Allied landings in Sicily, and in support of the land forces in Sicily and in Italy proper, in the weeks after. As ops in the Mediterranean counted only two-thirds—a bargain to aircrew at that—we finished, alive and unharmed, at thirty-four trips.

Thus I was particularly interested in one film, "Death by Moonlight"—because I had been part of what it was about—and because it had generated by far the largest number of letters to the CBC, and the angriest.

That widespread anger was rooted in the film's central theme—that bomber crews were lied to, made dupes of, led to believe they were bombing only essential industries when the hidden purpose was to kill civilians. Terence McKenna approached the subject by way of another piece of British deceit (as the film was pleased to represent it). The solemn music of the soundtrack rising behind him, he said, "The British high command knew how few bomber crews would survive. It deliberately hid the truth. That's not all that was concealed. Crews and the public were told the bombing targets were German factories and military installations. In fact, in 1942 a secret plan was adopted. Germany would be crushed by the deliberate annihilation of its civilians. Few airmen would ever learn of that plan. . . ."

The claim that survival rates were concealed can be ignored as hokum journalism. The BBC famously reported bomber sorties beginning "X number of bombers attacked [insert name of city] last night. . ." and ending "Y number of our aircraft are missing [or failed to return]." Consequently, when the aircraft of Bomber Command were mainly four-engined, multiplying the number lost by seven would provide anyone, enemy included, with a roughly accurate guide to the loss of crew. At best, the allegation that Bomber Command knew how few would survive and cruelly hid the figures from aircrew was a touch of fiction intended to highlight the wickedness of "British High Command".

The so-called secret plan of the McKennas' rich collection of conspiracy theories was no more secret than *all* military plans, ever, in wartime. Also it represented more an acceptance of reality than a fiendish departure in which killing people for the sake of killing people would replace efforts at destroying steel mills, ball-bearing works, munitions factories, oil storages, centres for research and development of missiles and the like. Nor did the plan spring into being in isolation. It went with the enlargement of the bomber force, as evidenced by the increase in Canadian squadrons from five to fifteen in less than a year and a half, and with the steady replacement of the remaining two-engined bombers with four-engined Lancasters and Halifaxes, which flew higher, faster and farther, and carried a greater weight of bombs. Not least in this upgrading was the installation in aircaft of a new navigational device called the Gee, which enabled navigators to find their way to targets as far into Germany as the industrial Ruhr Valley, more surely than before.

What the producers of "Death by Moonlight" found convenient to skip over was the context in which all this planned intensification of bombing came about. The time was the low point for the Allies. It was also a point at which Bomber Command, the only force capable of carrying the war into Germany, had to recognize itself caught between unacceptable casualties when visibility permitted some slight hope of finding targets by sight, and being ineffectual in conditions of fog, rain, industrial haze, and smokescreens put out by the defenders.

Area bombing essentially involved putting a large number of heavy bombers, roughly like waves in a stream, through an area containing a strategic objective or objectives, in as short a space of time as possible.

Certainly the planners accepted the killing of civilians—as civilians have been killed in all bombing raids before or since, including those raids with supposedly "smart bombs" in the recent war in the Persian Gulf. One estimate of the bombing in the Gulf was that more than half the bombs missed the designated target .

Certainly it was true at Hiroshima and Nagasaki with the atomic bomb. Certainly it was the fundamental principle on which the policy of deterrence rested during the Cold War—Mutual Assured Destruction. Certainly it was used before the Second World War, by Germany in Spain, and the Italians in Abyssinia, for example, and in The Netherlands and England, by Germany in the early days of the Second World War.

But area bombing did not mean the abandonment of attacks on industry for the sake of levelling streets of houses. Had that been the goal, there were cities that were easier to reach than in such a conglomeration of smokestack industry as Essen, Duisburg, Bochum, Düsseldorf, Dortmund and the Ruhr Valley as a whole. That, as *The Valour and the Horror* itself said, constituted "the heartland of German industry", and was, with Berlin, the most heavily defended part of the country.

The proposition that, after the "secret order" came into effect, bombing was directed at obliterating cities for the purpose of doing so, rather than at precise targets, does not accord with an important fact. Gee, in 1943, was only the beginning of efforts to develop new equipment for finding more precise targets, and new ways of marking them once found. Had indiscriminate bombing been good enough, that would have had no purpose.

Did Bomber Command crews not know that dropping incendiaries on built-up areas killed people, as implied in Terence McKenna's claim that aircrew were deceived? The proposition that they did *not* know was made explicit in a letter from Brian McKenna to *Maclean's* magazine complaining about a column I had written. "In the film," he said, "*we gave the crews the benefit of the doubt* [my italics] whether they knew their missions included the deliberate killing of civilians. " Thus, if they knew, they (along with Bomber Harris) were murderers. That, of course, would make them ineligible to be portrayed as heroes.

In addition to its rank arrogance, that absolution was remarkably self-interested. The insistent theme in all three segments of *The Valour and the Horror* was, in true populist fashion, that the people who *took* orders were Good Guys; the Bad Guys lied to them, duped them, hid information from them and, by incompetence, often wantonly threw away their lives. The plot line would be ruined if there were no Good Guys. Hence the benefit of the doubt.

Among other items to make total innocence questionable is the fact that Bomber Command aircraft carried aiming-point cameras that operated automatically with the pressing of the bomb-release button. Not only were the resulting pictures available, but crews were encouraged to look at them, to know what their bombs did. Another point the film did not touch is that the civilian populations of all participating countries, including Canada, were scarcely kept in the dark—not with radio stations and newspapers announcing, sometimes every few days, that this, that or the other city in Germany had been bombed. There was no rioting in the streets in protest.

Max Hastings, editor of *The Daily Telegraph* in London, is the author of books on two of the three *Valour and the Horror* topics—Normandy and Bomber Command. He is not a great fan of Bomber Harris, or of the bombing policy (at least as executed late in the war, the period that included Dresden). He is also cited by Brian McKenna as an author who generally endorsed "Death by Moonlight". But that is not all the story. Hastings was one of several writers Arnie Gelbart of Galafilm sought out for comment on the film series when complaints to the CBC began rising in the spring of 1992. In Hastings's judgement, considering the historical record, the viewpoint in "Death by Moonlight" fell within the parameters of responsible debate. In Britain, where reconstructing the Second World War has become virtually a literary industry, that covers a lot of ground. But Hastings had reservations—about, for example, the treatment of Harris as the villain of the piece, given that Harris at all times was a subordinate who did not make policy but executed it. Hastings also felt the nuances of policy had not been sufficiently examined. However, the crucial reservation concerned the purpose of the bomber offensive—represented in the film to be, again in the film's own words, "the deliberate annihilation of civilians". Although many Germans were killed, the aims of the bomber offensive were to break the will of the people to fight and to destroy Germany's war industries.

Both those, as deserves to be noted, were aims which the populations of all Allied countries, Canada included, overwhelmingly supported, and even applauded, at the time. Also to say the basic purpose of bombing was misinterpreted constitutes no mild dissent but attacks the core of the film.

Another English author from whom Galafilm solicited endorsement—so persistently that he finally hung up—was Martin Middlebrook. His work includes a series of books which carefully reconstruct several individual raids of more than usual importance, including the disastrous Nuremberg raid of March 1944, which occupied a large part of the "Death by Moonlight" story. (A list produced by Galafilm itself shows Middlebrook prominent among the sources the film-makers relied on.) Middlebrook gave this evaluation of that film: "My view of this is very simple. I think the Bomber Command episode was a gross distortion of the very complex subject which was Bomber Command's war over a period of six years. Whether that distortion was the result of incompetence or of deliberate malice, I cannot judge."

Hardly any of this background, of which there is much more, was gone into by the big players in the media during the period of the ecstatic reviews, and the complacent waiting-out of the storm of veterans' letters. But then a new player entered the scene. Jack Marshall—a tough-nut senator from Newfoundland, an army veteran, a survivor of the D-Day landings—decided that the war veterans angered at the errors, biases, omissions and distortions deserved a forum somewhere—and elected to make his committee the place.

Boom. Suddenly, *The Valour and the Horror* was transformed from a subject of indifference in the country's major newsrooms into an imperative national issue. Senator Marshall's Veterans' Affairs subcommittee (of the Standing Senate Committee on Social Affairs, Science and Technology) was proposing to hear the complaints of veterans, the opinions of historians and the arguments of producers and distributors about the quality of what had been put before the public, with extensive publicity, at a cost of more than $3 million of mainly public money, as incontestable, newly revealed truth. And, well, said the media, that was one of *us* they were daring to discuss. Media hands went up in horror and indignation at the thought.

That way, it was declared, lay the end of freedom of expression, of the fundamental rights "those gallant boys" (not many of whom thought of themselves as either gallant or boys) had fought and died to preserve, blah, blah, blah. Mind you, if the journalism community itself had shown more interest in the quality of journalism delivered to the public—in this case by the largest journalistic enterprise in the country—there would have been no need, room or justification for the Senate subcommittee to intervene.

Obviously people generally are free to say, "We do not criticize our own." But freedom of the press does not confer on media the unique constitutional privilege of adding, "and no one else may", and expecting to be heeded. But that is precisely what the whole loud outcry against censorship and the supposed stifling of freedom of expression was about. Consider just the first lines of an editorial in *The Windsor Star*:

"The Senate, not questions about how Canada fought the Second World War, is what should be muzzled in the controversy over The Valour and the Horror."

Others may have phrased it more diplomatically, but that point of view was not exclusive to the Windsor paper—that Marshall and his little band of senators were dabbling in the affairs of journalism, where they had no business, and should close the door, give a respectful tug to the collective forelock and back off. In the name of freedom of expression, a large part of the media in Canada, particularly in central Canada, was complaining about a subcommittee of the Senate giving a lot of angered veterans a chance to exercise theirs.

The Ottawa *Citizen* shed a fat crocodile tear over Marshall & Co. ever having come into the matter. "The distressing thing about the controversial Senate subcommittee hearings," it said, ". . . is that they weren't necessary. The same outcome—lively public debate about Canada's role in the Second World War—was possible without abusing legislative power. . . ." Marshall's band wasn't legislating anything; it was enquiring into an expenditure of some $3 million of public money and what it bought.

In the same vein, the Montreal *Gazette* said, "If a journalist gets something wrong . . . the way to set the record straight . . . is to enter the public arena and make one's own case. This can be done in many ways, from letters to the newspapers, all the way up to books and competing television films. . . ." *The Toronto Star* found it "disturbingly unclear where such Orwellian hearings . . . might go. Will Marshall's committee try to ban or censor the series and a related book? Will it call for heads to roll at the CBC or Film Board? Will it put a damper on future documentaries?"

The short answer to editorials about abuse of power, censorship and attacks on freedom of expression is the one Douglas Fisher, Ottawa's best-informed commentator on Parliament, gave to a reporter for *The Hill Times*, the newspaper for people whose lives revolve around Parliament Hill: "That's crap. All this [the subcommittee] is is a forum for people to present their views."

No less false than the talk of censorship and the rest were the editorial suggestions that public debate afforded a readily available, effective way of challenging the opinions of the country's public television network, joined, as it was, in fraternal solidarity with much of the rest of the country's press. For a start, freedom of expression does not exist—not in today's world—without carriers through which it may be exercised. Without the ability to reply *in kind*, being free to speak is an exercise in frustration akin to Shirley Valentine's talking to her wall.

The Globe and Mail, in an inspired demonstration of editorial hypocrisy, said, "Certainly the merits of The Valour and the Horror have been debated at length in the newspapers." That was enough to make a plaster statue gag. The paper was contrasting its enlightened self with the CBC, usually its great and good friend, which had apologized—apologized, mind!—for the flaws its own ombudsman had found in the series.

There was little enough debate initiated or accepted by newspapers in the beginning, and no more later than could be avoided without declaring an outright ban against the Senate subcommittee and a few 1940s-vintage journalists still in practice, such as Doug Fisher and Charles Lynch, who were prepared to say the films had an unacceptably high hogwash content.

Without the outcry, there is no reason to believe there would have been an internal inquiry at the CBC by William Morgan, the man appointed for the purpose of providing the corporation with an appearance of public accountability. It is unlikely there would have been a review of the series by the CRTC, the regulatory body that superintends all broadcasting, which became another, though minor, participant in the public debate. Those things took place because enough people who felt a bad product had been dumped on them found a quite different forum in which they could make themselves heard.

In any case, how many letters to the editor—edited to the bone, as they usually are—equate with twelve hours of prime-time national television, thoroughly hyped in advance by complaisant television critics to bring in audiences calculated (with questionable reliability) at two million for each film? How many copies would a book on the same three episodes of the war sell in Canada—five thousand? Twenty-five hundred? Five hundred? How ready would the CBC and the National Film Board be to finance and market a second series to correct the shortcomings of the first?

Obviously, *The Globe and Mail* carried news stories and commentaries on the issue before and after the Marshall subcommittee took up the subject. However, virtually nothing, certainly nothing of the paper's origination, dealt with the other side of the matter—whether the films were good as *journalism*, to which the *Globe* has always been assumed to aspire. What was demonstrated was media solidarity at work. It was only when Gérard Veilleux decided, on the evidence of the ombudsman, that the series did not measure up to the in-house journalism standard, and apologized, that much of the media turned and attacked him. He had let the side down.

A contribution to that chastening of the CBC president was provided by William Thorsell, editor-in-chief at the *Globe*, in a signed Saturday piece headed "Slavish defence of conventional wisdom shows up CBC's stupidity." In it he expressed himself profoundly depressed by Veilleux's "response to the controversy" (or, as an editorial had phrased it, the "abject disavowal of the series").

A few days later—all of this nearly a full year after *The Valour and the Horror* was first aired—Thorsell replied loftily to an Ottawa reader whose long and critical letter seemingly piqued him, "I do not sit in judgment over the particulars of the case."

Confusing, that. How does a newspaper editor judge between an "abject disavowal" and a richly merited apology for a piece of substandard work, without having sat in judgement over the particulars? Does that imply—which would be even more profoundly depressing—that an acknowledgement of fallibility in journalism is contemptible, deserving to be interpreted as a cowardly giving-way to blackmail? That was the slippery innuendo slipped into an editorial—that CBC management somehow saw Marshall, a Conservative, as the cat's paw of a Conservative and therefore hostile government. And that perhaps —wonderful word, "perhaps"—the CBC accordingly had thrown in its hand with an eye "on the $50 million supplementary allocation it has been angling for since spring, but has yet to receive." The editorial offered no scrap of evidence.

But quite a few strange things were being said by editorialists in the frenzy that followed the critical report of the CBC ombudsman, and the apology to viewers. Norman Webster, the editor of the Montreal *Gazette*, spoke of the disgraceful performance of the CBC, which, in his words, included the ombudsman's having produced "one of the most pitiful, inadequate, lightweight, pettifogging, truly embarrassing reports since the Vatican condemned Galileo. " He also gave the paper's readers his personal assurance that "almost every challenge to The Valour and the Horror is inconsequential." But then, perhaps he too had not sat in judgement on the particulars of the case.

The Globe and Mail, frothing slightly about the lips, dismissed criticism of the series with the words "the documentary is chastized for unsupported allegations, quotations taken out of context, and some minor errors of fact." It would be difficult to say under which of those headings the following would come: in the film "Death by Moonlight", a dramatic few lines spoken by the actor portraying Harris, the leader of Bomber Command and the villain of the piece, were "We shall destroy Germany's will to fight. Now that we have the planes and crews, in 1943 and 1944 we shall drop one and a quarter million tons of bombs, render 25 million Germans homeless, kill 900,000, and seriously injure one million."

In a statement subsequent to his report, Morgan said those words were taken in slightly altered form from an official document, "Estimate of the Effects of Anglo-American Bomber Offensive against Germany", and officially identified as "Note by the Chief of the Air Staff". The chief of the air staff was not Harris but Sir Charles Portal. The figures given, as is clear from the title, relate not just to the RAF (which encompassed the RCAF) but to the RAF and USAF *combined.* Whether or not Harris assisted in the preparation of that strategic assessment, which is not clear, that was not sufficient warrant, to the ombudsman's mind, for giving an actor lines that came from a document signed by someone else, and then describing them "as the boast of a man now free to deliberately target German civilians."

The question for editors in general must be "Can journalism, for its own sake, afford to be quite so cavalier in its attitude towards fact and context and attribution as some of you editors have made it seem in your arguments about freedom of press and the not-very-evident threat to it in this case?"

The Chronicle of Higher Education is not a publication that is on my regular reading list, but someone brought to my attention an item in the issue of November 18, 1992, at precisely the time when the editorial frenzy over the film series was at its peak, under the heading "Point of View". The writer was Dan T. Carter, a professor of history at Emory University, near Atlanta, Georgia. The whole piece was piquantly relevant to our situation. What follows is just one paragraph.

> As scholars and teachers, we cannot hope to challenge mass paranoia or outlandish conspiracy theories if we accept the notion that one version of reality, past or present, is as "truthful" as another; that our choices between different descriptions of reality are to be made simply on the basis of which version is more witty or interesting or cleverly constructed. The distinction between fact and fiction is essential both to our sanity and to our ability to make moral judgments. We may never know the truth, the whole truth, and nothing but the truth, but we have to believe that some descriptions of our past and our present conditions are more truthful than others. Oliver Stone's *JFK* is dramatically more compelling and infinitely more imaginative than the Warren Commission's plodding assessment of the weight of evidence. For all its many failings and shortcomings, however, the commission's report is more faithful to reality than Mr. Stone's film.

In the Canadian row over the merits of *The Valour and the Horror*, most editors in our largest newspapers demonstrated a profound attachment to the notion that one version of reality is as truthful as another. The attitude displayed was tantamount in the circumstances to saying that freedom of the press extends beyond an assured right to publish—which of course was exercised without interference in this case—to include an equally assured right not to be replied to later.

The Globe and Mail shortly before had published an editorial lesson on rights for beginners, not directly related to The Valour and the

Horror but embracing the same subject matter. It said that "10 years after the Charter of Rights and Freedoms, a century after John Stuart Mill, two centuries after the [U.S.] Bill of Rights, three centuries after Milton", a lot of people still did not, or would not, understand what free speech meant.

That did not say much except that freedom of speech, including print, is not a new concept. But, along with saying that many people still do not understand what it means, the *Globe* editorialist might have added that many people evidently still do not understand what it doesn't mean. For instance, John Stuart Mill writing on liberty said "The beliefs which we have most warrant for, have no safeguard to rest on but a standing invitation to the whole world to prove them unfounded." *Question:* How do a lot of individual Canadians go about making a case for unfoundedness in something broadcast as fact to millions, if the supposedly competing media decide to confine them to the letters columns?

Mill also said this: "To call any proposition certain, while there is anyone who would deny its certainty, if permitted. . .is to assume that we, and those who agree with us, are the judges of certainty, and judges without hearing the other side." *Question:* How do individuals get to enjoy freedom of speech remotely equal in potency with those who enjoy great platforms, if they can't make themselves heard because the media are not open to them? What we have here may be known as the Liebling proposition, that freedom of the press belongs to the man who owns one.

Mill also said, "Wrong opinions and practices gradually yield to fact and argument, but facts and arguments, to produce any effect on the mind, must be brought before it." *Question:* How, in a television age, are facts and arguments opposed to television's own to be brought to the public mind to produce that beneficial result? Television has no regular avenue of reply.

As for the U.S. Bill of Rights, the philosophical basis for constitutionalized freedom of the press was that an independent, numerous, diverse and disputatious press would provide a vehicle for every shade of opinion, from all of which the public would define truth. *Question:* What relevance has that today, when a very much smaller press, based upon larger units, increasingly leans to mutual reinforcement?

Milton? His most famous observation to which the *Globe*'s reference might be related was "Though all the winds of doctrine were let loose to play upon the earth, so Truth be in the field, we do injuriously, by licensing and prohibiting, to misdoubt her strength. Let her and Falsehood grapple; who ever knew Truth put to the worse in free and open encounter?"

"Licensing and prohibiting" implies censorship, prior restraint—stopping people from talking before they start. That has nothing to do with what we have been talking about here, which is the right to quarrel with what has been said once the sayer has said it. The question here is, where are Truth and Falsehood to find the mat on which to grapple in "free and open encounter", so that Truth may prevail, if the media themselves do not provide it?

The idea that a handful of persons with a sense of mission, a talent for propaganda and access to a medium of mass communications can be allowed not only to deliver their message, but to deliver it assured that the otherwise-minded cannot exercise an equal right of dissent, simply won't wash. Television, radio, newspapers, magazines, the works, would do themselves a great favour by diverting to their own performance, individually and collectively, a share of the judgementalism they bring to other institutions in our public life, notably government at all levels. If they do not, they invite others, such as Senate subcommittees, to do so.

When the CBC ombudsman's report eventually was produced, in truncated form, it was vigorously rejected not just by the film-makers but, more remarkably, by the CBC's own production staff. That was an act of solidarity with their friends the McKennas, but it was also a conspicuous act of nose-thumbing at all the viewers who had had the effrontery to complain.

With that—and notwithstanding Gérard Veilleux's public apology for the flaws which, in the ombudsman's words, caused the series not to measure up to corporate standards—within three weeks management and the McKennas were discussing how they could go about getting the films back on the air for a third run. In his public apology, Veilleux had said the series would not run again without changes to correct the flaws. Patrick Watson, chairman of the board, had said long before the ombudsman even set up shop that if errors were demonstrated, they would be corrected.

NINE
CHILL OR BE CHILLED

LUCAS A. POWE, JR., AN AMERICAN AUTHORITY ON WHAT is known generically in the United States as First Amendment law, has said that people in his country read more about libel than any other form of non-criminal law. The explanation is not that libel is so common; in fact, he says in *The Fourth Estate and the Constitution: Freedom of the Press in America* that it makes "an insignificant blip in the statistics of American courts". Rather, it is so much brought to public attention because libel affects the press "and the press assumes, with becoming myopia, that anything that affects it is important to us, too."

That same assumption, and the myopia that goes with it, are no less present in Canada. That is why everyone who has read, seen or heard the news at all in at least a decade may have some glimmering recollection of the term "chill effect", in another context than that of winter temperatures and biting winds.

The most common definition of libel chill is a fear induced in the media at the thought of being tied up in court forever and at great expense because someone who is (a) litigious and (b) rich has taken offence at something being made public. Thus a crimp is put upon freedom of the press, the crimp of fear, which may cause the withholding of information the public should have. It lies, of course, with those who complain of the chill to say what information the public should have.

What the argument omits is the fact that persons who are not at all litigious by nature, and not rich, may feel they have been gratuitously defamed, but may suffer a similar chill at the thought of going up against a large media corporation to seek redress. The press myopia has the curious effect of blanking out the second part of this double standard.

Nor is that all. *Any* proceeding which challenges an assumed right of the press to do anything may bring forth dark mutterings about an intrusion on the constitutional guarantee of a free press. A court grants an injunction to delay—not to ban, although it's usually so described—the broadcast of something because it might influence a jury at a trial. That may be represented as instilling fear in the hearts of producers, which may cause them to back off from doing the fearless, challenging documentary they have in mind. What of the right of the person on trial to be judged by an unprejudiced jury? Tough. The right of the public to know—nowhere defined—must take precedence if freedom is to prevail. Better a man be in the hoosegow than the media become self-censoring, backing away from subjects because of imposed timidity.

No one, of course, is obliged to believe the plaint without reservation, or to sympathize with it. Every time an editor takes pencil in hand, or rather manoeuvres the cursor of the computer, to consign the next several paragraphs to the now-metaphorical wastebasket, he or she is censoring—in this case the writer. It is called editing. Such cutting is done for all sorts of reasons, from the simple one of space or time, to the editor's having found the information improbable, morally offensive or biased—all qualitative judgements.

Some prominent persons who have been known to react badly to things published about them—the Reichmann family, for example, or Conrad Black—have become themselves living symbols of chill not surpassed by Frosty the Snowman. They have money, they are considered to have easily bruised sensitivities, and they may at any time, it is feared, use the first to demand salve for the second. Chill is everywhere—and the sensitivities of the media to it are tender.

Undoubtedly libel chill occurs, but even hearsay accounts are not readily found. The likeliest explanations for this are that the persons abandoning the story were never really sure whether they were experiencing an unwarranted chill or just an attack of sound judgement, or that acknowledging a story withheld might invite accusations of having chickened out. What stories there are about chills that worked crop up mainly in affidavits supplied by press people in support of press defendants in defamation suits. One such account is to be found in an affidavit prepared by Linden MacIntyre, a senior on-air and off-air public affairs journalist at CBC-TV, on behalf of the defence in a suit that eventually was settled out of court. The case was Coates *vs.* the Ottawa *Citizen*, a defamation suit by former Defence minister Robert Coates against the Southam company's newspaper in the capital. MacIntyre offered, as an example of how the press could become self-censoring, a story in which he had been involved.

The essence of it was this: a Romanian secret agent infiltrated a Canadian government agency and procured nuclear secrets—a story that to MacIntyre's mind was very much in the public interest and deserving to be broadcast, which, on the face of it, would seem to be the case. The difficulty was the program's inability to ascertain to the point of provability whether the information it had was good, or whether the story, in whole or in part, was CIA "disinformation"—the bureaucratic term for what was called in the days of Dr. Joseph Goebbels, the world's great disinformer, "the Big Lie".

MacIntyre said in the affidavit that he felt journalism had "become an exercise primarily directed at the avoidance of libel laws as opposed to being primarily directed at communication in the public interest." No matter how much one may agree with that—I do hardly at all—it would still merit at least a quiet "Yes, but. . . ." The deterrent was fear of being sued. The necessary grounds for that suit would be damage to reputation. Consequently what was at issue was whether the news medium, having decided independently what constituted the public interest, then had the right to decide, also independently, that someone's reputation—someone *else's* reputation—was worth risking for it.

The orthodox media response to that kind of rumination is to say that the aggrieved party would be able to win compensation in the courts if the facts alleged turned out not to be capable of proof. However, that skips lightly over the fact that the first effect would be to put a perhaps innocent party to the necessity of doing precisely what the broadcaster objected to—facing the chilling prospect of being endlessly and expensively tied up in the courts. Moreover, if the "public interest" truly meant that an imminent threat to public safety existed, the communicator had a moral obligation to ignore the chill and get the matter out in the open as soon as possible. The decision would not be easy; the question is whether it ought to be. What is virtually guaranteed is that too many wrong decisions, arrived at by confusing the media interest with the public interest, or exaggerating the public interest at the expense of the individual interest, will result in more and more chill-inducing damages awards. Juries everywhere these days are not notably sympathetic to the media.

Freedom of the press, whether constitutionally guaranteed or simply established in common law, is a warrant to put in print or on air almost anything the publisher or broadcaster is prepared to take responsibility for. In other words, it is not necessary, before going ahead, to submit material to be read for acceptability, or to apply for a licence to publish, or even to get an informal nod of approval anywhere.

Except in extraordinary circumstances—such as a court intervening to say that this or that should not be published *at this time*—there is no prior restraint, as the term is. After the event, things are different; that is where accountability comes in. Freedom of the press does not mean press immunity from criticism, questioning or full-blown public denunciation. More important, it does not supersede the civil law which recognizes defamation as a tort, defined as a wrongful act which results in injury to another person's bodily well-being, property or reputation, among other things.

What the undoubted bulk of journalists regard as the most galling aspect of the Canadian law is that the one unfailing defence in libel—obviously not the only defence—is the defence of justification. What justifies is truth—but the defendant must be able to prove it. That reverse onus, as it is called, is the reverse of what applies in most damage suits, in which the party claiming injury is left to make his or her case that injury actually was done and by what fault of the defendant.

The Canadian law has defenders among some journalists and lawyers, who say in effect that a little bit of chill encourages further effort to nail things down, and so improves accuracy. The evidence that it actually does so is at best patchy but it is difficult to argue that *easing* the law would make anything better.

The reverse onus has gone from U.S. law, but while it remained an interesting sidelight was cast upon it by a highly successful libel lawyer, E. Douglas Hamilton, who looked after the legal troubles of *The New York Herald Tribune* over a period of twenty-nine years. During that time, Hamilton lost only one contested case, in 1939. The plaintiff was awarded damages of $2,500, reduced on appeal to $1,000.

The story is briefly told in *The Paper: The Life and Death of The*

New York Herald Tribune, a superb portrait of a much-admired newspaper by Richard Kluger. Hamilton did not like settlements out of court; he thought they could only encourage others to try their hand. Whether or not he, as a courtroom lawyer, ever found the reverse onus irksome, he nevertheless acknowledged the legal logic in it. His view, as recounted by Kluger, was that "the publisher of a libel is standing in the shoes of a prosecutor since he is accusing someone of bad conduct, while the person named in the publication is, as he should be, presumed innocent of the accusation." That is a restatement, in terms of civil law, of a fundamental proposition of criminal law.

Another relevant consideration in the matter of onus is that the news media are in the business of selling information which they want their viewers, listeners and readers to believe is at all times as true as they can make it. It seems somehow inconsistent to argue that the law should be written to relieve them of the responsibility of defending their product in court. Obviously doing away with the reverse onus would remove a considerable element of the chill to which the press claim such extreme susceptibility; whether the inhibition is quite what it is made out to be, or warrants a greater degree of protection being provided, are a couple of other matters.

One celebrated case of demonstrated libel chill was the great political scandal in Britain in the early 1960s. The three principals in the affair—with a rich supporting cast, including a marijuana dealer picturesquely known as Johnny Shit—were John Profumo, the Secretary of State for War; Yevgeny Ivanov, an assistant naval attaché at the Soviet embassy in London; and Christine Keeler, euphemistically described as a model. The first two from time to time shared the bed of the third, although not together.

What made the story more than merely piquant was the Cold War, which at that point was at its coldest. Any pillow talk that took place could have encompassed the deployment of submarines or nuclear missiles, or other national defence secrets. (Nuclear missiles seem an improbable subject of conversation in the circumstances, but in the depths of the Cold War a lot of improbable scenarios received serious consideration.)

The story, as related by Phillip Knightley and Caroline Kennedy in *Affair of State* (published by Jonathan Cape in London, 1987), was scarcely unknown in Fleet Street long before it eventually broke—but not first in the press. The *Sunday Pictorial* had the tale, or a version of it, complete, initialled page by page by Christine Keeler herself as staff writers put her verbal reflections into *Sunday Pictorial* words. The *News of the World* had it too, at least in outline; Keeler had gone there from the *Pictorial* looking for a better offer, but the *News of the World*, not usually known for its lack of interest in a juicy yarn, refused to get into a bidding war. Very much guarded rumours had even appeared in print.

However, the facts remained unpublished until a front-bench Labour MP, George Wigg, in opposition, sprang enough of the story under the protection of parliamentary privilege to ensure that the rest must follow. Profumo was first to respond; he acknowledged that he and Keeler were on friendly terms, but assured the House that there had been no impropriety. When that was shown not to be pure fact, it gave rise to a couplet defining parliamentary sensibilities in such matters: "To lie in the nude is at worst rather crude, but to lie in the House is obscene." Profumo soon resigned.

When Wigg spoke, he said every Member of Parliament and of the parliamentary press had heard rumour upon rumour. But the press, he said, had shown itself willing to wound—an apparent reference to the guarded bits that had appeared—but not to kill. He went on: "These great press lords, these men who control the great instruments of public opinion and of power, do not have the guts to discharge the duty that they are now claiming for themselves."

It was not an unfair comment. If the possibility existed that information had gone from the Secretary of State for War, via a shared lover, to an intelligence-gatherer for the Soviet Union—which, as it happened, was the naval attaché's real role—the security of not just Britain but perhaps others might have been endangered. The press had had the information in their hands, and presumably had seen the implicaitons they were quick enough to announce once the story became public; this reluctance to publish showed either the lack of guts alleged by the Labour MP, or an inactive sense of public responsibility.

At times, a rare story comes along that can't *not* be published. An editor then must take a calculated risk and go to press with it even if it represents probable truth rather than provable truth. Truth, of course, is not always easy to assess, because often considerable effort is expended to keep it from getting out. The editor who makes the decision must accept the risk of having to pay for it if the facts do not persuade a court. After all, the other side of the coin of freedom of the press is responsibility.

Freedom of the press first became a constitutional right in the still-new United States, in 1791, phrased in the First Amendment simply as "Congress shall make no law . . . abridging freedom of speech or of the press." Since 1925, the same guarantee has existed in state law. But the idea was not new even in 1791. Although the revolution in the Thirteen Colonies was in rejection of the government and laws of England, the makers of the U.S. constitution borrowed freely from the thinking of Whig radicals in England. The proposition that all men are created equal and the idea of a constitution based upon checks and balances derived from the writings of the English philosopher John Locke. In 1769, twenty-two years before the First Amendment was proclaimed, the English jurist Sir William Blackstone had already written in his *Commentaries on the Laws of England*: "The liberty of the press is indeed essential to the nature of a free state, but this consists in laying no previous restraint upon publications, and not from censure . . . when published."

From the beginning, the spectrum of debate in the United States on freedom of the press has run mainly from very little restraint to none. The subject is rich in lore. The quotation from Thomas Jefferson most favoured by the press is that, the basis of government being the opinion of the people, "were it left to me to decide whether we should have a government without newspapers, or newspapers without a government, I should not hesitate a moment to prefer the latter." He also said that government should intervene to regulate people only when they did something, not when they said something. On the other hand, as recorded in *Jefferson & Civil Liberties: The Darker Side*, by Leonard W. Levy (Quadrangle, 1973), he also said that the press, while free of censorship, must remain "responsible for abuse of an unrestrained freedom to publish". And once he was even moved to write to the governor of Pennsylvania to say—which sounds like a hint—that "a few prosecutions of the most prominent offenders would have a wholesome effect in restoring the integrity of the presses." The states at the time were not constrained, as Washington was, by the First Amendment.

First Amendment law has never been a neglected subject in the American press, but there probably has never been a time when it was more to the forefront in the news than in the 1960s and 1970s. It is mostly in terms of the changes that occurred then that unfavourable contrasts are made by Canadian journalists with Canadian law. The lifting of restraints was the theme of the time, and First Amendment law was not excluded.

Of the three most notable decisions, the first, in 1964, was *The New York Times* vs. Sullivan, which was rooted in neither the newspaper's own reporting nor its commentary, but in a full-page advertisement taken by a black civil rights organization in Alabama. As it was not news material, it had not been read for libel—although even today, the supposed defamation it contained scarcely leaps out at the lay reader. Even more oddly, the original plaintiff—L.B. Sullivan, the police commissioner in Montgomery, the state capital—was nowhere mentioned in the ad, either by name or by office. Nevertheless, his lawyers argued that there were damning references to police actions, and that as he was the responsible officer, they reflected on him. He was awarded $500,000 in the Supreme Court of Alabama.

On the *Times*'s appeal, eventually to the U.S. Supreme Court, a decision was rendered that made it virtually impossible for a public official to sue successfully for defamation arising from anything written or published about his or her performance of official duties. Henceforth, it would be necessary for the plaintiff to prove not only that there was untruth—the reverse of our law—but that the untruth resulted from either reckless disregard of the truth, or malice. Because they can only exist in someone else's head, malice and reckless disregard are difficult to prove.

The other two most notable cases, which extended the same conditions to a class loosely defined as "public persons", were Associated Press vs. Walker, and Gertz vs. Robert Welch.

Walker was a retired major-general in the U.S. Army and a raging anti-Communist. Injudicious public comments about the Cold War while he was on duty in Europe caused him to be brought home; when he accused President John F. Kennedy of collaborating with the international Communist conspiracy, he was hustled into retirement.

On a September night in 1962, U.S. federal marshals ringed the administration building as the first black student, James Meredith, was enrolled at the University of Mississippi. According to the Associated

Press, Walker assumed command of a mob of protesters and led them through the grey fog of tear gas in attacks on the marshals. Two men, one a French journalist, were killed that night. I was there; it is an indelible memory. The general succeeded in his suit in a lower court, $500,000 worth, but the U.S. Supreme Court, in June 1967, said a public person—which it found Walker to be—was on a different footing from a private one, and had to establish malice or reckless disregard, just as was set out for public officials.

The circumstances were turned around in Gertz vs. Robert Welch in 1974. Elmer Gertz, a Chicago lawyer, sued a monthly publication, *American Opinion*, put out by the John Birch Society, a rabidly anti-Communist organization backed by Welch. The magazine had called Gertz a Leninist and a Communist-fronter, a euphemism for the more popular "commie stooge". *American Opinion* sought shelter in the Walker decision. It argued in court that he was a public person, and therefore would need to show actual malice on the part of the publisher. But the Supreme Court found otherwise; Gertz was well known as a lawyer but had not thrust himself into the public eye; if he was there, it was not by his design.

As a sidelight indicative of the trend of the time, Justice William O. Douglas said in a separate decision that all discussion of public affairs should be shielded from libel—and he emphasized that, by public affairs, he did not mean politics alone but "science, economics, business, art, literature. . . . Indeed, any matter of sufficient general interest to prompt media attention, may be said to be a public affair." It would take a decision of some supreme court to work out the full ramifications of that, but one thing is certain: for the media, it would do wonders in relieving libel chill. Whether making access to the courts more difficult for so many people seeking redress for loss of reputation would contribute greatly to civilized public discourse is less certain.

Apart from the sixties' and seventies' initiatives of the U.S. Supreme Court, which came as merely gratifying add-ons to the much earlier elimination of the reverse-onus provision in libel law, the U.S. holds another source of envy for Canadian journalists. That is the cosy "shield laws" which some states have adopted, which are represented by media people as desirable not for *their* benefit, perish the thought, but for the benefit of public knowledge. (On matters of press freedom, the press like to speak on behalf of the public, the public voice having been delegated to them at a time and by a process no one ever ventures to explain.)

Shield laws protect media from having to disclose their sources. The rationale is that important information—about criminal activity, say, or a scandal in government—may have been obtained only on the reporter's pledge not to name the informant. If the reporter cannot give the source that assurance of anonymity, so the argument runs, the information may remain forever hidden. Furthermore, if a reporter breaks a promise, or is *made* to break it, word will get about that all journalists are untrustworthy, useful sources will dry up and everyone will suffer. But it is more a private interest than a public one that is being argued. There is no question about the right of the media to publish unsourced information. That goes with freedom of the press, and is done all the time; quite often the best quotations, which is to say the most vicious, come from people who "spoke on the condition of anonymity". It is only when the unsourced material becomes relevant to some legal proceeding that the media, somewhat in contradiction of their usual full-disclosure doctrine, proclaim an exception—their own. Sources are sacred.

The circumstances in which identification of sources becomes an issue come about something like this: first, assume the subject of some published or broadcast disclosure has become important to a civil or criminal proceeding. The reporter's name is on the story, but the only attribution of the material in question is to a "source". The reporter can tell everything that he or she knows firsthand, but cannot testify to what the source provided, beyond the fact that, with whatever double-checking was done, it seemed to be true.

The lawyers for either or both sides want the source called to be examined and cross-examined. The judge agrees; the source's testimony is needed. Consequently, an order of the court is given that says the reporter must produce the name or. . . . Or, as the Criminal Code puts it, "everyone who, without lawful excuse, disobeys a lawful order made by a court of justice, is guilty of an indictable offence and is liable to imprisonment for two years." Does the reporter at that point—a court attendant at each elbow—go marching off reciting, "It is a far, far better thing that I do than I have ever done . . . ," or quietly rat on the source?

A difficult choice. If the source can be persuaded that anonymity is less important after a lapse of time than when the promise was given, fine. If not, which should prevail—the perceived need of the justice system, or an assumed right of a free press? The journalist's options are few and painful. In fact, if the commitment was firm and clear on both sides, the options come down to one—to start reciting the Dickens bit.

The assumed rights of the press also cross with the authority of the courts when a judge decides that exceptional circumstances warrant a curtailment of reporting—as in the recent Ontario cases of Karla Homolka and her estranged husband, Paul Teale, and charges of manslaughter and murder. Mr. Justice Francis Kovacs, without closing the court to reporters, placed a ban on the immediate publication of the evidence in the trial of Karla Homolka lest a jury in the subsequent trial of her husband might be prejudiced by it. The case had generated volumes of sensational coverage even long before the arrests were made. The media reaction to the holding up of evidence was intense and self-righteously indignant. This was proclaimed as a denial, not just of press freedom, but of a fundamental of the justice system, namely that justice must be *seen* to be done. (Debatable, that; it is nowhere written that the press have to be present for justice to be seen to be done.)

John Miller, chairman of the school of journalism at Ryerson Polytechnic University in Toronto and a former senior newsroom executive at *The Toronto Star*, was one who took a much cooler view—and attracted sour comments for it. His point was that the press were largely responsible for creating the exceptional circumstances cited by the judge, by excesses committed in the coverage before the trial of either accused.

However, worse than that lapse, Miller had taken a swipe at the pretensions of the media to be the collective surrogate of the people, by quoting some observations of David Lepofsky, a constitutional lawyer in the department of the Ontario attorney general, to a conference in England in 1991. These were some of Lepofsky's words: "News organizations will appear in court from time to time and assert . . . that they are attempting to enforce the public's right. Yet they secure no prior authorization from the public before doing so. Many members of the public may well not agree with the positions purportedly being advanced in their name. . . . News outlets, like the producers of any product or service consumed by the public, can be properly seen as private operations. . . ."

Therefore—not in Lepofsky's words, but in mine—their claims as emissaries of the people to be somehow *different*, somehow removed from the legal strictures that apply to others, are unwarranted pretensions if not actual delusions of grandeur—and a demonstration of a thoroughgoing double standard.

Through much of the reporting and commentary on the judge's stay order there ran a fine thread of suggestion that this sort of thing would never be tolerated in the United States and, accordingly, should not be accepted in this country. American reporters, from Buffalo and other nearby border points, were quoted to that effect, properly aghast at the thought. What was more surprising was that various domestic editorials seemed to accept, not just in that case but in subsequent others in which less substantial delays were imposed, that Canadians had some catching up to do. How so, and why?

Two facts underlie this excursion into American law. The first is that to look at press law *without* looking south would be difficult. As a constitutional concept, it began there. There are two hundred years of American jurisprudence relating to the press—and there can't be many fewer books on it than there are seats in Maple Leaf Gardens. The inclusion of freedom of the press in the constitution of Canada dates only from 1982. Before that we were not without freedom of the press—it was honoured no less or more than now, in common law—but it was not written down until it was included in our charter as a fundamental freedom.

The second fact is that, now that we have freedom of the press in our constitution just like the Americans, the thinking of Canadian journalism has turned to the development of a body of press law that will also be just like the Americans'. What has helped that along, on top of the inbred Canadian leaning to copy-cattism, is the fact that the generation now dominant in journalism became politically aware at the same time as those radical changes in press law—and everything else—were occurring in our all-purpose role model to the south. Their attitudes generally came from there.

But the notion that we need made-in-America press law rests on thin logic.

Freedom of the press was conceived in the United States around the idea of an independent, numerous and disputatious press as the collective monitor that would bring every possible viewpoint to bear on the performance of government, not so much to keep it honest as to keep it democratic. The press would be the people's watchdog and informant. Such outside surveillance is valuable in a system in which the executive of government does not sit in the legislature—as it does in the parliamentary system—where it is answerable on a day-to-day basis to the direct representatives of the people. Therefore, the power conferred on the U.S. press in 1791, by way of an irrevocable freedom to publish without interference, had a recognized rationale and purpose.

If the Canadian federal-provincial conferees who produced the Charter of Rights in 1982 decided what freedom of the press was *for*, beyond perhaps the gratification of the media, they did not say. Certainly the U.S. reasons for special treatment do not apply in Canada, and the assumptions on which the U.S. First Amendment was based have become, by the nineties, too ludicrous to be taken seriously. The Canadian media are neither numerous nor, as to ownership, diverse. As to their being disputatious, at least among themselves, every influence is in the opposite direction—to become more and more alike.

These facts deserve to be recognized, if only to bring another light to bear on current strivings to bring our media law more into conformity with America's. At one time, for a small example, Canadians—journalists included—took pride in the fact that we did not have American-style trial-by-media, with pre-trial displays of rumour, speculations and suspicions making it difficult to find jurors whose minds were not at least pre-inclined, if not made up. But the trend now has become to denounce any effort to prevent trial-by-media as a denial of the *media's* rights.

A particular example of an effort to bring Canadian media law more into conformity with the American version, again seemingly inspired by the coming of the charter, was in a brief presented to the Ontario government in early 1991 by a group, mainly of periodical writers and writers of books, calling itself Writers to Reform the Libel Law.

The title of their petition, "A Dangerous Silence", suggested that quantities of information the public should have had were not written, or at least not published, because of the suppressive effect of the law of defamation on "the free expression of ideas, the free flow of facts".

"We are writers," they said, "who have joined together in a common cause—the reform of the libel and slander laws of Ontario—because these laws are outdated, unworkable, and unfair, and because they interfere with the free flow of information necessary in a democratic society." They went on to say, "It is our challenge and our pleasure to bring forward new ideas, raise new issues, root in the past for the origin and meaning of current circumstances and for clues about the future. Unfortunately . . . it has become progressively more difficult for us to do those things."

That makes a strange complaint. The law in Ontario—or anywhere else in Canada—has not noticeably been amended backwards at any recent time; that cannot be what is making the writers' task "progressively more difficult", if anything is. There has never been a legal restriction against recording facts in print or on the air; it is only after the event that there may be trouble, if the authenticity of the asserted facts is challenged. If life has become more difficult for writers, perhaps the blame lies not with the law but with the writers themselves, and their publishers. If the subjects chosen and the treatment given them have become more aggressive, more accusatory, more judgemental, more intrusive into people's lives—more risk-taking, in fact—this results from decisions the writers have made freely. Thus the argument becomes "We want to do things our way and we want some protection taken from people we write about and given to us to reduce our risk." That is an argument they are free to make, but, stated baldly like that, it is much more readily identifiable as a self-interested aim rather than the high-minded, disinterested, service-to-the-public goal they profess it to be.

The Writers to Reform the Libel Law enumerated in their brief some of the ways in which they found the law irksome. "The libel law," they said, ". . . makes it possible to sue over everything from a slur to a song, from an assault on a person's character to a well-documented report on a public corporation's misbehavior. There is no definition of libel. There is no definition of a reputation and what it is worth. There are no guidelines as to which complaints are trivial and which are worth a court's time."

Well, yes—up to a point. But there are reliable clues to where the lines are drawn. For instance, one definition of "slur" is "to calumniate", which in turn is defined as "to make false and malicious statements", a useful guide. There is also the long-standing, informal definition of libel which says, sexist pronouns and all: "Any printed (or broadcast) words, picture, cartoon, or caricature which tend to lower a person in the estimation of right-thinking men, or cause him to be shunned and avoided, or expose him to hatred, contempt or ridicule, or to disparage him in his office, trade or calling, constitutes a libel."

But a song as a cause of action? Why not? Nancy White, who writes and sings her own songs, did one on CBC "Sunday Morning", the network's heavyweight radio public affairs show, that contained in the refrain the line "The cesspool that is Parliament today." Good, clean fun; ho, ho, ho. Great stuff for alleviating public cynicism and distrust. Parliament, of course, does not sue. Still, try that one on, say, the private life of the moderator of the United Church, or the business ethics of the Toronto Dominion Bank, and wait for the writs to arrive straight from the lawyers' smoking word processors.

The writers who signed the brief to the Ontario government were only sixteen in number, but they had the support of significant groups of Canadians who live by writing; including the Canadian Association of Journalists, the Periodical Writers' Association, the Writers' Union and the Canadian Centre of International PEN. Most, if not all, of the sixteen signatories had firsthand knowledge of the discomfort of being exposed to a suit, or the threat of a suit, for defamation. No one can doubt their sincerity. Still, the proposition underlying the argument for a more accommodating media law is not easy to swallow, because it takes from the side that is, in effect, the accused, and gives to the side that is, in effect, the accuser. In exchange for the perhaps illusory benefit to be realized from the exposure of more injustices, illegalities and lapses of trust, we would lose the perhaps salutary discomfort of occasional chills to the media. In the climate of recent times, the merits of chill-free journalism—or even chill-freer journalism—do not stick out all over.

TEN
THE RISE OF YESTERDAY'S KIDS

IN MAY 1991, WHEN DAVID HALTON WAS ON THE POINT of moving from Ottawa to Washington as chief correspondent for the CBC, he was interviewed by Charles Lewis in the Ottawa *Citizen*. The piece was titled, "The CBC's Nice Guy". Lewis found him low-keyed, unopinionated and someone who "unlike a lot of his colleagues, usually leaves the conclusions . . . up to the viewers," all of which was true. However, on the subject of political journalism Halton proved unreluctant to express opinion, and opinion unlikely to enhance his standing as a nice guy in the eyes of those colleagues Lewis referred to. There was, he said, a younger school of reporters in Ottawa who considered politicians villains and approached journalism from a very adversarial vantage point. They failed to consider in making their frequently critical judgements the problems of those on the other side—"to put themselves in the boots of the person they're reporting on." They needed a dose of humility in dealing with other people.

Hallelujah, brother.

However, his was a distinctly minority view amid the Ottawa media horde, who scrupulously observe in all questions of criticism the biblical admonition that it is more blessed to give than to receive.

Still, Halton is not alone. There are others following Canadian political reporting close up who also are unhappy with the tendency to look upon politicians as the foe, to consider mutually tolerant relationships with politicians as incapable of being maintained except at the expense of journalistic independence and to see the natural condition between the two as a war in which the media must be on endless search-and-destroy missions.

Douglas Fisher, for years the Ottawa columnist for the *Sun* newspapers in Toronto, Edmonton, Calgary and Ottawa, came to political columning by the roundabout route of first becoming a CCF Member of Parliament. In 1957, when the Liberals were defeated after an unbroken run since 1935 and John Diefenbaker became prime minister, one of the big stories for Canadians who had television sets—the medium had not yet reached a state of total dominance—was the defeat of the great C.D. Howe, the Liberals' Minister of Everything, as he sometimes was called, by an unknown schoolteacher at Ontario's Lakehead, Douglas Fisher.

Long before he went to Ottawa, Fisher was already a news junkie. Consequently, he soon began to look attentively at the parliamentary press gallery and what it did, and occasionally to comment on it—not always to applause from its members. Looking now from journalism onto politics, Fisher thinks that it is "essential to be aware of the media, because politics more and more *is* the media, and the media, politics." Partly that is due to the close relationship that has developed between the media and pressure groups, which has made both of them players in the game—as opponents of government. "All these groups," he says, "have learned how to lobby and raise hell and they're remorseless. They have channels. They have their television. They see government. And they take aim. They want funds. They want legislation. And they know how to put on all the dog-and-pony shows. They know how to run picket lines, press conferences and all that kind of thing. And [everything they find wrong] tends to be charged against government."

The cheapest and easiest way of doing that, in Fisher's view, is "to kick the hell out of the prime minister", the most visible symbol of The Government and therefore the person most Canadians with a beef against The Government will most like to see the hell kicked out of. As Fisher puts it, "It all adds up."

His samples of recent great exponents of that cheap and easy strategy include, from within politics, Sheila Copps, who parlayed leadership of the Rat Pack in the 1984–88 House of Commons into deputy-leadership of the Liberal opposition, and deputy prime-ministership in the Chrétien government. Others on his short list were Dennis McDermott and Shirley Carr, presidents in that order of the Canadian Labour Congress before the coming of the less raucous Bob White, former head of the Canadian Auto Workers.

What political journalists of Fisher's stripe find sadly perplexing is that so many of the newer breed of reporters are indifferent to politics. They are more ambitious, more inclined to look upon assignment to Ottawa as a way-stop on the road to positions in management, but less informed about and interested in what is, or ought to be, a significant aspect of what they are there for. "A part of this," he says, "is the turnover; they don't stay long. The other part—how do I describe it?—there is more politics, in an odd kind of way; politics has really been popularized enormously since Diefenbaker's day in terms of where it fits in television and radio newscasts and so on. But I find there are very few of the younger reporters who are much interested in it. When I look around the gallery and think of the people I bump into and talk to, I find very few real fans, people who, in a sense, live it."

That is a long way from saying that they do not try to influence politics according to their own beliefs—and prejudices.

During the Mulroney years, Fisher was one journalist who saw the prime minister more than occasionally, and not always for set-piece interviews, but to talk politics. For this he once was denounced to his own editors in Toronto by a colleague who said, according to the word that came back to Fisher, "He *talks* with him; he often *talks* with the guy." To that, Fisher says: "I thought, 'What the hell do you do? If I was to be convicted of talking to politicians . . . [the sentence is broken off]. I just spent two hours this morning bullshitting with a prominent Grit. Where would I be if I didn't?' "

It is part of Fisher's day, first thing when he gets downtown in the morning, to go to a table just inside the door of the cafeteria in the West Block of the Parliament Buildings, where two or three politicians, elected and unelected, are likely on any day to stop by. By ancient dictate of the trade, talking with garden-variety MPs and miscellaneous persons in political jobs was part of political reporting. But it is no longer considered an essential, and more often is looked upon as something akin to consorting with the enemy. Obviously, talking with ordinary politicians and persons on their staffs does not carry the same stigma of toadying subservience as does sharing a prime minister's trust; nevertheless, it is considered mildly déclassé and Simply Not Done—at least, not in public—by the best people. But in fact, the best people do it, although they do not take out ads to say so.

To Anthony Westell, there is something posturing about the sort of macho journalism that postulates all politicians as—to borrow Halton's term—villains. "There is a lot of pretence about this adversary role," Westell says. "The more successful media writers don't subscribe to it. Nobody supposes that Jeffrey Simpson doesn't have confidential relations with politicians, or David Halton. People who are well known in the business obviously do have off-the-record or confidential relationships with politicians." But journalists of the sort he describes are a handful, and not the ones most readers of newspapers and magazines, or watchers of television, get their news from.

Halton—like Joe Schlesinger, his successor as chief correspondent in Ottawa—delivered more rounded accounts of situations and events than hard news reports. Craig Oliver, CTV's Ottawa bureau chief, is another of the same. So was Westell himself, successively bureau chief for *The Globe and Mail* and bureau chief and columnist for *The Toronto Star* before going to Carleton University's school of journalism, from which he retired as director in 1992. Westell does not pretend to understand altogether how or why the antipathy of so many journalists towards the politicians they report upon has come about. But there are, he says, several possibilities to consider:

> Maybe this generation of politicians is much worse than previous generations. It's possible; I don't think it is true, but it is possible. Maybe it's that we've had good times that ran from 1945 to 1970, or something like that, and after that it has been mostly downhill and people resent the fact that politicians aren't delivering what they thought they ought to deliver. I think there is some truth in that. The thing about the proposition is, who is it who creates the expectation? It is journalists who lead people to believe that "this" is what the politicians ought to be able to produce, and when, and when they can't, the public blame [the politicians] for it. . . . What we used to call the revolution of rising expectations—all that came to a nasty end. . . . [But] it is still flickering, so it is supposed to be still there. People still have not got over the fact that the government cannot deliver endless prosperity, peace, happiness. The good life.

A complicating factor, which Westell might have added but did not, is that Canada has a political party—the New Democrats—that has very much lived off the fostering of unreal expectations. Because the

NDP has never held power in Ottawa, and because many journalists have an underlying sympathy towards its philosophy, it has never had to submit to the same sort of critical scrutiny as the Liberal and, particularly, the Conservative parties. Consequently, it was only when Bob Rae became head of the first NDP government in Ontario and had to make a sharp about-turn in economic policy that it was exposed for all to see that the federal party's political/economic policy—a sort of shopping basket of interest-group demands, with something for all—could not be made to work in bad times and with huge debts to be taken into account.

As is inescapable in any conversation on the connection between the media and the state of cynicism in the country, the proliferation of the so-called interest groups and their interaction with the media become part of the story. They got their great boost early in the Trudeau regime, when "participatory democracy" suddenly sprang to prominence as the magic phrase in politics. With a view to enabling various groups to make themselves heard in competition with other, better-off interests, government in effect raised critics against itself—native groups, women's groups, environmental groups, among others. This too was a product of its time, and perhaps a noble thought. But whether it made government demonstrably more democratic, or merely more difficult and less workable, is another matter. Certainly it shifted the role of watchdog over the performance of government from the elected representatives of the people to unelected, self-appointed bodies representative only of their own prejudices.

"About the same time [as the good times began to dwindle]," Westell said, "the old parties began to decline. . . . If you had a cause you wanted to promote, you didn't join a party, you joined a coalition, had a demonstration, went to the media. . . . The destruction, or at least the weakening, of the federal political parties in brokering the interests of the regions, partly due to the rise of the advocacy groups, has created a whole lot—and Ottawa has acquired a whole lot—of enemies. . . ."

With that, there has been a growing belief among media people that effective opposition, especially to a government with a solid majority, lies not in the parliamentary opposition but in themselves. The government of the day, according to that creed, becomes accountable primarily to the media, and only through their filter to the public.

"The argument I make," Westell says, "is that if the media see themselves as the opposition, the government is at a hopeless disadvantage. In everything it says, it is not speaking to the electorate, but speaking to it through the opposition. It has another effect, and that is to destroy the notion of parliamentary debate. The press or the media simply push aside the . . . opposition and take over the role themselves, so that instead of being concerned primarily with the reporting of a debate in Parliament between different points of view, they become one of the sides in the argument."

Mike Duffy, host of "Sunday Edition" on CTV stations and others across Canada, agrees with Halton, his former colleague at CBC-TV News, that the adversarial attitude is overdone, that too many young journalists are too judgemental and that there is a marked failure ever to put themselves in the shoes of the people they write and broadcast about so glibly. Duffy speaks of "young people who want to change the world, seeking careers in journalism as a vehicle to do that, instead of going off to become foreign missionaries and bring the word of God to the heathen."

He, like most journalists, accepts as a given that political journalists and politicians will look at the same things from different viewpoints. The politician, in government or in opposition, has a natural and legitimate desire to present in the best light possible whatever his or her party is trying to do.

"I," he says, "am the last one to suggest that everyone should go around being naïve and Pollyanna-ish, but I think there is a balance. The idea of an adversarial relationship has been taken too far. I think a lot is lost by the assumption that everything a politician does is somehow bizarre, corrupt or wrong." He goes on, more strongly even than Fisher, on the point that political journalists often are not attuned to politics: "One of the terrible things is that a lot of people who are now covering politics in this country hate politics and politicians. The view that many journalists hold about politics, the negative view, does not serve the country well or the readers, because it means to me that they only ever go and look for bad news. . . . If that is all you ever read in the pages of your newspaper or see on television, then the public comes to the view that that's all it is. I think that leads to the sense of national malaise, that 'They're all crooks,' and 'What does it matter who is in power, anyway; just worry about yourself as a citizen, and beggar your neighbour.' "

It is sometimes argued by journalists, in defence of an untrusting attitude towards politicians, that the journalists would otherwise be tools in the hands of people whose wish is to manipulate them. Duffy tells a story from the 1980 election campaign that reflects another side. That was the election that returned Pierre Trudeau to the prime-ministership after the Liberal defeat the year before. The place was Cape Breton.

"Trudeau," he recalls, "came down with a goodie to announce—$25 million or some such for a local project, perhaps one of the several upgradings of Sysco steel. He made his announcement and, when everyone came down from the platform, some reporters gathered around the local candidate to see what he had to say about it. And somebody suggested to him that $25 million was chickenfeed. The candidate guessed that was right; it really was chickenfeed.

"Well, everybody walked away and the journalists began laughing, 'Well, there's our lead. Trudeau comes and makes an announcement and the local candidate says it's chickenfeed.' Well, he was a new politician who was set up, and the journalists walked away and laughed. . . . They got the quote and hung it on him. None of the context was put in the news reports—that the word 'chickenfeed' had been first used by the reporter and he just agreed. . . ."

Duffy says his sense of some of his younger colleagues is that they tell themselves, "There is only one way to look at politicians, and that is down."

Now, to this group of senior journalists, all knowledgeable about the ways of both media and politicians in Ottawa, we add a fifth of similar characteristics but of a newer vintage—Wendy Mesley, anchor of CBC's "Sunday Report" and holder of other occasional chairperson spots, but before that an Ottawa-based national affairs correspondent. Thus—like bottles of the same wine but of different years, set up for what is called a vertical tasting—we have Fisher, seventies; Westell, sixties; Halton, fifties; and Duffy and Mesley further down the vintage list.

All these several conversations occurred while the Conservatives were already reaching for the bottom in public opinon polls. Mesley's assessment of the reporter's job then, and presumably now, is that it is "to report on what the government is doing, and to put it into context as fairly and as fully as possible. . . ." She went on: "Just because the policy or position bears a government stamp does not make it inherently evil, just as not all opposition stands are automatically righteous. Even if they were all evil, or all good, it is not the role of the reporter to rule on them. I believe our role is to give people enough unbiased information so they can make up their own minds."

However, there is a "however".

"While I don't think we should be judgemental," she said, "I do think we need to watch against being used as a propaganda arm of the government. I do think reporters should act as government watchdogs. We should be skeptical about what governments say and do, and we should be constantly on the lookout against being used or taken in. Part of being a politician," she says, "is selling yourself and your party platform. And most politicians see nothing wrong with covering up shortcomings and overstating the good parts. Manipulating the press is part of a press attaché's job, and parties in power usually have more staff and more money and other resources to try to manipulate us with. So, yes, we must be especially vigilant. Besides, it is nearly always the parties in power that initiate the legislation that affects people's lives."

All of those points are valid. Government does most of the governing, but that is what it was elected for. Also, it has more of the wherewithal to get its message across. If a prime minister calls a press conference, it is obligatory that reporters attend, not out of any duty to the prime minister but because the reporter's home office will demand it. But between the top and the bottom of our vertical sampling there is a clear difference of emphasis. Mesley clearly is more wary of government, more sensitive to the danger of being manipulated and more confident of the non-malignant influence of the combined media and pressure groups on the efficacy of government.

What has changed most in media–government relations is the reporter—better educated, less experienced, more transient in the political assignment, less deeply interested, infinitely more dedicated to personal causes and, accordingly, more dogmatic. The bulk of reporting from Ottawa today, and most of the editing in the home offices, is done by persons who grew up in the sixties and seventies, a period of social revolution rooted in the United States but enthusiastically imported to Canada by young people (and by some elders who let their thinning hair grow long, wore jeans and chains, and left their shirts open to the navel to show off the chains and went around asking plaintively, "What does youth *want*?", to which there was no answer, because youth knew that if you had to ask, you wouldn't understand anyway).

The objective was to leave behind a lot of burdensome baggage, as exemplified by the famous words—among not very many—of Timothy Leary, Harvard professor and self-appointed preceptor of the burgeoning culture: "Tune in, turn on, drop out." What you dropped out of, or were emancipated from, included institutions of all kinds—starting out with big government, which was to be made somehow to yield power to the people, most of whom thought they already had it.

The future would bring a more co-operative society, organized at the foundation level, perhaps, as communes of like-minded, mutually reinforcing individuals who together would build their own shelter, grow their own chemical-free rutabagas, mill their own wheat germ, weave their own linsey-woolsey for clothes and bake their own hash-enhanced chocolate chip cookies.

To have a cause, or causes, imported or not, was the thing, and if the Canadian government chose not to involve the country in the Vietnam war, that was no fault of the people who wanted to demonstrate against it. All the popular causes, in their different ways, represented street politics versus elected politics, "the people" pushing against resistant government, or what could be represented as resistant government.

In 1990, Harper & Row caused a flutter in the U.S. academic community by publishing *Tenured Radicals: How Politics Has Corrupted Our Higher Education*, by Roger Kimball, managing editor of *The New Criterion*, a monthly magazine of the arts. In his preface, Kimball said this:

> It has often been observed that yesterday's student radical is today's tenured professor or academic dean. The point of this observation is not to suggest that our campuses are littered with political agitators. In comparison to the situation that prevailed in 1968, when colleges and universities across the country were scenes of violent demonstrations, the academy today seems positively sedate. Yet if the undergraduate population has moved quietly to the Right in recent years, the men and women who are paid to introduce students to the great works and ideas of our civilization have by and large remained true to the

> emancipationist ideology of the Sixties. Indeed, it is important to appreciate the extent to which the radical vision of the Sixties has not so much been abandoned as internalized by many who came of age then and who now teach at and administer our institutions of higher education.

The thesis of *Tenured Radicals* is that the teaching of the humanities in many, perhaps most, colleges and universities has been debased, and "the ideals of objectivity and disinterested pursuit of knowledge" not just disowned but "pilloried as products of a repressive bourgeois society." At the instance of now-tenured one-time students, the great works of Western civilization have been subordinated in curriculums to "more women's literature for feminists, black literature for blacks, gay literature for homosexuals, and so on." He went on: "The idea of literary quality that transcends the contingencies of race, gender, and the like, or that transcends the ephemeral attractions of popular entertainment, is excoriated as naïve, deliberately deceptive, or worse."

Traits of the sixties are plentiful in today's political journalism. Products of that era, now in their forties, fifties and even a little more, have been largely responsible for setting the current prosecutorial style of political reporting. Journalism, after all, provides no less attractive a vantage point than the professor's lectern for persons with a self-assigned mission to put the world to rights. Another side of that generation's personality reflected in today's journalism is a "cynical assumption that corruption is rampant in the establishment".

Those words—used to describe one reporter's viewpoint, but broadly applicable—are from a 1982 judgment in the Supreme Court of British Columbia in a defamation suit brought by the provincial deputy attorney general of the time, Richard Vogel, against the CBC. Preliminary to making the second-largest Canadian award of damages for defamation to that date, Justice William Esson wrote a devastating analysis, amounting to an exposé of an exposé, of the motives and methods behind a piece of investigative journalism that was foreseen from the beginning to be a blockbuster—and was, although not quite in the way anticipated. (The court's award was $125,000, paltry by current standards.) What his judgment defined was a scandal. Any equivalent *political* scandal would be publicized across the country the next day, even if based on a document far less authoritative than the judgment of a court. It contained such phrases as "deceptive methods", "deceitful implications", "another piece of deception", "facts which were fabrications", "exercise in deception", "that message was quite untrue", "it is of course a falsehood", "false innuendoes" and "at least a deceptive half-truth", among others. Although the suit involved the largest media entity in the country—the CBC—the judgment was reported cursorily outside British Columbia, as just another court item.

The story begins with Chris Bird, a reporter with experience at the Victoria *Daily Colonist* and the Vancouver *Province*, being hired by CBC Vancouver. After a stint on a commentary show called "Pacific Report", he was assigned to the six o'clock news show, which was running a poor second in the ratings to its CTV rival. It was thought that Bird would ferret out more hard news, and give the show more kick. He did, but not without help from his superiors.

Bird had more than just an interest in investigative reporting; with it went, in Judge Esson's words, "a romantic view of the investigative reporter as society's bulwark against corruption" and "a sourly cynical assumption that corruption is rampant in the Establishment and that all attempts to maintain privacy and confidentiality are part of a conspiracy to suppress the truth." Those characteristics inclined Bird to regard as a hero of sorts anyone within the system who would leak information—and disinclined to accept that such information might be unreliable for a number of reasons, including that the leaker might have a not altogether disinterested reason for leaking it.

CBC Vancouver's six o'clock news show on March 6, 1980, led off, *bang*, with the anchor, Bill Good, Jr., saying, "British Columbia's deputy attorney general has interfered with the judicial system. Tonight, a detailed report." Behind Good was a still shot of Richard Vogel looking appropriately worried and harassed. The picture had been taken several weeks earlier and the look had nothing to do with the story about to be unfolded.

Chris Bird was brought on, shirt-sleeves rolled up, leaning on his typewriter, properly reporter-style. He ticked off three cases in which Vogel had "influenced, or tried to influence, the course of justice." He added that the deputy attorney general "has certain discretionary powers in deciding whether court cases should proceed or be halted", added that "these powers are supposed to be exercised in the public interest" and added further that "it seems Vogel took advantage of those powers in these specific cases." The implied motive was to assist friends.

The first instance concerned a lawyer in the Kootenays, known to Vogel, who himself had practised there before moving to Vancouver. The original charges were of impaired driving and refusal to take a breathalyzer test. When the case came to the provincial court, those charges were superseded by one of dangerous driving, to which the plea was guilty. Subsequently, application was made by the accused's lawyer for an absolute discharge, to which the prosecution did not object, and the judge acceded. The questionable circumstance was that the absolute discharge granted on that third charge could not have been given on the original two.

Just before the deputy attorney general's suit came to trial, the CBC acknowledged that there was no substance to that alleged interference and promised an on-air apology.

The second of the alleged interferences also involved a driving offence, this time the impairment of a seventeen-year-old student. Vogel in the beginning was inclined to the argument of the defence counsel that the case might be "diverted", a recognized proceeding in which persons charged, especially young ones with no previous record of trouble, may be spared trial; instead, the offender submits to an educational program, community work and other conditions. That proposal was vigorously disputed by, among others, the chief Crown prosecutor in the Vancouver district, Bruce Donald. Vogel yielded and the hearing went ahead. The trial judge dismissed the charge on the ground that the breathalyzer evidence was inconclusive.

The internal debate was resumed on the question of appeal. Vogel, although not certain the court's decision was warranted, decided that it offended no legal principle and was within the customary discretion of a judge. Consequently, it would not be justifiable to put the youth to the necessity of facing another court.

The allegation of the broadcast was once more interference to help friends. The producers paid a private investigator $2,200 to dig up information to demonstrate that Vogel and his wife were friends of the youth's parents. The wives of the two men played tennis together; the sons went to the same private school; there was no doubt, Bird said in the broadcast, about the friendly relationship. But as it turned out, there was more than a doubt. The two men knew one another, the judge said, but that was all. It perhaps might provide a ground for *thinking* Vogel had acted as he did to do a favour for a friend, but none for saying he had. As to the tennis, which was suggested as a particular bond, Mrs. Vogel not only did not play tennis, but had never met the youth's mother.

The third episode in the saga was of a different order—harking back to a major news story of the recent past. As shown in the transcript introduced in court, Bird said in introducing it,:

> Wendy King was the high-class hooker whose name was linked with former B.C. chief justice John Farris. Farris resigned abruptly in the fall of 1978 after he was heard on a police wiretap talking to the prostitute. Wendy King was charged with keeping a common bawdy-house, and there were fears that the Chief Justice might have to be called as a witness. Even before the charge was laid, Vogel told senior Vancouver police officials he would stay any subpoena that might be issued for Farris . . . even though he doesn't have that power. . . . And he said he'd block any attempt by the prosecution to call the former chief justice as a witness. . . . The police and prosecutors were furious.

Vogel's intervention was represented as assistance to a friend, or an "associate", as the term was. Vogel's explanation for his decision was that there was no reason to believe Farris had any evidence to give that would advance the prosecution's case, and that issuing a subpoena to effect an indirect purpose—to embarrass the chief justice because of his position—would be improper. Justice Esson concluded that Vogel's view "was based on proper grounds".

As to the friendship (or associateship) of Vogel and Farris, he said: "That Mr. Vogel and Farris . . . were not friends was virtually conceded at trial. Bird said in testimony that the word 'associates' . . . was intended to describe the relationship. That, he said, was a conclusion he came to because he understood that both were, or had been, members of the legal profession, the Liberal Party and the Canadian Bar Association." Judge Esson observed drily that if they *were* members of those bodies, they were bodies of rather large membership. The nub of his conclusion in the Farris–King matter was that the defendants, the CBC, "while not abandoning their position on the record, did not attempt to support, in evidence or argument, the imputation that the plaintiff [Vogel] had interfered or attempted to interfere, with the course of justice. . . ."

To the journalistic eye—specifically, mine—the crucial passage in the whole story began when Bird, on air, introduced "a letter marked 'Private and Confidential' that Bruce Donald, the chief prosecutor in the Vancouver district, had written to the provincial attorney general. In the letter [Bird quoting] the prosecutor said, 'If the information I have been given is true, it would appear there is the suggestion of the intention to interfere with the administration of justice.'"

To the camera, Bird said, "But despite his letter attorney prosecutor Donald didn't want to talk to us. . . ." A short clip followed of Bird asking questions of Donald, the last of them shouted through a door as Donald closed it behind him. The answers were all to one effect: "No comment."

Pure theatre.

Didn't want to talk? Donald not only had been willing to talk, but was Bird's tipster, his source, his Deep Throat, the person who had provided the seed for each of the three alleged instances of interference. They had met and talked over a period of weeks, after a first luncheon meeting at which Bird's purpose was to find if there was more to the recently completed bawdy-house case. Donald had dropped a hint that there just might be—on misconduct by the deputy attorney general involving interference with justice, not confined to one case.

They talked thereafter in the prosecutor's car, parked in quiet corners of Vancouver's Stanley Park or driving in parts of the city where neither was likely to be recognized. To a meeting on Bird's boat, Donald brought his office file, from which Bird was allowed to make notes. When Donald hesitated to give Bird a copy of his letter to the attorney general, it was arranged that he would leave one in a plain brown envelope in a locker at the bus depot. Bird would find the key on the flange of an I-shaped beam in an unfinished building nearby. Bird found the wrong beam and, on it, an old furniture-store invoice. After puzzling over that for a time, trying to determine what message it was intended to convey, he telephoned his source and got new directions.

It would be foolish to say that the investigation was not careless, but it was diligent in that much ingenuity and effort went into trying to make the allegations of interference stand up. The carelessness was at the end—in deciding to go ahead with a story that had gaping holes in it. In the dangerous-driving case, at least one member of the news team, Bird aside, knew before the program went to air that they lacked supporting evidence. Bird's investigation had included the use of a body-pack (i.e., hidden recording equipment) in separate interviews with several Crown counsel who had been close to the case. The interviewees had given detailed accounts of the how, what and why of the court proceeding. They had denied knowledge of any involvement by the deputy attorney general.

To one interview, Bird also took a bogus script intended to make a reader believe that the CBC already had the goods on the deputy attorney general and was set to go to air. The jig being up anyway, the evident thought was, the interviewee would be encouraged to open up and tell all. The lawyer to whom it was given not only said flat out that Vogel had not called him, but added that the CBC would be taking a risk if it went ahead with the script as shown him, because it was defamatory. Yet it was only when the libel suit was about to come to court that the CBC backed off its original position, which had been the traditional one—"We stand by our story"—and offered to make amends to Vogel over that one episode.

The records of the case tell a story of stubborn effort all round at CBC Vancouver to get this story to air. But the news business is not confined to the work and responsibilities of reporters, editors or producers; when there is a high risk of costly consequences, persons right up to the top of the management tree usually are brought in before the ultimate decision—to go or not to go—is taken.

Although he did not have many sympathetic words for Bird, Judge Esson found his blind faith in the tips given him "perhaps understandable" considering his relative inexperience and cynical turn of mind towards all things establishmentarian. But, he went on, "what is not understandable is that his superiors should have permitted such material to be broadcast without subjecting it to scrutiny by someone who could view it objectively; someone who was not committed in advance to a 'scandal theory'."

On March 5, the day the program was scheduled to run, there was a CBC meeting presided over by Len Lauk, director, Pacific region. Others taking part were Gordon Craig, director of television; William Sheehan, program director; William Donovan, area producer; Paul Waters, the executive producer who oversaw the making of the show;

and Colin King, a producer on loan from Toronto who, with Waters and Bird, had written the script. And, of course, Chris Bird.

All had an inkling that the whole enterprise hung on one source, and that the source was in some way connected with the Ministry of the Attorney-General—which might have suggested caution in case the tips were the product of a private feud. Bird was not pushed to divulge more because he was known to be touchy about being asked about sources and details of evidence. Lauk said lightly that they would have to accept for the time being that their source was "the tooth fairy".

The one consequential decision taken at the meeting was that the running of the show would be postponed a day to permit a local lawyer to look it over; the script or the tape may have been vetted earlier in Toronto, but that is unclear. The delay created a small embarrassment because the CBC's correspondent at the legislature had already been told to pass the word around to members of both government and opposition to be on the lookout for a political blockbuster that night. Now it would not be available.

Predictably, given the imperishable faith of the media in the truth of any blockbuster put out by a leading member of the fraternity, the pack was out in full cry the day after the story ran. The rush was not to question the facts but to solidify them. The late Marjorie Nichols, hard-headed as she was, wrote the next day in her legislature column in *The Vancouver Sun* of her distress because Vogel and his wife were her friends, but said, in the end, "Dick Vogel must be relieved of his responsibilities. Fired. Canned. Terminated. Take your pick." The CBC helped feed the excitement; the same night the show ran and the night after, it carried stories on "The National" to bring the Vancouver blockbuster to the rest of the country. Unsurprisingly, the story was *the* news in Vancouver, and played prominently in print and broadcast news elsewhere.

The media attention to Judge Esson's decision in the ensuing libel case was in sharp contrast. The day after it was delivered, the *Toronto Star* covered the story in sixty-six words, the Halifax *Chronicle-Herald* in forty-four. In every paper in a small sample—those two plus the Montreal *Gazette*, the Ottawa *Citizen*, the *Winnipeg Free Press* and the *Calgary Herald*—the story led with the amount of the damages. The misstatements of fact, the deceptions, the damaging innuendoes, the misrepresentations, the dismissal of information that did not support the thesis, all got short shrift. It demonstrated a remarkable double standard: political scandals are news, media scandals are not.

Fifteen days after the judgment came down, Canadian Press carried an economically written follow-up item. It reported the CBC's Pacific region director, Len Lauk, saying he and others involved had been disciplined for their parts in what he had already called "a bonehead blunder". The story did not say how or by whom they had been disciplined. He said he had offered his resignation, but it had been refused. Lauk later retired in Vancouver. William Sheehan, who was second-in-command, has since died. Gordon Craig later went to TSN, the sports network. William Donovan, the area producer, remained with the CBC and eventually was promoted to Maritimes regional director. Paul Waters, the executive producer who oversaw the making of the program, and Colin King, who assisted in writing the script, also remained with the CBC, although they subsequently moved on.

Chris Bird was fired—evidence of a curious form of business administration in which responsibility runs from the bottom up.

The larger question is whether the media as a whole, if they take seriously what they do, ought to reward bad practice within the fraternity by shutting their eyes to it and pretending it never happened.

If misstatements of fact, evasions and lies make news in every *political* context—and an extraordinary amount of effort is expended in detecting them, sometimes even where they do not exist—can the media be indifferent to the same in their own domain without raising doubts about their sincerity?

William Thorsell, editor-in-chief of *The Globe and Mail*, touched on that question, though not at all in relation to CBC's Vancouver blockbuster, more than a decade later, in delivering the annual Clissold Lecture at the Graduate School of Journalism, University of Western Ontario, in April 1991. More than a month later, some thoughts from that speech were carried over into the regular Saturday column he writes at the bottom of his own editorial page.

The general theme was that newspapers, which are having to run ever faster to replace readers who either die or simply turn elsewhere for their information, must find ways to make themselves compellingly worth the time of busy people. They should be educational for people who want to know. And they should break out of the mould of recording what went wrong yesterday, and look more deeply at what went right and why. It was in that vein that he produced an old chestnut of the trade, imported from Fleet Street in London—perhaps via a column in *Maclean's* magazine. He said at the university, and repeated in slightly different form in the newspaper:

> When we speak so reverentially of investigative journalism, we mean uncovering something that has gone wrong—the wronger the better—growing out of a classic but intellectually careless aphorism that it is the role of journalists "to comfort the afflicted and afflict the comfortable". Why in principle would we want to afflict the comfortable? This has long provided a convenient rationale for reporting for journalists who can't easily articulate broader reasons for what they do. As a result, we tend to be somewhat like fundamental preachers in our concentration on the evils of the world, ponderously finger-wagging from page one right through columns, editorials and reviews. There is certainly a role for us on this pulpit, uncovering evil and righting wrongs, but it is much too narrow a perch to carry the weight [of our striving] for a larger, loyal audience. . . .

Right. Pity his newsroom management appeared not to have read it.

ELEVEN

AFFLICT AND BE AFFLICTED

IN POLITICS AND IN POLITICAL JOURNALISM, COMFORT IS measured in numbers. A government has a comfortable majority. A comfortable lead in public opinion polls is a harbinger of more comfort to come. Benjamin Disraeli, twice Britain's prime minister in the second half of the nineteenth century, said, "A majority is always the best repartee"—the equivalent of saying that having the numbers saves a lot of unnecessary parliamentary argy-bargy, a great comfort.

In Alberta, the Conservatives by 1990 had been comfortable to the point of satiety, provincially and federally, for years, and Donald Getty—following the more successful Peter Lougheed, who had started that comfortable reign—had two winning elections behind him and a lineup in the legislature of fifty-nine Conservatives to face sixteen New Democrats and eight Liberals. Then, on November 22, 1990, two visitors arrived on his doorstep, agents of William Thorsell, editor of *The Globe and Mail* and non-believer in that vainglorious and fatuous old chestnut about afflicting the comfortable. When they left, the comfortable premier was feeling so afflicted that he eventually sued.

The visitors were the *Globe*'s resident correspondent in Alberta, then Miro Cernetig, and Peter Moon, an investigative reporter from Toronto. They were there to talk about how the premier managed on his salary to pay his household bills, and about some oil leases which they acknowledged, in the subsequent stories, that Alberta's conflict-of-interest rules did not forbid him to have. But, as Moon put it to the premier, questions on both subjects were "really, really bugging our people in Toronto"—not, obviously, the people of Toronto at large, but his editors.

If the premier was living beyond his disclosed income, how was he doing so? Had he bought his own house? And why, when he wanted a mortgage, had he gone to a small lending firm, of which some of the directors were "influential provincial Progressive Conservatives", instead of to a bank? That last was asked although they knew the interest rate on the loan was at the going market rate, not at a bargain rate that would suggest a favour given or a return favour anticipated. What they also knew, but did not say in so many words, was that, considering the province's long-standing Tory sympathies, especially in the business community, it probably would have been a neat trick to find a lending firm, banks included, *without* Conservatives on the board.

Getty's answer was simple. He had been buying a house at the time, needed a mortgage, and was asked for his business. Someone evidently known to him in the small firm, perhaps one of those influential Progressive Conservatives, had told him, "You know, we do mortgages." His first reply was to say no, he was going to the Royal Bank because that was his bank. On second thought, he agreed, having been assured that the rate would be competitive. And why not? Would Roy Romanow in Saskatchewan be expected to answer for it if he got a car loan at the local co-op, which almost certainly would have a New Democrat or two on the board?

The assignment given the *Globe*'s two reporters was twofold. First, they were to ascertain whether, or in what degree, the premier of Alberta was in a conflict of interest in bringing in, and eventually seeing passed, legislation to assist the province's oil industry at a time when he himself had an investment in that industry. The second was to see if the suspicion that existed in the minds of newsroom editors that he was living beyond his visible income was sustainable. The first of these, related entirely to a matter of public business, was clearly a justifiable subject of journalistic inquiry. The second was much less so.

In the matter of a conflict of interest, the newspaper was able to demonstrate in some detail that Getty did indeed have an investment in three producing oil wells, although it was neither a large investment nor a hugely rewarding one. But the fact of his having such an investment was already on the public record. His government's program of assistance to the oil industry, the province's most valuable, was very much on the public record; $1-billion programs do not pass unnoticed. But the legislation to bring the program into being had not been pushed singlehandedly through the legislature by the Conservative majority.

In the second inquiry, the total achievement, assuming some people are influenced by what they read and hear in the media, may have been that a newspaper suspicion was translated into more widely held suspicion. The question of the loan illustrates the point that an obsession with finding something wrong, and the wronger the better, tilts the perspective. A mortgage on a private residence has nothing to do with the public business, unless it can be demonstrated that something has been lost to the public interest as a result. In the subsequent stories the *Globe* did not come close to demonstrating anything of the sort, although the writers went to the length of introducing this absurdity into their third story in pursuit of a sinister link: "An investigation . . . found that some of the directors [of the lending firm] also worked on behalf of Donald Cormie and his now-collapsed Principal Group empire, as advisers or lobbyists who *unsuccessfully* approached Mr. Getty's government for financial help." That was to say what? That the premier sought out his lender looking for a sweetheart deal in return for having turned down some of the firm's directors on another occasion?

The premier had some observations to make before the hour-long interview came to an end. Moon, who did most of the talking for his side, brought with him a set of printed questions which he referred to as his script. Whether by design or by a coincidence of unlike personalities, Moon and Cernetig played a sort of bad cop/good cop routine. Moon was the bad cop—fawning at times, blaming the editors in Toronto for the terrible questions he was asking, even as he asked them. The younger Cernetig had a relatively minor role as the good cop. His questions were fewer and less loaded, and he occasionally addressed the premier respectfully as "sir" or "Mr. Getty".

The style of the interview—"there are rumours out there, and they're not nice rumours"—was to suggest that Edmonton was seething with tales that needed to be refuted. The two evident underlying premises were, first, that the premier had done something, probably several somethings, quite improper in a person in public life, and, second, that he was somehow accountable to the editors of *The Globe and Mail* in Toronto. Getty was confronted with "scuttlebutt on the street", "bad rumours around Edmonton", "nasty rumours", "nasty suspicions" and "whispering in our ears", none of them identified as to either origin or content. He was also confronted with another version of the editors being bugged by unanswered questions—"in Toronto, they're jumping up and down saying, 'He's got to have a secret slush fund.' "

The interview came near the end of the investigation, which is standard practice. The more information is collected beforehand, the better equipped the interrogators are to dig into the substance of the issue, and the fewer loose ends are likely to be left in case they get only one crack at the central figure. Although some inquiries remained to be done after the Thursday interview, the first stories in the series were delivered extraordinarily quickly, in time for the first to meet the late-afternoon Friday deadline for the Saturday paper.

Saturday is a good day to launch a scandal series. For one reason, because, for most newspapers, the Saturday paper has the largest circulation in the week. The more exposure, the more other media will be inclined to follow. Although the *Globe*'s exposé did not really take hold as a full-blown National Story—too provincial—it was not for lack of effort. The Moon–Cernetig series, all days, news and commentary combined, ran to 448 column inches of type, roughly equivalent to three and a half full pages, free of all ads and everything else. Small wars have been covered in less.

The prime commentary, an even more than usually sanctimonious editorial, was headed "Time for Mr. Getty to tighten the conflict rules"—a curiously mild point to make after two months of investigative journalism, but bold in a way as well, considering that the investigation had not succeeded in demonstrating that the old rules had permitted any grievous wrong to occur. The editorial acknowledged that the applicable rules, however deficient in its eyes, had been observed. "The issue is not," it said, "whether Mr. Getty contravened his province's standards. The issue turns on the less-than-exacting nature of those standards, which are of sufficient breadth to allow ministers to influence public policy that may affect their personal investments."

Well, yes—but to say that the law against holding up stagecoaches is not sufficient to safeguard against the crime would not make a good argument for convicting anyone for having committed it. Perhaps Alberta's rules on conflict of interest needed to be amended, but that was not what those 448 inches of type were about.

Along with delivering its little sermon against neglect of standards, the editorial had one suggestion on how the province, once home to the

Globe's editor, might set its feet on the path of political virtue. In order to satisfy the public interest, without requiring ministers to divest themselves of all assets on taking office (which might drive many worthwhile people from even thinking about politics), what was needed was—the keenness of the insight takes the very breath away—a blind trust! But a better one. A properly structured blind trust.

Spake the *Globe*: "Allowing that the question of what exactly constitutes a conflict can sometimes be difficult to evaluate, the best remedy for clearing up the confusion is for ministers to place their assets in a blind trust that is structured to contain a much wider array of investments than appears to be held in Mr. Getty's trust. . . . The instrument of the properly structured blind trust [undefined] administered at arm's length from the owner of the assets it contains [the philosophy of every blind trust ever devised], is an adequate response [it isn't] to that concern"—the concern, again, being the danger of turning good prospective candidates away from politics. The editorial prattling on about this paragon of blind trusts: "It enables the senior elected official to retain his or her assets, while insulating the official from the reality and the perception of a conflict of interest."

With that, all that remains for journalism to do is devise a way to inculcate in editorial writers an awareness of the reality and the perception of baloney when they are producing it—allowing for the fact that what does and does not constitute baloney in the writing of editorials can sometimes can be difficult to evaluate.

The blind trust is no answer for the senior elected official, or anyone else, whose assets are in property—a farm or a ranch, for instance, or oil leases, the core of the whole supposed conflict of interest the editorial was maundering on about.

The value of physical assets, no less than paper assets, is capable of being affected by something done or not done by government. The difference is that physical assets cannot be put out of sight in a blind trust. Five hundred hectares of grassland, with or without the more mobile cattle on them, will not fit in a trust administrator's vault. Neither will oil wells. Divestiture, even temporarily, of the knowledge of owning a physical something is just not possible.

That leaves disclosure as an alternative—a public acknowledgement of ownership. The proposition behind it is that the declaration of an interest is sufficient notice to anyone on the lookout for conflicts. When the financial interest of the person in government is known and the performance of that person in office is known (or knowable), the one can be judged against the other—assuming those doing the judging can do it without yielding to anti-political or pro-scandal bias.

A disclosure arrangement, adequate or not, had been in effect in Alberta since at least 1975, when the original 1973 conflict-of-interest code was amended and extended to encompass not just ministers but senior civil servants as well. The portion directed at land holdings demanded the filing of "a legal description of all lands in Alberta including mineral rights, in which they or their families have a direct or indirect interest whether as owner, lessee, mortgagee, unpaid vendor, shareholder of a private company, or otherwise." And Getty had complied.

It was in this prescribed disclosure statement that Cernetig found that Getty had an investment in some oil and gas property, and that the extent of it had been increased during his time in office. That was where the whole story began.

In their long interview with the premier, and in the first story of their series, Moon and Cernetig made a point of saying that the disclosure form did not identify the premier's "partners" in this investment. Whether or not the others were partners in any strict sense is another question—presumably several people, or groups of people, can have investments in the same enterprise without there being a unity between them—but an answer to the mystery of the missing partners, sufficient or not, was not hard to find. I got one by calling Michael Ritter, Alberta's parliamentary counsel, who said the rule as it had been interpreted did not demand that partners be individually named, just that an identified partnership must be declared.

Moon and Cernetig did not have the names before the interviews and they did not get them there. Getty said he did not know. If he and the others were not involved together, there was no reason why he should. They still did not have them in time for the first story on Saturday, which said they were missing. However, they did have a list of eight names, some personal, some corporate, typed and photocopied on paper without letterhead, that ran alongside the last story in the series on the following Wednesday.

At one side, under "Name of beneficiary", were four names of evidently individual investors, three business names and one trustee. The trustee beneficiary, the text said, was Lloyd W. McLaren, acting for Getty. This "Edmonton group", as the Moon–Cernetig story described it, had a one-third interest with two small companies, each of which had the same in oil rights on the whole 1,620 hectares involved. Getty's share in this oil venture was 6 per cent in a one-third interest in rights to 1,620 hectares. That, then, was the kernel of the conflict-of-interest side of the *Globe*'s investigation.

The lead story in *The Globe and Mail*'s series began with these two paragraphs:

> Premier Donald Getty has been a little-known, but successful, speculator in Alberta's oil business while holding the province's top government post.
>
> In a five-year period, during which his Progressive Conservative government introduced royalty cuts to save oil companies more than a billion dollars, Mr. Getty almost doubled his personal stake in Alberta's oil and gas lands.

The story went on to say, in sharp contrast to the preceding references to the "successful speculator" and the premier's having "almost doubled his personal stake in Alberta's oil and gas lands", that the sale of oil netted him a profit of "at least $60,000". That amount, which on the figures presented equally well could have been described as "at most", necessarily included whatever benefit the government program conferred on his investment. The program applied to the industry as a whole. Further, it covered five years. The writer of a letter to the editor of the newspaper was moved to say that, if Getty was a successful speculator, he was not at a rate averaging $12,000 a year a "spectacularly successful speculator."

Observing the proclaimed media commitment to fairness and balance, the *Globe*'s writers then turned to an unnamed industry source, who said that the premier's interests were "nickel and dime" compared with those of the big players in the oil business, and that no doubt it was the good of the industry he had in mind when the 1986 royalty assistance was introduced. Balancing that balance, another expert was introduced to say, "You'd hate to think there was a situation where the premier has a direct working interest in wells that might end up in discussion in cabinet."

The first of two lay views on the matter is that oil-investing is, or has been, endemic in a stratum of Alberta society which encompasses politicians of all parties and just about everyone with a few dollars to invest. Perhaps Getty would have been wiser to remove himself from it when he became premier, although it is difficult to say why; he had not hidden the fact. The other is that *The Globe and Mail* succeeded—448 inches of type and all—in proving nothing except that he had investments there, which was already on record.

Obviously reporting on so elusive a matter as conflict of interest needs to take likelihood into account. That in turn must recognize that at a certain point a government program becomes so large—in breadth of application, money involved and surrounding circumstances—that one cannot rationally believe that a minor private interest was a serious motivating influence in its formulation.

In 1986, according to the Energy Resources Conservation Board in Calgary, there were 23,000 wells producing oil in the province. Some of those were doing, perhaps, a dozen barrels a day, a few as many as 1,000. Different means were provided in the program to assist small companies and large, and it was calculated that $1 billion would be disbursed in outright contributions to cash flow on the one hand, and in royalty and other tax incentives on the other.

Obviously any overlap of private and public interests in government invites legitimate enquiry to ascertain if the one has influenced the other. But recent political journalism has made a fetish of conflict of interest, so that not just the thing itself is newsworthy, or even just the appearance of it, but the possibility of the appearance of the likelihood of an actuality. One need not prove that any thing occurred—just that it might have. Or could have. Perhaps.

In 1986, Alberta's energy industry, the province's big revenue earner, was in a bad way. Ian Doig, publisher of *Doig's Digest*—a respected newsletter analysing Canadian oil and gas affairs—has not been an admirer of handouts to the industry by either federal or provincial governments. Of the curtailment in 1989 of the Alberta Royalty Tax Credits (ARTC) program, one of the vehicles used in the Billion Dollar

Package, he wrote with evident satisfaction that junior producers who had been finding their rewards mainly in grants would now have to use the same ingenuity to find them in the ground. But at the earlier date, in 1986, he recognized the industry's hard times.

He said then that a price of $20 (U.S.) a barrel would have been better all round—better for the industry's bottom line, and for government, to which it would have meant more revenue in and less money out. But in the tenth month of the (mostly Middle East oil producers') price upheaval, "the human pain became too much." The immediate short-term thrust of the policy was "to stop the bleeding of jobs by increasing activity." From the heady days of the 1970s, when oil prices seemed to have no ceiling, the industry had suffered a sharp downturn, made worse by the severe general recession of 1981–82. It enjoyed a brief recovery and then, when oil prices crashed by more than half between late 1985 and 1986, fell upon even worse days. Thousands of skilled jobs were being lost and the economies of not just Alberta but other parts of the country as well were severely affected.

The speculation *The Globe and Mail*'s heavily played series dangled before readers was that a connection could have—not had, but could have—existed between that very large public program and a very small private interest. It is one thing to say that the subject was a legitimate something for news-gatherers to look into. It is another to say that the published result reasonably reflected what was found. At the point when an investigation is to be translated into publication, there are questions that reason suggests need to be asked: has a clear case been made to support the premise? Is the story fully documented or something less than that, and, if the latter, how much less? What is the story worth to the public interest; will it do more to inform than simply to create cynicism? And where does it belong in the whole run of the day's news—top of page one, lead item in broadcast news, or somewhere down the way?

Another question which deserves to be asked is whether the premise is being allowed to dictate the conclusion. Stories which are within the control of editors and reporters—stories that are not simply about happenings—obviously spring from some sort of premise; the subject needs to be enquired into for this, this and this reason. But it is sometimes difficult to let go when it has not panned out. That is particularly true with investigations in which a lot of time and money have been invested. Also, investigations naturally spread out as they go along, throwing up a lot of marginalia, more decorative perhaps than important or strictly relevant; this extra bulk can create an illusion of weight, and result in a story surviving into print or onto the air that might better have been abandoned.

An example of marginalia in the *Globe*'s Getty series was a piece in the November 26, 1990, issue which reported, with an air of significance, that earlier in the year the premier had taken out a one-year mortgage "with a subsidiary of the Canadian Imperial Bank of Commerce . . . the Alberta government's principal banker". The writers acknowledged that the mortgage was at the prevailing rate, so the story was purely decorative, adding perhaps a note of intrigue but saying nothing. The bank had done Getty no favour, he had done the bank none. Given the suggestion earlier of something suspicious in his *not* having gone to a bank but to an independent lender for a mortgage some years before, the option left would seem to be to pay cash—which could be counted on to excite worse suspicion.

It was also journalistic embroidery to say in another story that "Mr. Getty has fared well in the residential real estate market." The following paragraph offered this as Exhibit A: "In 1970, he bought a four-bedroom house in Edmonton for $60,500, paid off the mortgage, and sold it in 1985 for $220,000 in cash." Holy cow! A cool $159,500 gain in just fifteen years! However, on that basis, everyone in Edmonton who bought and sold a house in the same period fared well—leaving aside, of course, the leaping inflation of the time.

Figures compiled by the Edmonton Real Estate Board indicate that, on average, selling prices between mid-year 1970 and mid-year 1985 rose by three and a half times. By that reckoning, the $220,000 realized on the Getty house was not out of line with the average selling price of any house bought for $60,500 in 1970—$211,750. More poignant is the fact that had he sold it at any time in the four years preceding 1985 or the five years after, he would have fared a lot better. The year 1985 was the trough of the market in Edmonton.

But the real subject of the Moon–Cernetig treatise on price trends in real estate was the premier's new home at Stettler, 140 kilometres southeast of Edmonton. Getty moved to Stettler to find a seat when, embarrassingly, he was defeated in Edmonton–Whitemud in the 1989 provincial election. Stettler was a natural place to go; he had been going there for duck-hunting for about twenty years. In the by-election that returned him to the assembly, he said, perhaps with the thought in mind of eventual retirement there, that if elected he would establish a year-round home in the constituency. He set out almost at once to redeem the promise, but, according to Moon and Cernetig, more things than the digging of a foundation began once he became Stettler's MLA.

For one, the provincial government had "dusted off a controversial plan to raise the level of Buffalo Lake, a project critics of Mr. Getty say may enhance property values in an area including the premier's property." The story went on, a few paragraphs later, to say that "since Mr. Getty arrived in Stettler, the town has been awarded the 1991 Alberta Summer Games, a $500,000 alcohol and drug-abuse treatment centre, and $750,000 in grants for new tennis courts and other recreational facilities. In addition, some highways in the area have been repaved, making the ride to Buffalo Lake (and Mr. Getty's home) smoother."

The local newspaper, *The Stettler Independent*, and Mayor Bob Stewart quickly had enough of stories following on the *Globe*'s heels, of Stettler as the pork-barrel capital of the province. "Everyone," said the mayor, "is taking a shot at us." The *Independent*, in a story by staff reporter Greg Knill headed "Gravy train not running through Stettler: Stewart", said the minutes of the Alberta Sports Council, which Knill had seen, showed that the decision to award the summer games to Stettler had been taken nearly a month before the May 9 by-election, while Getty was still in that politicians' limbo—without a seat.

In addition the $500,000 alcohol and drug-treatment centre was not a treatment centre but a storefront in a strip mall serving as a counselling and education office, with a reading room stocked with books and pamphlets of a sort that might be used in a high school. Lance Penney, the area supervisor for the Alberta Alcohol and Drug Abuse Commission, told the *Independent*'s reporter, if he found a treatment clinic in the community, to let him know—he would like to see one.

The idea of pumping water from the Red Deer River into Buffalo Lake to stabilize its level had been around for years. From about the beginning of the eighties it had been discussed seriously, with marked differences of opinion about its utility and desirability. Still more recently there had been studies and reports, with opinions pro and con on effects on the environment and on the possibility of a more constant lake attracting more tourists. But the implied relationship between a dormant scheme having been "dusted off" and any effect on property values around where the premier lived was scoffed at by Robert Willis, publisher of the *Independent* at the time. He said, "Some of these sensational reporters, I think, thought, 'Well, here's an opportunity for us to swing this one across the country.' He [Getty] is miles from the lake. He's up on a high hill and he can see the lake, but he's so far away his property value wouldn't be increased by the lake coming in. [It would] have to come up in length five miles before it was close."

The repaving that would make "the ride to Buffalo Lake (and Mr. Getty's home) smoother" was in the cards before Getty had reason to think about running anywhere except in Edmonton–Whitemud. The provincial government earlier had spent more than $1 million improving a provincial campsite and park on the shores of the lake; that in itself constituted good reason for improving the highway.

How all these frilly bits related to the governing of the province, the premier's oil investments or the general state of his financial health is not luminously clear. They were by-products turned up along the way in a long search for material to fatten a hypothesis. They are also characteristic of much investigative reporting in that much of what was asserted came unburdened by any sort of identification as to origin.

Anonymity in journalism is only sometimes for the protection of the source. It is also a convenience to the reporter, because the people who come up with the most damning quotations have a curious way of also being the ones who "spoke on condition he/she not be identified". Also, "sources" sounds sexy. Like the term "investigative reporting", "sources" has an intriguing touch of mystery, of men in 1930s-style fedoras, whispering dark secrets to the reporter in dark alleys. It hypes the story.

Nine of what might be called original sources were identified by name in the *Globe*'s entire Getty series. Four of those spoke on the premier's horse-racing interest, a story marginal to the main theme. A fifth was Robert Willis, the Stettler publisher.

The first of two named sources who came close to the primary issues was Tony Galishoff, a spokesman for the Alberta Energy Department. He said, in about so many words, that a general program of assistance to the industry introduced by the government in 1986 was open to all oil companies, but policy forbade the release of information related to specific wells, because it might be used for commercial advantage. The second was René Rutter, a pumps maintenance man in the area in which Getty had invested, who said, in total, "You're kidding. I've been here for nine years, and I never heard that before."

The other two named sources, and the only two substantial ones, were Lloyd McLaren, an Edmonton oil man, keeper of Getty's blind trust and a friend and mentor for more than twenty years, and Getty himself. As for the rest, it was all:

"One industry source said. . . ."
"Another said. . . ."
"The source said. . . ."
"Industry experts and business leaders interviewed by the *Globe* said. . . ."
"Said an oil industry expert. . . ."
"Another oil industry executive. . . ."
"The details of activity on the Premier's oil and gas lands described by industry sources. . . ."
"Industry experts and government officials all said. . . ."
"Oil industry experts [were surprised to learn]. . . ."
"A source who has been associated with. . . ."
"Mr. Getty was estimated by one analyst to have made. . . ."
"Critics of Mr. Getty say. . . ."
"Most residents [of Stettler] believe. . . ."
"The townspeople described the premier as. . . ."
"Says one visitor to the Getty home. . . ."
"A resident of the complex [in which Getty, earlier, had a condo in Palm Springs, California] said. . . ."
"Many local real estate people think. . . ."
"Confidential provincial Progressive Conservative documents show. . . ."
"Said an oil industry expert. . . ."
"Another oil industry executive. . . ."
"The details described by industry sources. . . ."
"One long-time oil man said. . . ."

"Industry sources say. . . ."
"One example cited by a source. . . ."
"An industry veteran said. . . ."
"The three wells . . . were described as a 'superb investment' by one analyst. . . ."

Six months after the event, Christopher Waddell, who, as national editor, necessarily would have been one of those described by Moon as jumping up and down in Toronto, sketched for me the origins of the series in which those sources played so large a part. It began, Waddell said, when Miro Cernetig's journalistic curiosity drove him to look up Getty's 1989 statement of land holdings. The practice in the office of the clerk of the assembly was to discard the last statement when a new one came in, and it was only when Cernetig received by chance, from an environmentalist, a copy of the *1986* statement that he found the premier's oil acreage had increased. The question then became, Waddell said, "whether it is appropriate for a premier to be making investments in oil and gas while he is premier."

That clearly was a plinth on which to base an inquiry. A subsidiary question that intrigued the editors—about a breach of the blind trust—was a shakier proposition. That overlooked the fact that disclosure of land holdings was required, therefore those were not *in* a blind trust; they were not required to be. And then there was the matter of the premier's private finances—the two houses, one in Edmonton, the other in Stettler, and the mortgages, and Getty's having had to scurry once to raise money to pay off a bank loan.

The reflection of the latter speculation was in a story at the end of the series, headed "Backers saved Getty over debt to bank", with a subhead "Edmonton oil man provided cash by purchasing land from premier". The essence of the story was that Getty at some earlier time had obtained a loan from an unnamed bank for which he had put up as security his half-share in some property outside Edmonton on which he stabled his horses. In 1988, the bank wanted whole or partial repayment and had gone so far as to try to find a buyer for the pledged property, but without success. At that point—this was reported as "The Globe and Mail has learned"—Lloyd McLaren and two other Edmonton oil men, Carl Guthrie and Trevor Cuthill, both old associates of the premier, came to his assistance and bought his half-share for $33,000. The implication seemed to be that some cronies had bailed out a political friend, perhaps with a thought to some future favour.

In fact, the details depicted an arrangement which, while no doubt welcome at the time, would not have incurred a great debt of gratitude. The half-share of a 44.5 acre (18.5 hectare) parcel of land that Getty had bought for $210,000 in 1981, during his time out of politics, was taken off his hands for $33,000 in 1988 and was back on the market in 1990 for $200,000, an offer of $150,000 already having been refused.

The response of other media to the *Globe*'s series was limited but immediate. CBC News reacted so quickly to the first story that Hugh Dunne, Getty's press secretary, was convinced that the newspaper had alerted the network to what was coming. Whether or not that was the case, both CBC and CTV had couriers at the *Globe and Mail* plant on Front Street in Toronto on Friday night, when the first edition of the Saturday paper became available. A crew from CBC was at the premier's Stettler home on the Saturday morning, shooting from the end of the driveway. On the eleven o'clock CBC news that night, Knowlton Nash introduced the item, "Don Getty says he has done nothing wrong, but the opposition thinks he should resign. *The Globe and Mail* reported today that Getty earned tens of thousands in the oil and gas business since becoming premier. . . ." With that, he brought on reporter Kevin Newman, strategically stationed beside nodding oil-lifters. "These," he said, "are the wells that have been producing oil, tens of thousands of dollars of profit, for Don Getty, since he became premier of Alberta. The *Globe* says these same wells qualified for tax breaks brought in by the Getty government. Officials say they cannot release documents which would detail if Getty received any royalties, and Don Getty isn't saying much. . . ."

That, allowing for slightly different words—"tens of thousands", for example, as a more dramatic, and less specific, substitute for "at least $60,000" in *five* years—was taken straight from the *Globe*, because the premier was doing more than just not saying much; to the CBC he wasn't saying anything. He had chased the crew away, annoyed to find people shooting his house without coming to the door to say who they were or what they were there for.

The CBC had just gone off down the road when CTV's Dana Lewis arrived. He also received a gruff reception, but had the good sense to say that naturally he would leave if asked, but that the story was already published and it might be generally useful, not least to the premier himself, to get some of his own comments on the record. . . . Lewis got a brief interview. Next day, there were bitter complaints of favouritism from the CBC.

Murdoch Davis, managing editor of *The Edmonton Journal*, was chagrined to see his newspaper beaten to a story on its own turf—which is not the same as saying he found it altogether right or entirely honest. The premier's having an interest in oil properties he viewed as a legitimate subject of journalism for the *Globe*, *The Edmonton Journal* or anyone. The *Journal*, he said, had been poking around in Getty's personal finances earlier, but had not pulled a story together. However, the bread-on-the-table bit—"that particular passage," Davis said, "I don't think the *Globe* can or should defend." It did, though.

The phrase came from a story headed "Getty's job 'Tough' on living standards". It began: "Donald Getty says his personal assets are dwindling and that being the premier of Alberta has hurt his standard of living. Since becoming premier, Mr. Getty has taken out two mortgages, totalling $550,000, and he said he has been forced to sell some of his Canada Savings Bonds and spend the interest on his bank term deposits to make ends meet."

"How do you put bread on the table?" Getty was reported as saying to *The Globe and Mail* in a frank, hour-long interview. "You sell off assets."

Five paragraphs farther on in the transcript of that interview, after giving Getty's salary as $98,193 (with which went an annual tax-free expense allowance of $19,167), the writers—double-bylined throughout the series—returned to the theme of hardship: "He said he took a major paycut to become premier. 'I was making, just so you know, probably six to seven hundred thousand dollars a year when I came back to government [in 1985]. How's that for a cut in salary? Tough on my family, very tough on my family, tough on our standard of living.'"

The Alberta media responded with ridicule—of the premier. An editorial cartoon in the tabloid *Edmonton Sun* showed him grimacing and saying as he put on a pair of shoes, "From Gucci to Florsheim! It can't get any worse," with a beggar in rags standing at his side saying, "Wanna bet?" The *Sun* also took an editorial cut at the premier for what it called his "insensitivity" in complaining of his circumstances, and suggested he and the Cabinet "take a good look at how the other 95% live." But the *Sun* was generally sympathetic. An *Edmonton Journal* cartoon showed the premier and his wife sitting down to a splendid dinner, with him lamenting, "The public expects me to divest this! Sell that! How am I supposed to put bread on the table?" and Mrs. Getty replying, "Ask the servants to bring another loaf, Don."

The Grande Prairie *Daily Herald-Tribune* said, "Just to make ends meet, Getty says he's had to take out mortgages totalling $550,000, cashed in his Canada Savings Bonds, and spent the interest on his term deposits. He also had to sell his condominium in Palm Springs . . . and is planning to sell his house in Edmonton. . . . It's the only way he's been able to put bread on the table." And the *Edson Report*, only one in a flock of others all in the same vein, said, "Does the premier expect us to believe he's had to 'sell off assets to put bread on the table'? That is one of the more ridiculous statements he's made."

Perhaps, but it wasn't his statement. In the reporting of what Getty supposedly said about putting bread on the table, two crucial words—"you say"—had been lopped off the front end. Getty was repeating a question that had been put to him by Moon. Christopher Waddell in effect defended the editing when he gave Sherry Aikenhead of *The Edmonton Journal* the stock answer newspapers use in such circumstances, "We stand by our reporter." His explanation to me six months later was essentially the same, but with some rationale added: Getty, someone not unaccustomed to being interviewed, had made the phrase his own when he chose to repeat it later, at a point removed from Moon's use of it. Therefore, in effect, the loss of the words "you say" was irrelevant.

The local media did not think so when the premier's office was smart enough to get the text of the interview out to editors around the province. A sharp change took place. The resentment directed at the premier for what seemed to be whining about the hardships of office was turned instead on the interloper.

The day after he read the transcript, Don Braid, political columnist for *The Calgary Herald*, expressed regret for the scorn with which he had commented on the bread-on-the-table line. The editing that made the phrase appear as Getty's own, spontaneously given, struck him as something a supermarket tabloid would be proud of. John Brown, *The*

Edmonton Journal's ombudsman, acknowledged that his own newspaper had absorbed some information from the *Globe*, but said, "It was unfortunate the public criticism of the Getty remark was based on what appeared in the *Globe*. The transcript does not give me the impression that Getty was whining. He gave frank answers to very personal questions. A less patient man might have refused to continue the interview. . . ."

Simon Blake, of *The Leduc Representative*, said, "I had a few guilty feelings after writing Sunday's column and then finding the premier had been a victim of dishonest journalism by The Toronto Globe and Mail." Douglas Stinson, editor of *The Camrose Canadian*, took the affair as an opportunity to read all journalism a lesson: reporters may believe what they like, "but if they can't prove it there's no story."

The question of putting bread on the table arose, first, on page fourteen of the forty-four-page transcript of the Moon–Cernetig interview, as provided by the premier's office. Unless by prior understanding, most interviews, as distinct from open press conferences, do not leave behind records to permit reliable comparisons to be made. However, in any contest for the most prolix, inarticulate, occasionally incomprehensible and generally bizarre interview, this one certainly would qualify, at least for the short list. In his meandering style, Peter Moon put the question to the premier.

> Moon: We sort of look at your salary as premier, and as far as we know that's your only source of income, because Mr. McLaren [Getty's trustee], you never asked for, and he's never given you, any money from the blind trust. And we've added up, and you're spending more than $85,000 a year just to meet the mortgages, the taxes, the utilities, the insurance, and we're saying, "Hey, how does he put bread on the table in the morning?"
> Getty: Well, that's because you end up selling assets that you've acquired over the years. I mean I had a home in Palm Springs I've sold.
> Moon: Yes, we know that.
> Getty: That gave me money and I've used it up.
> Moon: Well, then, how would you buy cereal tomorrow morning?
> Moon [later]: I don't know how you live on your premier's salary.
> Getty: I either live on your [*sic*] premier's salary or on assets that you've accumulated and that you have to liquidate over time. That's what happens to you.

Moon: The assets, are they in the form of—how can I phrase this? Please don't be offended because we've got to still go back to our editors about it. . . . Those assets, are they in the form of Canada Savings Bonds you get interest on?
Getty: Some are.
Moon: So it doesn't have to go down to blind trust? I mean, just keeping it in the bank in a savings account, I mean, I think . . . ?
Getty: Some are term deposits. . . .
Moon: And I guess a guy's got to question, I know what the answer's going to be and I'll try to be. . . . But in Toronto, they're jumping up and down saying, "He's got to have a secret slush fund. He's got. . . . He's got a trust account." It goes on like that. Do you have anything like that?
Cernetig: The other thing, Mr. Getty, is we're not trying anything crooked. And that may be hard for you to believe, but that's true. And I think if you read them [the coming stories] you'll find out.
Getty: We'll wait and see. I think, frankly guys. . . . You know, you get up and look in the mirror in the morning, don't you think "what a ['s' word deleted in transcript] job I have? [The "I" here plainly referred to the writers' own ruminations in front of the mirror.]
Moon: No, because sometimes we're right. I have put people in jail. I've had people put out of political office over the years. And I've broken up all sorts of criminal scandals. And some of the things I've done, I'm proud of. Others I haven't enjoyed looking back at because there was no story at the end. . . . But you can't do the good things that journalism does . . . without getting close to the line you're referring to. And I accepted that. We're not a profession, that's what I'm saying. But we're part of—we're part of the Fourth Estate, if you like, and that's what it is. We really should have to put up with each other.
Getty: Well yes, I'm putting up with you.
Moon: Thank you very much. You were very good to us, and I thank you for that.
Getty: You're welcome.

A year to the day after the interview, the Edmonton firm of McLennan Ross, barristers and solicitors, gave notice that their client, Donald R. Getty, was suing for defamation. Damages were claimed in the amount of $1 million. By mid-year 1994, the case still had not come to court.

TWELVE

PUBLIC INQUIRY, PRIVATE INJUSTICE

SINCLAIR STEVENS, IN THE OPINION OF PUBLIC SERVANTS who worked with him in the federal Department of Regional Industrial Expansion, was the best minister the department had had in their experience. They said he created more jobs than all previous ministers together because he was bold in making decisions.

The authority for those statements is Mr. Justice W.D. Parker, the former chief justice of the trial division of the Supreme Court of Ontario, who conducted the long public inquiry into allegations against Stevens of conflict of interest—no fewer than 146 of them—all of which originated in the media. Judge Parker found the minister in breach of the government's code of ethics in 14 instances, including several in which there had been no prior allegations at all, but which emerged as gratuitous by-products of the inquiry itself.

Stevens had resigned from the Mulroney Cabinet before the inquiry began, confident he would be exonerated. Notwithstanding the damaging report, he was ready to run again in the 1988 general election, at which the Conservatives were re-elected for a second term. However, Prime Minister Brian Mulroney refused to sign his nomination papers, the equivalent to Stevens of being publicly disowned by his own party.

The Stevens Affair, as it became known, was the greatest scandal of the Mulroney years. Judge Parker later—and perhaps at the time—thought the inquiry, at least in certain respects, unnecessary and a waste of public money. Early in the same interview during which he commented on the view of Stevens within the department, I asked Judge Parker what he thought of the whole process of the public inquiry, based as it was on allegations derived entirely from newspapers, magazines, radio broadcasts and television broadcasts, each with its own standards and methods in information gathering. Those reports, swept up from across the country and made available all in one piece in a commission document, could only have the effect, as I saw it, of giving them the weight in the public mind of formal "charges", as in a criminal trial.

"I think that process is wrong, really," he said, "to throw [the whole subject matter] onto a public inquiry when there are many allegations that were made that there was a reasonable explanation for. They could have been looked at in a parliamentary committee. . . . Some of those things, they may have looked suspicious, but once you looked at them there was nothing to them. Nobody had benefited, nobody did anything wrong. The feeling I got from the bureaucrats, the people in the department, they would set up an agenda for a Cabinet minister, and they would present him with his options.

"I was amazed at how good and sensible they were," he continued. "They would say, 'You can do this and this. If you do this, these are the good points, and these are the bad points.' And he just had to make a decision. . . . So many of the decisions that were in dispute, he had accepted on the recommendations of the staff. And that staff, when they gave evidence, impressed me. I thought they were sensible with the solutions they put out for the man and, as a matter of fact, the people who worked for the government, the bureaucratic staff, they were not all that critical of Sinclair Stevens. They said he was the best minister they ever had for their department. He created more jobs than all the other ministers put together previously because he took chances. To call a public inquiry into things like that, where it was clear from their own record he had followed recommendations of the department, I thought was a waste of public money. . . ."

I am not a lawyer or a judge, and am neither equipped or inclined to set myself up as a court of appeal in the Stevens Affair. However, I am comfortable, especially with a later, unrelated judgment of the Supreme Court of Canada to refer to, in saying that it's a queer process and a queer sort of justice that prosecutes but doesn't charge, judges but doesn't convict, and punishes—sometimes seriously and lastingly—but doesn't sentence.

There are two sorts of public inquiry. First, and with a long tradition, there is the inquiry created by government to explore some large matter of public policy. The most notable recent example of that species is the inquiry presided over by Donald Macdonald, a Minister of Finance in the Trudeau period, to report on Canada's economic future. Its best-remembered product was the recommendation that Canada seek a free trade agreement with the United States.

The other sort, as exemplified by the Stevens inquiry, is one in which a matter that focuses on an individual and bears a distinct resemblance to something to be found in the Criminal Code has neither been disposed of where it should have been—in this case, in Parliament—nor made subject to a criminal charge and sent to the courts.

The inquiry looks like a trial and often has a judge presiding, under the title of "commissioner of inquiry". The resemblance is heightened, particularly in circumstances of political scandal, by intense media coverage. In the inquiry into the Stevens Affair, the media had a peculiar interest, having themselves produced the indictments which led to the inquiry. It consequently was engaged in confirming or not confirming proclaimed facts—but not in publicly examining the sources, or questioning the integrity of the means by which they were arrived at. Some of those allegations were identifiable on sight as irresponsible, based on no original research, and libellous.

But, resemblances notwithstanding, a public inquiry is not a trial. It does not convict and sentence, for example. However, whether that, in the end, is to the good of the individual involved is questionable. Meanwhile the looser procedure affords that person less protection. In a criminal proceeding the persons who collect the evidence are the police, but they do not put anyone in a courtroom on their own. Their evidence most often is examined in the office of a Crown attorney to ensure that there is enough substance to warrant a criminal charge. Not all of those 146 allegations against Sinclair Stevens, as Judge Parker said, had substance at all, yet there they were, in their impressive number, and any reporter covering the inquiry was entitled to write or broadcast that "Under this heading alone [naming one] there are thirty, fifty or however many allegations. . . ." And the reader or listener was no less free to say, "Wow, fifty allegations under one heading alone; this guy really must have been fiddling the system."

Also, the inquiry proceeds under much less demanding rules concerning the admissibility of circumstantial or hearsay evidence, and without the choice an accused has in a criminal trial of remaining silent, or of speaking in his or her own defence at the cost then of being open to cross-examination. Another important difference is that, while a trial proceeds for the purpose of deciding guilt or innocence according to the law as laid down in statutes, a public inquiry labours under terms of reference drafted for the occasion in Cabinet. The terms given the Parker Commission were, in at least two respects, sloppily drawn. The following, with a couple of inconsequential edits, are the terms of reference that brought the Stevens inquiry into being:

> The committee of the Privy Council, on the recommendation of the Prime Minister, advise that pursuant to Section 37 of the Judge's Act, the Honorable William Dickens Parker be authorized to act as a commissioner . . . under Part 1 of the Inquiries Act and under the great seal of Canada . . . to inquire into and report on (a) the facts following allegations of conflict of interest made in various newspapers, electronic media, and the House of Commons . . . whether the Honorable Sinclair M. Stevens was in real or apparent conflict of interest, as defined by the Conflict of Interest and Post-Employment Code for Public Office Holders. . . .

Straightforward enough once the overburden of official language is cleared away, no? Not really. What does the phrase "the facts *following* allegations" mean? Does "following" in that context mean after *in time*, or as a consequence of, or perhaps incidental to? Or does it simply suggest, without actually saying so, that the inquiry might also look into the methodology of the media in developing those allegations? Or, if not the allegations and their substance, what? That wording gave the commission considerable trouble. And how far into the future should "following" be assumed to run? It was that question, although not alone, which led the commission to go beyond the allegations handed it to consider and finally report upon five "minglings" of interest which had not been alleged by anyone but which arose from evidence produced incidentally along the way.

As for allegations "in various newspapers, electronic media, and the House", the last could be considered to be there only for the sake of comprehensiveness. Almost every word spoken in the House was an extrapolation from what the other two, the print and electronic media, had put in the public domain.

But the worst problem left the commission was to decide how to carry out the principal task assigned it—"to inquire into and report on" whether Sinclair Stevens was in "real or apparent conflict of interest as defined by the Conflict of Interest and Post-Employment Code for Public Office Holders." Conflict of interest—real, apparent, supposed, or any other species—turned out not to be defined in the code. Rules had been laid down for the avoidance of it, but someone had neglected to state with precision what it was. The result was that Judge Parker was left not just to decide—again to borrow the language of the criminal courts—if the accused was guilty or not guilty, but also what he was guilty or not guilty *of*. Thus the media were effectively the prosecution, and the commissioner was both the law adjudicator and the lawmaker.

The footings on which the Stevens Affair was erected were laid down on page one of *The Globe and Mail*, March 27, 1986, under the double byline of Michael Harris and David Stewart-Patterson, both then members of the newspaper's Ottawa bureau. A five-column heading at the top of the page said, "Hyundai-linked bank lent to Stevens firm" and a three-column underline read, "Minister drew car plants to Canada." The following are the first three paragraphs of the story itself:

> A South Korean bank with close ties to the Hyundai business group lent $3.6 million in 1983 to a company controlled by Sinclair Stevens, who as Minister of Regional Industrial Expansion, was later instrumental in bringing the Korean automaker into Canada.
>
> The loans from Hanil Bank Canada remained in place after Mr. Stevens put his controlling interest in York Centre Corp. into a blind trust when he became a cabinet minister in September, 1984.
>
> When the Korean bank granted the loans in May and October of 1983, Mr. Stevens was chairman of the company, which has experienced cash-flow problems over the past four years. York Centre said that two of the loans were repaid last year and replaced with new borrowing from the Canadian Imperial Bank of Commerce, but one is still outstanding with a balance at March 1 of $775,000.

The story went on to say that Stevens, through his chief-of-staff, Effie Triantafilopoulos, recalled a loan from the Korean bank but was hazy about the details. When asked whether the loans represented a conflict of interest, Ms. Triantafilopoulos replied, "I presented him with the facts you gave me and he just looked blank and said, 'I don't know how Hyundai could be involved with Hanil.'" He was not alone in that, as we will see.

She also said the minister had no personal dealings with the bank, a point affirmed by Ted Rowe, president of York Centre, who said he himself had arranged the loan with Arnold Denton, vice-president for corporate loans at the Korean bank's Canadian subsidiary. Rowe knew Denton and said that, if Denton had been with any other of the seventy-odd foreign banks in Canada, he probably would have gone to him, "because Arnold is a good guy and wanted to do some business."

Nowhere, other than in that question asked of the minister's chief-of-staff, did the *Globe*'s reporters use the phrase "conflict of interest". But more than just a whiff of the accusation was present; the story would have been pointless unless they had something like that in mind. It existed more positively in a reference to "the parts plant Mr. Stevens negotiated with Hyundai for his own riding" and in the comment of "one source", not otherwise identified, who said the governments in Ottawa and in Quebec had given Hyundai a "sweetheart deal" to locate a much larger full assembly plant in Bromont, Quebec.

Those were the essentials of the *Globe*'s original Hanil-Hyundai story—the loans from the Canadian subsidiary of the Korean bank; Hyundai's first manufacturing venture in Canada, a $25-million parts plant in the minister's own constituency of York-Peel, just north of Toronto; and finally, the leap into actual car-assembly at a new plant at Bromont, with financial assistance from two governments.

My own reaction on reading and rereading that story was that, although evidently patiently researched, it did not quite make the case that the paper implied but hesitated to state explicitly. Stevens was not a minister of anything at the time the loans from the Hanil bank were obtained; he was in the parliamentary opposition, therefore without administrative authority over anything. The money had come from a legitimate source at an apparently conventional rate for the time. Of the $3.6 million obtained, $2.8 million had been repaid. There was nothing to suggest—and nothing *was* suggested, then or later—that the loan had been forgiven or that it would not continue to be paid down. What the story inspired most was a puzzled "So what?"

From everything that could be seen, the response in Parliament and the other media was similar. True, the House had recessed for Easter just as the story broke, but when the session resumed there was just one question at the Commons Question Period, no more than the knee-jerk reaction of any parliamentary opposition to any scandalous allegation in any major news medium against any government. The media pack, usually so easily aroused, scarcely twitched. The story to all appearances was dead.

An unrelated second story in the *Globe*—unrelated except that it applied to the same minister—brought the first back to vigorous life, sprouting new allegations of wrongdoing in all directions. Fifty allegations—nearly one-third of all those gathered up by the Parker Commission on all aspects of its several-sided inquiry—related to a Hanil-Hyundai connection. Most of those were broadcast or published during the issue's second life, after the original story had been left seemingly for dead. With a second exposé to buttress the first, all restraint was let go, as attention returned to the supposed sweetheart deal that had led to Hyundai's setting up as a car-maker in Canada.

The deal was described in various stories as a $300-million something; among the terms used were "the forgiveness of the $300 million obligation", the minister's having "personally got the company off the hook for $300 million", his having given up "a legally binding undertaking with respect to the purchase of $300 million worth of Canadian goods" and his having "unilaterally broke[n] the agreement with Hyundai with respect to the $300 million". Another way of phrasing the thought was to translate the supposed $300 million into lost jobs in Canada—"10,000 jobs", "10,000 to 15,000", "the possible destruction of 4,000 existing jobs". The claim that Hyundai had been "released" was based on an alleged commitment to export $300 million of Canadian goods, in an earlier agreement from the time when Korea needed special approval to do business in Canada. It entered Canada under those original terms as a trader in general merchandise, not as a car-maker, and the understanding was that it would export Canadian-made goods to at least half the value of what it imported.

There never was a $300-million commitment, demanded by Canada or accepted by Hyundai, to do anything. That figure was someone's calculation, based on one unusual year's experience, of the value of the made-in-Canada goods the company *would* have had to export under the terms of the old agreement. But as an auto assembler it needed to import the parts it proposed to assemble, which changed the import-export ratio. On the other hand, Canada was now getting about a thousand well-paying new jobs in Quebec.

That was the reality of the would-have-been from which the $300 million was fabricated—along with such allegations, from the commission's collected allegations, as a concession granted as "some sort of kickback", "not with the full public interest in mind", "a way of returning a favor", "the forgiveness of the $300 million obligation", "for his [the minister's] own personal interest", and the rest. . . .

The first words of the Parker Commission's conclusions on the "Allegations Relating to Hyundai"—all fifty of them—were these:

> The . . . evidence establishes beyond doubt that the allegations involving Mr. Stevens' dealings with Hyundai were without foundation. In fact, it would be accurate to say that there is a complete absence of evidence that Mr. Stevens had any personal pecuniary interest in Hyundai or that he stood to gain in any way by giving Hyundai special treatment. This is amply demonstrated by the remote nature of the relationship between the Hanil Bank and Hyundai. Further, the extensive evidence involving the benefits received by Hyundai established that, in each case, Mr. Stevens acted entirely properly within the scope of his public duty and on the advice of his department.

Except for a reference to a parts plant at Newmarket, Ontario, that "Mr. Stevens negotiated for his own riding", not itself a trifling exception, *The Globe and Mail*'s facts were far more reliable than those in the reporting that followed. This is common; the originators of a story do the research which the followers use as a platform to build on, sometimes with reckless abandon. However, the facts gathered by Harris and Stewart-Patterson did not quite add up to what their story implied. The relationship between Hyundai and the Hanil Bank was not that of "a major shareholder", far less "*the* major shareholder", as some reports not only implied but stated as fact. Neither was the relationship between the bank and Hyundai known to Stevens. Nor was the relationship known to many others before the *Globe* asked Stevens's chief-of-staff about it. The commissioner's report said, "Even the Hyundai (Canada) representatives who appeared before the inquiry were unaware of this relationship. Therefore, there can be no doubt Mr. Stevens could not and did not seek to exploit a relationship of which he was unaware."

Although not phrased as such, those conclusions constituted a rebuke to the media for the reporting on that whole section of the affair. The *Globe*'s main fault was to have put in the public domain a story that was essentially a by-product of a larger investigation it was engaged in, and one in which the two-and-two of its facts made eight. The results of the larger investigation became public a month later. On April 29, 1986, the paper—again at the top of page one, with the same double byline, Michael Harris and David Stewart-Patterson—ran a story headed "Stevens' wife got year of free interest on loan." These were the first paragraphs:

> Noreen Stevens, wife of Industry Minister Sinclair Stevens, negotiated a year's free interest on a $2.6 million loan in the course of refinancing her husband's cash-starved business interests last May.
>
> The loan came from a source suggested by Frank Stronach, chairman of Magna International Inc., whom she also approached but who refused to get involved in the deal.
>
> Anton Czapka, co-founder of Magna with Mr. Stronach, lent the money through 622109 Ontario Ltd. It charged no interest for the first year of the five-year mortgage loan to Cardiff Investments Ltd., the real-estate arm of York Centre Corp. With interest on the loan at 12 percent, the concession was worth $314,400. . . .

In simplest form—the loan arrangement that became central to the Parker Commission's inquiry was anything but simple—Noreen Stevens, a lawyer and businesswoman, had been in search of cash to sustain the Stevenses' York Centre group of companies. The companies were, in the later words of the Parker inquiry's report, "In a collective sense . . . in a condition of financial peril" at the time the loan was arranged. The search led her to Frank Stronach, the spectacularly successful manufacturer of automobile components; she had met Stronach, a neighbour, in the 1970s through a common interest in the Big Brother movement.

Her husband became acquainted with him only later, but had become a keen admirer of Stronach's business philosophy—to the point of consulting him on the new Conservative government's privatization program and recommending his appointment to the board of the Canadian Development Investment Corporation.

Stronach referred Noreen Stevens to Anton Czapka, who had been associated with him in Magna from the beginning, still had an office at its headquarters in Markham, Ontario, and continued as a consultant. Czapka, who has since died, had resigned as a director and executive officer in 1981 and subsequently sold much of his stock, and was close to retiring altogether. Czapka undeniably was still involved with the affairs of Magna, but the relationship was not so close as much of the reporting conveniently made it. His interest, which became an eminently successful one, had turned to real estate. Mrs. Stevens put up as surety for the loan six properties, four of them with industrial buildings on them, which Czapka himself evaluated at $3.1 million. The loan, $2.62 million, was for five years, with interest becoming payable one year from the date the agreement was signed.

Among the curiosities of the arrangement, which quickly was translated into another "sweetheart deal" in the follow-on reporting to the *Globe*'s original, was that the parties signed two documents in short order which conveyed to the lay eye different impressions about the year's "free interest". The first, signed on April 19, 1985, said the amount of the loan would be $2.62 million, the interest at 12 per cent, to begin after the first anniversary of the loan, payable yearly, term five years, at the end of which the whole principal would fall due, subject to partial payments in the interim on the sale of real estate. That might be taken to say that the loan would run for five years but the interest would apply to only four.

The second, the formal agreement signed May 15, 1985 (the effective date of the loan), said, "The corporation [Czapka] has advanced $2,620, 000 to the owner [Mrs. Stevens] on the security of mortgages . . . on the lands and premises listed . . . with interest commencing after May 15, 1986, at 12 percent per annum, payable annually for a term of five years." That said, at least to the lay eye, that the interest was payable for five years, presumably picking up the first payment at the end. Thus there was no interest-free year at all. But no, evidently not;

it was no more than an instance of imprecise drafting, as the Parker Commission report, in its several references to "an interest-free year", seems to have seen it.

While the Stevens stories still occupied Question Period in the House of Commons, I talked with David Stewart-Patterson about the affair, because it seemed to me that the circuit had not been completed; it had not been demonstrated conclusively that a private benefit had been gained at the one end, or a reciprocal favour done at the other. (That proved to be a naïve belief on my part when Judge Parker's definitions of real and apparent conflict of interest came out. No demonstrable transfer of benefit needed to appear at all.) My question to Stewart-Patterson was "What is the importance of the fact that Magna International got grants and loans and other forms of assistance from the Department [of Regional Industrial Expansion] to build two plants in Cape Breton? What is the association between that and the loan?" He replied, "As far as I am concerned, the important association there is to point out the fact that the company does business with her husband's department. Now, a lot of the political opposition have been trying to stretch that further into saying that Magna is collecting a benefit . . . and similarly trying to say that the loan constituted a benefit that came from . . . that can be linked to Magna, and that, in so doing, trying to put together a circle that completes the necessary ingredients for a criminal charge."

Whether or not anyone was trying to bring about a criminal charge may be questioned, but what Stewart-Patterson skipped over, presumably in loyalty to his trade, was the fact that efforts to push the story were much more apparent in the media than in the parliamentary opposition. Commission counsel, in preparing lists of possible witnesses in advance of the inquiry, interviewed all the Members of Parliament who had participated in the to-and-fro in the Commons, and some but not all of the newspeople who had written a line or broadcast a few words on the subject. The MPs had virtually no information of their own.

As described to me in the early days of the inquiry by David Scott, the commission counsel, the purpose of the interviews with the MPs was "to see if they had any first-hand information". In the end, only two MPs were called, and they to testify on peripheral matters. Of the media, the managing editor of *The Globe and Mail*, Geoffrey Stevens (no relation to the minister), and three reporters would not agree to be interviewed because the paper already had been served with notice of a libel action by the Stevenses. (Eight years later, it had not proceeded.) However, the four subsequently became minor witnesses in the inquiry itself. As for the remainder of the journalists who had reported or commented on the matter, what the commission's interviewers found, in Scott's words, was that "most were simply repeating with appropriate adjectival add-ons what the original reporters dug up."

However, not all those add-ons were innocuous, especially in light of the fact that they were rooted in no more substantial evidence than was available to any bus-rider in the country. For example, consider this, unattributed, in the commission's sub-category of "Epithets": "Sinclair Stevens has no standard of morality whatsoever when it comes to his role as a minister of the Crown." Or this, under the simple title of "Other allegations": "The Minister instituted a true system of pay-offs, suggesting to businesses that want government contracts and grants, that they must first provide financing to York Centre." Those statements, without hard proof, would be libellous.

As in the Hyundai dealings, what was implicit in those allegations, again lacking documentation but now on a much broader scale, was a sinister linkage. Relative specifically to the dealings between the minister and Magna, the underlying innuendo was that the $64.2 million of assistance from the government to the company to set up plants in Cape Breton was related to the $2.6-million loan made to Mrs. Stevens by Anton Czapka, encouraged by Frank Stronach. That—although it suggested not just one but two criminal charges might be warranted—overlooked several important points.

First, the Department of Regional Industrial Expansion was in the business of fostering such expansion, particularly in areas of chronic unemployment, by means of grants, loans and similar assistance to induce companies to create new plants in designated locations, or expand existing ones. Certainly Cape Breton was one of those locations. Parliament repeatedly had voted money precisely for that purpose.

Secondly, it was Stevens's Liberal predecessor in the department, Edward Lumley, who first picked the burgeoning Magna as the chosen instrument through which to stimulate growth in the Canadian auto parts industry. The loans, credits and grants of Stevens's time were not the first to Magna. In January 1984, just before Parliament was dissolved for the general election at which the change of government occurred, Lumley discussed with Stronach plans for the future. A memorandum of understanding resulted, as a framework for further assistance in pursuit of the government's objective. That memorandum continued to be in effect under Stevens.

Thirdly, Frank Stronach, having been receptive in the beginning to the idea of locating a plant or two, or a plant and a training school, in Cape Breton, had become hesitant. There was resistance within the company to what some saw as a departure from the fundamental corporate policy of concentrating expansion along the line of Ontario's Highway 401, the better to serve an auto industry in Canada and the United States working to a just-in-time parts delivery system. Stevens had to work to secure what he wanted, and felt it an achievement when agreement was reached. In other words, policy ruled—not an exchange of favours.

Only here and there did the media show interest in such considerations as those, or even whether Czapka had secured for himself, in the loan agreement, enough compensation to account for his having entered into it without a hidden motive. For example, a "Schedule A" attached to the full agreement, which I obtained through Access to Information, listed six properties pledged by Mrs. Stevens with a total value of $3,106,000, which was Czapka's figure. A note below said, "The corporation [Czapka] to be entitled to all net sale proceeds up to [the] above evaluation, and any excess realized over such amount to be shared equally between the corporation and the owner [Mrs. Stevens]." That in itself made no trifling assurance to the lender.

It is true that some of those properties were encumbered with mortgages which would reduce their realizable worth in the event of a sale in the short term. However, Czapka's own analysis, as determined by the inquiry, focused on the prospect of increased cash flow from higher rents raising the property values, which would ensure a short-term paydown, and on the division of proceeds in case a sale for any reason became unavoidable.

His interest rate, at 12 per cent, was a fraction better—for him—than the going loan rate as reported by Harris and Stewart-Patterson, 11.5 to 11.75 per cent. To lend to Mrs. Stevens, he borrowed from his bank. Obviously an old and good customer—his personal wealth was estimated at about $15 million—and with a "comfort letter" from Magna, he was able to borrow at 10.5 per cent, which gave him a further little cushion. But much more important to his security was his having become a business partner, and one with a lot of weight, as is evident in the first four clauses in the May 15 agreement:

> 1. Except for managing and renting the said land, the Owner [Mrs. Stevens] will not mortgage, sell, or deal with the said lands without the consent of the Corporation [Czapka].
> 2. The owner will use its best efforts to increase all rental values from the said lands and abide by all instructions the Corporation at any time gives to it.
> 3. In the event at any time the Corporation wishes to assume complete control and operation of all or any part of the said lands, the Owner shall surrender the same to it and execute any appropriate power of attorney to enable the Corporation to deal with the said lands or any part thereof.
> 4. Commencing June 30, 1985, the Owner shall thereafter render quarterly financial reports to the Corporation of all income and expenses relating to the said lands or shall render more frequent reports if requested to do so by the corporation.

It became part of the inquiry to ask why Magna provided Czapka with a comfort letter. A comfort letter is a simple device whereby a lender, in this case Czapka's bank, is assured that if its borrower can't make good, the writer of the comfort letter will. In other words, Magna was providing backup for Czapka's borrowing, a round-about procedure but a further illustration of Anton Czapka's sharp eye for business. Judge Parker said in his report that there was insufficient evidence for him to conclude that the comfort letter was other than part of a "genuine commercial arrangement" between Magna, Czapka and the bank. "The evidence," he said, "falls short of establishing that the arrangement was a ruse to disguise Magna's financing of the . . . loan."

The report did not find fault with Czapka's rationale in making the loan. It said the premise was that "property values would rise, interest rates would drop, and rents would increase", thus permitting the Stevens companies "to pay down prior mortgages and carry his mortgage." It went on, "I am unable to conclude that these expectations were unreasonable . . . and subsequent events seem to have proven him correct. Interest rates have dropped, rents have risen, and so perhaps has the value of the properties. . . . Obviously the transaction was not a gift to the borrowers."

Although finding that the Czapka loan was *not* a sweetheart deal, the report did so for a reason more terminological than either political or financial. It was that the description was imprecisely applied, "there being no evidence of collusion or that the terms [of the loan] were detrimental or disadvantageous to a third party." It went on to say that "the terms of the transaction were unusually beneficial to the borrowers" and "afforded the borrowers and their parent and affiliated companies substantial and timely relief." But then, loans usually *are* for substantial and timely relief—the more substantial and timely, the better—which does not make them illegal, improper or even questionable.

At the time the loan story first bloomed, and later, I put to several persons knowledgeable about real estate transactions, first the facts about the loan as set out in the *Globe*'s original story, and later those in the formal Stevens–Czapka agreement. The general reaction was not to denounce the loan as a sweetheart deal, but to say that it was not out of keeping with other private commercial property deals they had seen; there were glimmerings of admiration for Czapka as a sharp operator who drove a hard bargain.

To my mind, the terms laid down by Czapka, with the prospects he foresaw for his investment, more than compensated for the year free of interest. The borrower needed money up front; the lender took prudent precautions to see that there was no great risk of his being a loser in the short run, and that he would probably be a substantial winner in the long run.

When I asked Judge Parker about that, I got a mild lesson in judicial practice. "You are now asking me," he said, "to justify my ruling. I don't think I should second-guess myself because I called it as I saw it at the time; judges do that. Well, judges make mistakes. I am not saying that was a mistake, but I don't think I should second-guess my ruling. That is why we have a court of appeal."

Mrs. Stevens obviously was indiscreet in seeking help in a substantial financial matter from the chairman of a company with which her husband carried on government business, friend and neighbour regardless. Nevertheless, that is not to say damage was done to the public interest, whatever the appearances. (Writers and broadcasters were virtually unanimous in finding those appearances blatantly bad, although not so bad that they couldn't be exaggerated. As time went on, a tendency developed to drop the "one year" from the endlessly repeated "$2.6 million loan free of interest for one year", and to use the quicker, slicker and inaccurate version "$2.6 million interest-free loan".)

The excitement in the press and Parliament about the loan had not quite died when Diane Francis, now editor of *The Financial Post*, then writing about Bay Street and business in general for *The Toronto Star*, produced the third major element in the Stevens Affair. This story was about Noreen Stevens and Ted Rowe, president of York Centre, having approached three big-name Bay Street brokers, well before her Czapka loan but on the same mission—looking for cash to sustain the Stevens companies through a bad patch. The meeting had been arranged for Mrs. Stevens by J. Trevor Eyton, president of Brascan. They talked about the possibilities of a share offering or arranging new loans. That would have been no more than a case of doing business as business is done, except for a political connection: the *Star* story in effect juxtaposed those talks and the appointment not long after of Eyton and three other "Brascan persons", as the Parker report called them, to the board of the Canadian Development Investment Corporation (CDIC), and the retaining of the three brokerage houses as advisers on the intended privatization of several publicly owned companies. Again, the matter was one of appearances, to which there was another side, scarcely touched upon by reporters and commentators following in Francis's wake and looking to feast on a new scandal.

Part of the other side was that nothing had come of Mrs. Stevens's mission; she left with the bad news that these financiers could do nothing for her troubled companies—which hardly suggests that the Bay Streeters were intimidated by the knowledge that, gee whiz, this was the wife of an important minister they were dealing with, or that they were obsequiously ready to do a favour in the prospect of some favour in return. Also, though it may be a quibble, the appointments were not made nor the contracts delivered by the minister, but by the CDIC. Moreover, Diane Francis herself observed that "as three of Canada's leading brokerage houses, the three firms were certainly among the likeliest candidates for these [advisory] contracts." Judge Parker's report, when it came out, said that "Mr. Eyton clearly was well-qualified for the CDIC position" and that there was nothing "improper or untoward in the award by the CDIC of the advisory contracts . . . or the fees paid."

But such considerations, by Judge Parker's definition of conflict of interest, were irrelevant. That the persons and companies might be qualified and competent for the jobs to which they were appointed, that nothing of tangible value to the Stevens companies came of the talks, and that Stevens had testified he thought his wife was simply seeking advice (which, from such sources, would be advice of value) did not matter. What mattered was that he *knew*. "Any finding of a real conflict of interest on the part of Mr. Stevens," the report said, "is dependent on Mr. Stevens' knowledge of those efforts." And, a few pages on, "I find that Mr. Stevens had knowledge of a private economic interest that was sufficient to influence the exercise of [his] public duties and responsibilities." Stevens, as minister responsible for the CDIC, knew that persons he was talking with in one context, his wife was talking with in another. Therefore, there was "a connection, or a nexus, with his . . . public duties . . . sufficient to influence . . . those duties," whether it influenced them or not.

The report was published on December 3, 1987, eighteen months after the inquiry began. Notwithstanding the fourteen findings of conflict of interest, it was not nearly so relentlessly condemning as the media in general were before, and as some remained after. A *Toronto Star* editorial spoke of it as a "searing indictment", which was a little strong. In fact, on the three main issues, Judge Parker had very little to say about identified wrongdoing.

These were the definitions of two main species of conflict he settled on after considering a number:

> 1) A real conflict of interest denotes a situation in which a minister of the Crown has knowledge of a private economic interest that is sufficient to influence the exercise of his or her public duties and responsibilities;
> 2) An apparent conflict of interest exists when there is a reasonable apprehension which reasonably well-informed persons could properly have, that a conflict of interest exists.

The proposition underlying the second is readily understandable—imagine putting all the circumstances of a decision taken by a minister or official before a reasonably well-informed person and asking, "Does all of that say to you that a self-interested motive may have entered into it?" If the person reasonably could be expected to answer yes, an apparent conflict of interest existed.

The rationale for determining a *real* conflict of interest is more difficult to get hold of, because it requires going into the mind of the individual concerned. What constitutes knowledge of a private economic interest? If the minister or official had considered the possibility and dismissed it, would that constitute knowledge, or simply an error of judgement in believing that no one else could see it in that light either? And who is to say at what point a private economic interest becomes sufficient to influence a person in the exercise of the duties and responsibilities of an office? One man might be ready to sell his dear old granny into slavery for $10,000, but it would be at least slightly unfair to translate that into a general rule.

Also, the definition is open-ended; nothing provably needs to have been done. In a slightly different context, Judge Parker quoted from the 1984 report of a task force on conflict of interest conducted by Michael Starr, who had been Minister of Labour in the Diefenbaker years, and Mitchell Sharp, who held several posts in the Pearson and Trudeau governments, including Minister of Finance. They said, "Private and public interests need not be in competition . . . for an ethical problem to exist . . . with the result that in serving the public purpose the individual benefits privately as well. . . . Conflict of interest can in some cases mean compatibility of interest."

But even in those presumably rare circumstances, a demonstrable benefit was seen at the end. In Judge Parker's definition, however, it was necessary only that a private economic interest *could* influence a decision, whether it did or not, whether it produced a benefit at the end or not. The triangular scenario in the Magna portion of the affair, as extracted by the commission from the media coverage, seemed to sketch a journey to nowhere. The grants and loans to Magna from Stevens' department were consistent with departmental policy. Frank Stronach's comfort letter to Anton Czapka was no more than a genuine commercial arrangement. The $2.6 million which Czapka lent Mrs. Stevens was not a gift. On top of all that—though Judge Parker did not accept it—Stevens had denied knowledge of his wife's efforts to raise money for the family firms, which she was running while he was in politics. The appearances were undeniably untidy, but the eventual report found the minister to be in breach of the code, not on appearances but on the *reality* of a conflict of interest.

When, in February 1992, Judge Parker was invited to appear before a joint committee of the Senate and House of Commons which had been appointed to study conflicts of interest, it was evident that his outsider's view as a jurist did not coincide with the insider views of quite a few of the parliamentarians, though they disagreed in an amiable manner. He, for example, believed that the blind trust, which had been the prescribed way to ward off allegations of conflicts, was a farce. The surer way, to his mind, was to require all investments and the like to be put on the public record, which would be accessible. That would allow the public to judge "whether you have done something wrong or not". The view that seemed to predominate among the committee members was that full disclosure or, worse, total divestiture, which has its advocates, would put a price on entering politics that many good people would not be prepared to accept. That would be to the country's loss.

Judge Parker acknowledged that in the inquiry—which he tartly reminded the committee "might have been avoided had you had some procedure in place earlier"—he had approached the subject from quite a different viewpoint. "We were then faced with allegations," he said. "They were dealt with as if it were a court. If you make allegations against a person you have to have some standard against which to compare the conduct. . . . As the commissioner, I picked one definition . . . which I thought was fair and reasonable. You may have different ideas; it's your duty to decide which one you want. . . . But I was approaching it—had to approach it—from the view of an inquiry as to what the public perception would be. By that time, the media were having a field day. They were pointing out the attitude of the public. . . ."

But that raises the point that a public inquiry is not designed to serve as an alternative form of court. It also raises a question that is central to this book: "From where does the public take the perceptions which become public attitudes, except from the media?" Undoubtedly there were a few people—there usually are—who settled in at the hearing room to follow the inquiry at first hand from end to end. But had the hearings been held in the SkyDome, filled to the brim each day with such dedicated followers, they still would have made a minute fraction of even the people of Toronto, far less the 27 million Canadians from coast to coast. Of however many of those were interested at all, the bulk necessarily received every scrap of their information from television, radio, newspapers and magazines. In this particular case those were the same sources from which the accusations came—accusations founded in many cases wholly on what the accusers had read or heard from other members of their own media fraternity. Thus the public attitudes which in Judge Parker's opinion the media reflected were in fact, by a circular process, their own.

In 1990, the Supreme Court of Canada produced a majority decision in a case called Starr vs. Houlden that may—or should—cause provincial and federal governments to draw back from the temptation to use the Inquiries Act as an easy way out of political embarrassments that ought to be disposed of within Parliament or sent to the courts to be dealt with according to the definitions, practices and penalties of the criminal courts.

There need be no doubt that getting the Stevens Affair out of Parliament was what the Mulroney government had first in mind in setting up the Parker Commission. However, on the other side of the argument, some allowance must be made for the fact that the climate in the House of Commons scarcely encouraged hope that a rational examination of the facts could be achieved there.

Sheila Copps and John Nunziata, charter members of the Liberals' Rat Pack of the day, had given a persuasive demonstration of that when they created a mêlée at a night sitting of an unrelated House committee at which Stevens appeared in the routine of being quizzed on the business of his department. John Turner, the Liberal leader of the opposition, was embarrassed the next day to hear and read accounts of Copps leaping over chairs to get at the minister, and Nunziata claiming he had been assaulted by Stevens's associate minister, André Bissonnette, when he too was in ostensibly innocent pursuit of the minister as he tried to make his way out.

However, the thought that the issue could be disposed of that discreetly was not only mistaken but out of touch. The last great quasi-criminal public inquiry in Ontario—the Grange Inquiry into the unexplained deaths of a number of infants in the Hospital for Sick Children—had found cable television rapping on the door of government the day after an inquiry was announced, seeking assent to its plan to cover the inquiry wall to wall. The Stevens inquiry was covered not only by television but by the print media, day after day, and by the larger media entities in relays of reporters.

The 1989 Patty Starr Affair was an embarrassment to the Liberal government of Ontario under Premier David Peterson, an embarrassment made worse by the fact that a provincial general election—which the Liberals, incidentally, would lose—lay just ahead. Patricia Starr was president of the board of the Toronto section of the National Council of Jewish Women in Canada, a registered charitable organization. A *Globe and Mail* story alleged that Ms. Starr had made political donations from money given to the charity. The announcement of an inquiry was made the day after a senior aide to the premier resigned after having revealed that Ms. Starr had arranged for his family to receive a new refrigerator and to have their house painted at no cost. The inquiry was to examine facts related to Ms. Starr's role as the Toronto head of the charitable organization, and to persons or firms she might have acted for, including a large Toronto property developer, Tridel Corporation Inc., and elected and appointed officials.

Before the inquiry even got going, the commissioner, Mr. Justice Lloyd W. Houlden, was asked to state a case dealing with the province's constitutional competence to establish the inquiry, and its potential effects on an individual and on individual rights under common law and under the Charter of Rights.

It was only after that application was refused, and two references made to provincial courts on appeal were both dismissed, that the matter reached the Supreme Court. The decision delivered there, in March 1990, was on the question of whether the order-in-council that created the inquiry was beyond the legal authority of the provincial government. The answer of Mr. Justice Antonio Lamer, with six others assenting, was yes. That being so, as the judge noted, he did not need to pronounce upon the other constitutional questions or the other issues raised by the appellants. But the reasons for judgment that prefaced that answer contain dozens of references to principles, applicable no less to the national government than to the provinces, that argue strongly against the use of public inquiries as a place to dump allegations of misconduct, which, if incapable of being resolved within Parliament itself, ought to be tried under the protections afforded an accused under the criminal law. These are examples of a general nature, some related to the case that was before the court, some not; some in Judge Lamer's own words, some his quotations from other sources. First, on the two forms of public inquiry, one on broad policy questions, the other as quasi-trials:

> Provinces should be given ample room . . . to establish public inquiries aimed at investigating, studying and recommending changes for the better government of their citizens. What a province must not do . . . is [to] enact a public inquiry, with all its coercive powers, as a substitute for an investigation [by police] and preliminary inquiry [in court] into specific individuals in respect of specific criminal offences. This is an interference with federal interests in the enactment of and provision for a system of criminal justice as embodied in the criminal code.

On the difference in circumstances between a person enmeshed in a public inquiry and a suspect or an accused in a criminal proceeding, he said: "The inquiry can compel a 'witness,' who is really one of the named 'suspects,' to answer questions under oath even though that person could not have been compelled to provide incriminating evidence against [herself/himself], in the course of a regular police investigation, during the course of a preliminary inquiry under the Code . . . or during the course of a trial. . . ." And: "A public inquiry is not the means by which investigations are carried out with respect to the commission of particular crimes. . . . Such an inquiry is a coercive procedure and is quite incompatible with our notion of justice in the investigation of a particular crime and the determination of actual or probable criminal or civil responsibility." And: "When the object is in substance a circumvention of the prescribed criminal procedure by the use of the inquiry technique with all the . . . serious consequences to the individuals affected, the . . . action will be invalid as being in violation of either the criminal procedure . . . or the substantive criminal law, or both. . . ."

And then there were observations on the different end-effects on the individual of having judgements of his or her performance, in office or out of it, made by a commissioner in a public inquiry, or a judge in a court of law: "The inquiry does not act as a criminal court or exercise criminal jurisdiction. . . . We are not here concerned with a criminal trial, structured as a dispute between two sides, the Crown and the accused. The function of the inquiry is merely to investigate and report; no person is accused; those who appear do so as witnesses. . . . The proceedings of the commission are not criminal proceedings in the sense that punishment is their aim. . . ."

Well, perhaps those are not the intended effects. But surely it is unrealistic, at least, to say, when 146 published allegations are brought to bear in a public inquiry that goes on for months in the brightest light of concentrated media attention, that there is no *accused*? And it is true that no mandate to punish is included in the jurisdiction of a public inquiry, but is punishment not, perhaps, the inescapable result?

The section of the Criminal Code to which the Supreme Court judgment in the Starr case pointed as the equivalent in law of the unstated purpose of quasi-trial public inquiries is Section 121, subsections (b) and (c). These two are mirror images, one related to persons having dealings with government, and the other to persons in government having dealings outside. The second, which brings us back directly to the Sinclair Stevens inquiry, says that "everyone commits an offence who, being an official of the government . . . accepts or offers . . . advantage or benefit of any kind directly or indirectly, by himself, or through a member of his family, or through anyone, for his benefit. . . ." The commission's definition in the Stevens affair stroked out actual advantage or benefit as an essential component, and added having knowledge sufficient (perhaps) to influence a decision. Thus the criminal law became less stringent than a rule of Parliament covering the same offence under no law at all—a strange situation.

Another case, tangentially related to the Stevens Affair, arose later but still had not come to court in early 1994. In March 1991, lawyers for Sinclair Stevens gave notice of a suit for defamation in the amount of $3 million—$1 million in general damages, $1 million for general damages by way of legal innuendo, special damages of $500,000 and the same amount in punitive damages. Defamation, more commonly called libel, alleges damage to reputation. The statement of claim said the defamation occurred in a broadcast on the previous December 4 conducted by talk-show host John Michael at station CKTB in St. Catharines, Ontario. Persons who know the show well say it is abrasive, abusive, given to extreme viewpoints, amounting to an exercise in political incorrectness, loved by some and hated by others. Attached to the statement of claim was "Schedule A", a fragmented transcript, or the transcript of a fragmented narrative, containing such comments apropos of the former minister as "the guy is corrupt", "wallowing in corruption", "the man's credibility is zero", "the man's credibility is shot", "crooked", and "politically bankrupt".

Three days later, the station broadcast an apology in which Michael said he had made statements which he wanted to retract. "I attacked his honesty and credibility in a way that was quite unwarranted. . . . While I had in mind the 1987 Parker Commission of Inquiry report that Mr. Stevens had been in a conflict-of-interest position when he was minister, I was not justified in attacking his basic honesty. . . ."

The apology and retraction were rebroadcast not quite two weeks later. However, lawyers for the radio station also said in their statement of reply: "Notwithstanding the apology, the defendants said that the words spoken by . . . John Michael during the said broadcast were nevertheless fair comment made without malice on a matter of public interest. In this connection the defendants plead and rely upon the analysis and conclusions set out in the final report of Chief Justice W.D. Parker in the Commission of Inquiry into the Facts of Allegations of Conflict of Interest Concerning the Honourable Sinclair M. Stevens."

It is to make no judgement of the substance of the case itself, pro or con, to say that reasonable inference from that reliance on the Parker Commission report seems to be "Your ground for suing for damage to reputation is not good because you have none left to damage."

Considering that much of the supposed evidence against Stevens was flawed, that it led via a flawed mandate to a commission of inquiry, a flawed means of dealing with such matters, as the Supreme Court found, and that commissions of inquiry were never intended to decide guilt and innocence, or to punish—what followed from the reporting of the Stevens Affair is a form of justice worth pondering—not least by news executives whose concentration on the good they do in bringing wrongdoing to light should not exclude consideration of the harm they do when they extrapolate extreme conclusions from insufficient facts.

THIRTEEN

BLESSED ARE THE PURE IN HEART

AT THE SAME TIME IN 1986–87 AS SINCLAIR STEVENS was being pursued, first by the media, then by the parliamentary opposition and finally by a judicial inquiry, a Toronto firm, Saturday Night Publishing Services, was doing business with several departments of the Ontario government.

Publishing Services was conceived as a contract publisher which would utilize the technical and editorial expertise collected around *Saturday Night* magazine to produce quality publications for other people. Leaving the government departments aside for the moment, it did so for, among others, *The Globe and Mail*'s *Report on Business* and *Destinations* magazines, the *Royal Bank Reporter*, the *CBC Radio Guide* and a management newsletter for the newsprint maker Abitibi-Price Inc.

Another and not necessarily secondary objective foreseen for Publishing Services was that it would produce a little something on its balance sheet to help ensure the survival of *Saturday Night* magazine itself. *Saturday Night*—a hundred years old in 1987—had always been a critical success, among the winners in the National Magazine Awards. Financially, it had never been a star.

Saturday Night, the magazine, of which Publishing Services became a subsidiary, had been owned since 1980 by Dascon Investments Limited of Toronto. Dascon in turn was owned by Norman Webster; his sister, Margaret Gallagher; and his brother, William. And Norman Webster at the time was the editor-in-chief of *The Globe and Mail*. As such, he was the next executive in line to the publisher, and the man responsible for the whole content of the newspaper, news and commentary alike.

That included, particularly, the editorial page. Most newspapers dote on their editorial pages and take them very seriously. It is on the editorial page that the newspaper sets out its own studied view of the world and everything in it, with emphasis on the practices and policies of domestic governments—federal, provincial and municipal. The editor-in-chief of *The Globe and Mail*, then, was writing and directing editorial comment on the performance of the government of Ontario—from which a firm of which he was a principal owner was deriving revenue.

Material obtained under the Ontario Freedom of Information and Protection of Privacy Act shows that the *Saturday Night* subsidiary held contracts with several ministries. On a three-year contract, the company did work for the Ministry of Tourism and Recreation worth $4,627.50 in the 1986–87 fiscal year. That jumped to $249,585.63 in the part of the next fiscal year before the company was sold and became King West Communications. The Ministry of Natural Resources paid the *Saturday Night* subsidiary $110,337 in 1983–84, $144,164 in 1984–85, $190,384 in 1985–86, $173,985 the next year and $150,287 in the year after that—a total of $769,157 over five years. There were also two smaller contracts, one for $47,385.55 with the Ministry of Education, for graphic design services in 1986–87, and another worth $10,840 with the Ministry of Community and Social Services. Webster left *The Globe and Mail* in February 1989.

Was there a conflict of interest? No; this was in the real world, away from politics. It was entirely an internal matter and the essential facts were known or knowable. They were known within *The Globe and Mail*, thus sanctioned as carrying no threat to the integrity of the newspaper. And they were knowable outside; *The Globe and Mail* itself had carried at least one story—that one in a supplement called *Marketing and Media*, under the heading "Contract work lucrative for Saturday Night"—which identified the relationship, via Dascon Investments, between Publishing Services and the *Globe*'s editor. (That it was lucrative seems to have been an understatement.)

The facts offended against no law or set of rules or code of ethics that I am aware of. And the editorial page, in its comments on the performance of the government of Ontario, was neither more complaisant nor more severe than ever.

However, the question is not what is done and not done in business.

Rather it is why so striking a difference should exist between standards in business—where people are assumed to be honest—and in politics—where, as soon as a question arises about the executive conduct of a minister, the minister is assumed guilty until proven innocent. (That in itself is more than just faintly ridiculous, considering that elected Canadians are simply ordinary Canadians except for the mistake of having allowed themselves to be elected—no less well motivated, no less desirous of the good opinion of their colleagues and countrymen, no less dedicated to the job and no less honest. What is supposed to have happened to them as a consequence of their having asked for, and been given, the trust of their local folk, and then having done well enough in Ottawa to become Cabinet ministers?)

If someone quietly—preferably hand cupped over mouth for greater dramatic effect—passed on to an Ottawa journalist a verbal sketch of circumstances equivalent to those cited here apropos of Norman Webster's business enterprise, but referring instead to a government minister—any minister—not only would the seed have been planted, but by next morning the plant would have put out roots from sea to sea. To say that the facts were known to the prime minister, and were thus tacitly approved, would do nothing except enlarge the story into one of conspiracy. That the essential facts were on the public record? Donald Getty's oil holdings were formally on the public record, but that did not divert *The Globe and Mail* from its mammoth series on how he managed to put bread on the table.

When it is suggested that good prospective candidates may be driven away from entering public life because it imposes standards that other Canadians are not expected to meet, the frequent answer from media people is "When has there ever been a shortage of candidates?" Perhaps. But an erosion of quality is highly probable over time. It is still a relatively new madness, this largely media-propagated idea that politicians at the rank of minister need closer surveillance than any of the rest of us because (a) they may at any time raid the public treasury in their assumed greed, and (b) they are supposed to serve as behavioural models for the citizenry at large. (The reasons are rather contradictory—constant suspects as national moral exemplars? Confusing.)

The Chrétien government's promise from the beginning was to bring in what it called grandly an "integrity package". That would include, along with new rules to govern lobbyists in relations with Parliament (and vice versa), new guidance, particularly for ministers, on what conflict of interest is and what precautions must be taken to avoid it. The appointment by Jean Chrétien of his former Cabinet colleague and mentor, Mitchell Sharp, as his adviser on ethical questions was an encouraging sign, considering Sharp's long parliamentary experience, and seemed to indicate a move in the direction of common sense and practicality, as distinct from a knee-jerk reaction to the usual vacuous media demand that the rules become ever "tougher" (presumable meaning: designed to entrap the unwary).

The government's first proposals were introduced too late to be looked at for this book; they still had a long way to go, beginning with consideration in committee, which would not be done in a day. It is to be hoped that, in following the process, "parliamentary observers"—a euphemism frequently used by the media for the simpler "we"—will be able to bring themselves to accept that politicians are Canadians indistinguishable from themselves, which is to say, not by definition crooks.

Some recent propositions related to conflict of interest were not so much wrong in principle as unrealistic. For example, if a minister had knowledge of something that *could* influence his decision in some matter before him, it was assumed to have done so—whether it had or hadn't. If the matter proceeded, a conflict had occurred. How was that to be proved on the one hand, or disproved on the other?

Then there is the mingling of interests, which might consist of a minister raising a private interest in a conversation about public business. Without professing knowledge of business life, which would be a lie, I would be pleased to have the chance to lay $100 on the proposition, if it could be proved, that dozens of such mingling conversations occur every day over lunch in downtowns all over the country—subsidized, even, by the federal tax system, although on a reduced scale since Paul Martin's first budget. They are not unknown to persons in the news business, including political reporters, who will be properly aghast—outwardly—to learn that some politicians also have the poor taste to lapse into such gaucherie.

The fact is that conflicts of interest occur everywhere, all the time and in all their several identified species. What is hard on politics and politicians is that they are hardly ever heard of in other contexts, which leads people to say such things as "Oh, politicians are just in it for what they can get out of it," and "They don't care about us; all they're interested in is lining their pockets."

But are reporters who take information highly critical of a third party, on a not-for attribution basis, guilty of a conflict of interest? News executives and news gatherers in the various media are always quick to argue the right of the public to know when they want access anywhere—for TV cameras in the courts, for instance—or when authority imposes any sort of restraint upon them. Is not that dedication to the public interest overlooked when relevant information is withheld, by private contract between reporter and source, because it is in the reporter's and the news organization's interest to withhold it? May not the source's identity be important to the validity of what is reported?

Or are Ottawa reporters who do occasional (or more than occasional) bits for the CBC compromised by knowing that the largest part of the corporation's revenue comes from the public treasury via an annual parliamentary appropriation—in other words, they they are deriving income from a publicly funded corporation which figures prominently in the budgetary considerations they report and comment upon?

Or, much more important, is the CBC itself in conflict of interest if it uses the plant, equipment and personnel given it to manage in the public interest to argue its corporate interest against a government whose fiscal policy is to reduce public expenditure all round? Obviously the CBC is free to make its case before any parliamentary committee, in briefs to the government, in hearings of the CRTC, from public platforms, by taking ads in the newspapers or by any other means. However, using privileged access to the public air to deliver a corporate message offends against, if nothing else, long-standing CBC policy applicable to others.

The CBC grew up with the idea that the "usurping of the airwaves for special-interest propaganda" could not be permitted. Those quoted words are from Herschel Hardin in *Closed Circuits: The Sellout of Canadian Television* (Douglas & McIntyre, 1985). What he was writing about had nothing to do with any use of the public air by the CBC for its own purposes, but with a series of commentaries of an editorial nature dropped into "Hockey Night in Canada" broadcasts sponsored at the time—1972–73—by Imperial Oil. The complaint was that a large corporation was being permitted to buy time to promote, not necessarily its products, but its business interests.

Hardin retrieved comments by the first chairman of the CBC, Leonard W. Brockington, in 1939, including the statement that "there should be in general no preference for any Canadian over his fellow Canadian" in access to the public air; an unequal right of free speech, in other words, was not to be bought from the public broadcaster.

That thought was taken up by the Board of Broadcast Governors, the first regulatory body over broadcasting in Canada (long since incorporated into today's CRTC), in a set of principles concerning controversial broadcasting, one of which said, "The air must not fall under the control of any individual or groups influential by reason of their wealth *or special position* [my italics]."

That rule is reflected almost exactly in the CBC's current guidebook, *Journalistic Standards and Practices*, under the heading "CBC Philosophy". It says: "The air waves must not fall under the control of any individuals or *groups influential because of their special position* [again, my italics]." Those last words clearly apply—or should apply—to all the personnel of the CBC, and certainly to persons in executive positions. They not only have a special position in deciding what does and does not go on the air, paid for or otherwise, but also have a distinct pecuniary interest, both collectively as a corporation and as individuals, in building up public pressure against government spending cuts, at least where they apply to the CBC.

The corporation's response to the first cuts in its parliamentary appropriation began with this woeful introduction by Peter Mansbridge: "Consider this. An average Canadian viewer will spend nine years in front of his television set, but the message he will be getting won't be Canadian. Your children will have watched twelve thousand hours of television by the time they are twelve. Ten thousand of those hours will be programs made by Americans, for Americans. That has many people concerned about Canada's cultural sovereignty."

Mansbridge was followed by a no less sombre Bill Cameron: "In this segment of the program we focus on a painful and, most people would say, crucial event in Canadian cultural history—the recent severe cuts to the Canadian Broadcasting Corporation. What we will be talking about is not just a loss of jobs for actors, writers, technicians and producers; we will be talking about what you'll be seeing on your television set as those cuts lead to less Canadian programming."

He, in turn, was followed by the CBC president at the time, Pierre Juneau, in what appeared to be a cut from some question-and-answer session. He said: "The CBC English-language television network will be able to program only one or two full twenty-episode series, such as "The Beachcombers". It won't be able to enrich and extend the successful but short-duration series, such as "Seeing Things". . . ."

Between miscellaneous shots—R.B. Bennett, silent and in black and white, Conservative prime minister in the early thirties when the foundations for the CBC were laid; the Parliament Buildings from the air; cameramen on the set in the early days of television—Karen Woolridge, actress; Don Shebib, independent producer; John Kennedy, head of CBC drama; and Robert Lantos, president of RSL Entertainment Corporation made their appearances to say their little bit, or to be interviewed.

> Mansbridge: Just how bad are the cuts; when will viewers see the differences and how will they see the differences?
> Kennedy: Well, the cuts, Peter, are very bad indeed. . . .
> Finally, Davidson Dunton, who was president of the CBC at the advent of television.
> Mansbridge: Mr. Dunton, clearly you, as one of the senior statesmen of television broadcasting in this country . . . have seen a lot of crises. . . . How would you rate this one?
> Dunton: About the biggest, I think. . . .

That, obviously, was not all that was said in almost fifteen minutes of television time. However, any pangs of conscience I might have over cutting short other comments are a good deal eased by the overall content, a mini-documentary of woe and a performed definition of the term "advocacy advertising". That was on December 14, 1984, and was not the peak of the corporation's use of news and public affairs programming as its own public platform.

That was reached in December 1990, when the chairman of the board, Patrick Watson, and the president, Gérard Veilleux, announced as economy measures the closing of eleven local stations across the country, and the elimination of 1,100 jobs, not all, obviously, from closing the stations.

It is routine practice, in print and broadcast journalism, to put the day's freshest and best goods in the front window—top of page one in print, top of the lineup in broadcast news. That day, at the CBC, the CBC itself became the biggest story in the world. My local "CBC-TV News" presented the story in its top spot and at considerable length, with extensive detail and some emotion. At ten o'clock, on "The National", it again occupied top spot, considerably fattened now by new material fitted in around the old. At the end, Peter Mansbridge introduced what was to come from the outside world with "Now for the rest of the news. . . ." It's a common enough phrase in television news, but this time it sounded as if he were about to sweep the newsroom floor to see what might be left that was worth mentioning on so momentous a day. No similar internal shakeups in companies, private or public, before or after, elicited anything like the solicitude the CBC lavished on itself.

The *whole* of "The Journal" was occupied with the trials of the corporation. Radio was still at it the following morning, and the story was still on the main news programs the next night. The theme was that "the corporation is . . . reeling from a . . . cutback that slashed 1,100 jobs and shut down eleven stations across the country. . . ." (That was to say the corporation and all in it were reeling from what the corporation had done to solve its problem of insufficient revenue—which problem, had it been able to detach its fascinated gaze from its own navel, the corporation would have recognized as widespread across the country.)

The makeup of "The Journal" that December 5, 1990, bore about the same relationship to the CBC's own requirements of balance within a single program as Cro-Magnon man bears to a twentieth-century scholar. This is what the CBC book of rules says: "Single programs dealing with a major controversial issue should give adequate recognition to the range of opinion on the subject. Fairness must be the guiding principle in presentation, so that the audience is enabled to make a judgment on the matter in question based on facts."

Balance on that issue of "The Journal" began with an interview between Bill Cameron, the host, and Gérard Veilleux; there could be no quarrel with that. They talked mainly about why the decision had been taken to do away with those eleven local stations rather than economize somewhere else. Veilleux said there was not really an option. The whole country depended on network production, therefore what was left was to "diminish the role of local television and concentrate on regional and national, and international" news.

That was followed by a panel of three men from cities in which the local CBC stations were listed to go—Kevin Peterson, publisher of *The Calgary Herald*, and Parker Barrs Donham, a Cape Breton–based senior writer for *Reader's Digest*—both familiar to conscientious followers of CBC radio and/or television in their localities—and Mayor John Millson, of Windsor, Ontario.

Cameron began with Peterson and the not-quite-question "There are a lot of unhappy people in Calgary tonight?" Peterson replied, "There are an awful lot of unhappy people in Calgary tonight." Barrs Donham, unprompted, said, "Well, I feel just exactly the same way. The notion that we [in Cape Breton] can be served in a regional program from [Halifax] is just false."

And Mayor Millson added, "Citizens in Windsor are just outraged."

That, of course, was not all, but it conveys the flavour.

Next came, by Cameron's description, a panel of "four veterans of the public-broadcasting debate". The four were Paul Rutherford, a history professor at the University of Toronto; Gerry Caplan, co-author with Pierre Sauvageau of the 1986 task force on broadcasting policy; Al Johnson, former president of the CBC; and Howard Aster, professor of political science at McMaster University and a former member of the CBC board of directors. Any producer who did not know that a panel so constituted would be unsympathetic to a "hostile" government cutting the parliamentary appropriation to the public broadcaster deserved to be fired for incompetence. Cameron began with Johnson.

> Cameron: Al Johnson, [he said as television interviewers do, as if the person opposite might not be quite sure of his or her own identity], the reaction here [at CBC headquarters] and in CBC stations across the country was, of course, grief and anger. You used to be president, what was your reaction?"
>
> Johnson: My reaction was, of course, one of grief and anger too. The fundamental issue of these cuts is the failure on the part of the

government to recognize the importance of the CBC as a central Canadian institution. When it comes right down to it, if you undermine the CBC you are undermining Canadian programming, and if you are undermining Canadian programming you are undermining the country as a whole.

Cameron: Gerry Caplan?

Caplan: I'm with Al. . . . I don't see how you can resist the argument that the government, doesn't give a damn about the CBC, doesn't understand public broadcasting, probably resents public broadcasting, and I don't know if it's too conspiratorial—maybe it implies too much intelligence on their part—to say that [with] the free trade deal, with the deregulation of airlines, with the railways being cut back, we now have a fissiparous Canada; we now barely have anything called Canada; we have east-west links that are shrivelled, we have north-south links that are strengthening, and a blow to the CBC is something we couldn't afford at this time. [All of this was said, full tilt, in one breath.]

Cameron: *Paul Rutherford . . . what is your reaction to that?*

Rutherford: Well, I'm sad at the human tragedy, and I'm not particularly pleased at another victory for the Tory agenda, but I do think that a streamlined CBC is a better CBC. The CBC should not have been in local and regional programming anyway. Its mandate is to provide a national service, in two languages, and now it can focus on that.

Cameron: Howard Aster; I am sure you have heard these arguments as well.

Aster: I have heard them often enough. And it's a very, very sad day for the CBC and also for Canada. The president, . . . I think, hit the nail on the head when he said this is a fundamental restructuring. . . . I think he was trying to be optimistic; I want to be pessimistic. The corporation is now significantly different from what it was yesterday. I would go further and I would say that it is on the way to a fundamental shakedown which will change it dramatically.

On this major controversial issue, to return to the CBC's rule on balance, the range of opinion on which the audience would be "enabled to make a judgment . . . based on facts" ran the gamut from vehemently pro-CBC, to warmly CBC, to merely pro-CBC. Score? CBC, 4; government, 0. A shut-out.

The question that remained, and remains, is "What are the facts of the CBC's loudly proclaimed downward slide towards destitution and oblivion?" That 1986 Caplan–Sauvageau report contained a table setting out what it called "CBC Resources", year by year for the preceding ten years, under headings for annual government appropriation, commercial revenues and the two combined. The figures were identified as having come from the Treasury Board, and, as figures provided by a government department for use in the report of a government-appointed task force, seemed likely to be reliable. Consequently, at intervals afterwards I asked the Treasury Board, and it consented, three times, to update the table into the present.

In 1982–83, just before the election of a Conservative government—and by Caplan's NDP reckoning about coincidental with the onset of our national decline to the point that "we now barely have anything called Canada"—the CBC's parliamentary appropriation, in current dollars, was $744.3 million, its net commercial revenue $143.9 million, and the total of the two $888.2 million. In 1992–93, the corresponding figures were $1,089.5 million, or nicely over the billion in the parliamentary appropriation, and $343.2 million in commercial revenue, for a total of $1,432.7 million.

Accordingly, in round figures and without allowing for the depreciated value of the dollar because of inflation, the CBC's annual income rose in the period from just under $900 million to slightly more than $1.4 billion, an increase of half a billion dollars. Those figures may not spell abundance, but—taking into account the coming of Telefilm Canada, which assists both public and private television with the costs of selected productions—neither do they denote ruin and disaster.

Comparing public and private corporations is an inexact business because their circumstances are not all the same. For example, the CBC has a parliamentary mandate to fulfil—services it is obliged to supply, such as radio and television in the far north, which are costly and yield relatively little commercial revenue. In that way, it is more confined in where it may seek economies in bad times.

On the other hand, some persons in the print media who are familiar with the figures in their own field look at those for the CBC and say they do not look all that bad. It is a curiosity in the whole issue of the CBC's supposed deprivation that the print media, which have suffered severe difficulties of their own and in some cases had to chop proportionately more jobs than the CBC, should be so lavish in their sympathy and so quick to accept the line that the CBC was the victim of a hostile government, bent on delivering it the death of a thousand cuts.

In broadcasting, tough times have not been confined to the public broadcaster. Neither have they been unique to Canada. Ken Auletta, in *Three Blind Mice: How the TV Networks Lost Their Way* (Random House, 1991), said the combined profits of ABC, CBS and NBC—with no hostile government to blame their troubles on—had dropped from $800 million in 1984 to $400 million by 1988. They had claimed more than nine out of every ten viewers fifteen years earlier; at the time of his writing, they had lost a third of their audience. The CBC had been no more immune to the influences of cable and the multiplication of channels, or to management miscalculations, than the old American networks.

Consequently, the extravagant pre-emption of news time for corporate special pleading not only clashed with the fundamental rule of no privileged access to the air for special interests, and with the policy dictating balance in discussion of controversial subjects, but also was of questionable wisdom. Reasonably minded persons might be led to ask themselves whether the government's alleged hostility might be not so much ingrained as in reciprocation of the corporation's own.

Thus to the third in this small series of Interesting Occurrences in the Media containing Intimations of Matters of Principle which, if Translated into a Political Context, Might Cause Eyebrows, Questions and perhaps even Nasty Allegations to be Raised. It relates to *The Toronto Star* and what may be a world-record longest-running preoccupation by any newspaper, anywhere, with a piece of highway. The *Star* as an advocate is nothing if not tenacious, and with this issue it was not only that but aroused.

My incomplete record of the volumes of editorials and news stories the *Star* carried on that patch of highway touches, at one end, January 1971, and at the other, September 1986. However, the latter had a reminiscent flavour, like the recollection of a battle lost. "Toronto City Council," it said, of something vaguely related that had arisen, "is acting like a spoiled child. . . . Such petty behavior comes as no surprise, however, since Council had all along chosen to ignore the fact that thousands of Metro area residents need or prefer to drive their cars to work in Toronto. This sort of anti-car mentality. . . ."

In mid-year 1971, which marked only the beginning of a new and fiercer phase, not the beginning of the controversy as a whole, a *Star* editorial asked sarcastically: "Where do we go from here? What do we do next? The provincial government in its wisdom has stopped the Great Northwest Road in its tracks, Goodbye Spadina Expressway. Hello . . . hello . . . hello to what?"

The subject was whether an expressway should be created, based upon the city's Spadina Avenue at its lower end and pushing up into the populous suburbs to the northwest; it would be a mate of sorts to a much earlier limited-access road to the northeast, the Don Valley Parkway. However, with work well under way, the provincial government yielded to inner-city environmentalists and cut the new Spadina extension short, within the city. To say that the *Star* was not content with the wisdom or even the rationality of that would be mild.

The progress of its campaign can be judged by just a few headings and short extracts. For instance, in rejection of a suggested substitute: "Stupid alternative" (August 24, 1971), "No alternative" (October 13, 1971), "Spadina: Finish it" (October 26, 1971). And an extract: "What was predicted in June would happen when the Spadina Expressway was halted is now beginning. Residential streets are made noisy and dangerous by being used as main avenues for which they were never intended. The Star predicted this would be the outcome of halting Spadina. . . ."

It did indeed—and the termination of the project unnecessarily lengthening the time people living in the suburbs spent getting to and from their jobs downtown, and the slower movement of goods between city and suburbs, and the harm that would be done to quiet urban neighbourhoods with more and more traffic dumped upon them.

Here are just a few more samples, picked at random from the many as the campaign went on. The first is from the rich 1972 crop: "One of the unfortunate features of the Spadina Expressway controversy is that the special cost-benefit analysis of the expressway . . . was not ready when the Ontario Municipal Board considered the matter and later when Premier Davis imposed his veto. . . ." "It seems . . . on the edge of being too late . . . that Toronto people have awakened from their lethargy over the killing of the Spadina Expressway. . . ." "Premier William Davis is caught on the horns of a dilemma. He's either got to help to finance the Spadina Expressway to bring cars and trucks into Toronto, or he's got to keep them out. He's rejected the expressway solution and the public would never accept a ban. So the entire northwest section of the city is condemned to present congestion and future chaos." "Why not roof over the entire 6.5 miles [10.4 kilometres, of what had been marked out for the expressway] . . . and plant grass and flowers and call it William Davis Park." ". . . an impenetrable maze of one-way roads", "the worst blunder in the history of Toronto transportation planning", "the Borough of York, frantic to stop traffic crawling through its residential streets" and on and on.

Enough. The question is: can a newspaper or any news medium be in conflict with itself? I think so. Certainly, if the blending of interests that the Parker Commission recognized as improper in persons in government also applied to the media, that would necessitate rigorous avoidance of comment on any matter concerning the public good that might be construed as advancing a corporate interest. Consider: if a tabloid newspaper sells a lot of copies on the subways, streetcars and commuter trains that serve a big city—as tabloids originally were designed to do—where will it stand on a municipal decision to build an expressway or a new subway line? Or where would a broadsheet, multi-section newspaper stand, being very much dependent on home-delivery customers because a fat newspaper is difficult to handle in a crowded streetcar? Would it have a leaning to an expressway, because trucks are needed to drop off bundles in thickly planted housing developments? Or would it support the subway line?

Long after the Spadina extension had faded in even the *Star*'s interest, I asked two or three Toronto newspeople, not of the *Star*, what they had made of the *Star*'s fervency. The nub of the common answer was "Oh, Bee Honderich needed to get his trucks up from the bottom of Yonge Street to the suburbs." That conclusion obviously rested on hearsay and willing belief rather than direct evidence. Still, it may not be irrelevant to note that when the *Star* built a new $400-million production plant to do everything a newspaper needs to have done before it is bundled into trucks for delivery, it chose to build it in the quarter that the Spadina Expressway would have run into. (The news department stayed downtown.)

Whatever the conclusion, the *Star*'s preoccupation with the subject cannot be said to reveal a conflict of interest. The points it argued for the expressway were valid whether one agreed with them or not. Many of its readers, especially in the suburbs, enthusiastically did. It may have gone a little lightly on a parallel interest of its own, but that does not imply something contrary to the public interest. Yet it *knew* that mixing, or appearing to mix, public and private interests could be troublesome. While I briefly performed as editorial-page editor there, I was asked to join a provincial commission under the former premier, John Robarts, which was to make some enquiries into wine-buying at the Ontario Liquor Commission; I had written quite a lot on the subject. I told Martin Goodman, the editor, about it and, before I had said whether I was inclined to accept or refuse, he said, "No. We might want to write about the LCBO and its wine lists at some time, and where would we be then?" He was right; if the commission included cases of wine that made everyone sick who tried them, and the paper wanted to take the commission's hide off for carelessness, an awkward situation would have been created.

The point is that conflicts of interest are tricky things—difficult to prove from the outside and not always easy on the inside to see in advance and to avoid. And they *do* occur in the private sector, not just the public; they simply are not taken with such exaggerated seriousness or subjected to the same public attention—a double standard. That is not to say missteps or actual wrongdoings should be winked at in the public sector, but that the facts of the matter warrant reporters and editors imposing on themselves a high standard of proof to ensure that racking scandals are not set off on fragile conclusions.

FOURTEEN

WHITHER ARE WE DRIFTING?

THE HEADING HERE IS NOT ORIGINAL, BUT IS STOLEN from a very old *Globe and Mail* editorial. It was memorable as a heading of genius—darkly portentous but funny; meaningless but compelling, because any reader who glanced at it and did not immediately turn away would have difficulty in not reading on to find out what in hell it was about. It is apt here for those characteristics, of course, but also because this chapter is a little bit about whither the news business is drifting and whence—and about some things in the travel from whence to whither that it would be a good idea to give up.

The big question hanging over the media as we near the end of the century is which of their components will last long into the next century, at least in their present form, and why. Prognoses, of course, are notoriously uncertain, no less about news entities than about people. More than twenty years ago, an unpublished professional study of Toronto's three big newspapers done for the *Star* is supposed to have concluded—I put it that way because I have not seen it—that within ten years only two would remain, one of which would be *The Toronto Sun*. All three, if not flourishing quite as they once did, are still going in the mid-nineties. But Canadian newspapers as a whole have not been doing well for some time. Advertising went down severely in the recession of the early eighties, and recovered, but not to the previous level. It went down again with the recession of the early nineties and in 1994 was still making a slow recovery, which may fail to recapture that second loss.

The reason for the *Sun*'s anticipated survival—in addition to the fact that it was making a satisfying profit—was that it had cut out as its own a distinct segment of the market, an Ordinary Canadians audience. As a tabloid it was easy to handle, it had a bit of an impertinent air to it, was readable, carried a number of good columns—chatty, controversial, occasionally outrageous and, as in the case of Douglas Fisher in Ottawa, authoritative. It was also strong in sports. A mixture.

The *Star* was the biggest seller of the three (then and since), with bountiful advertising (still, but relatively less so), never stingy about going after a story, anywhere. It played to a slightly liberal-left audience and was known, within and without, for its dedication to causes—social programs and economic nationalism being two—and for never letting go any story with a trace of drama in it without extracting the last drop.

The Globe and Mail, which looked at the time the likeliest candidate for the chop, was still striving to grow up to its boast of being Canada's National Newspaper.

In the interval since, the *Sun* has lost some of its bounce, the *Star* has seemed to wallow a little in the early nineties, as if not quite sure where it should be going, and *The Globe and Mail*, still expensively reaching an audience even in small communities across the country, has succeeded in establishing itself as the country's one really national newspaper, and the best overall, but with a weakness for slanted stories in political contexts—slanted to accord not with the paper's editorial policy, but with the writers' and newsroom editors' own biases. If those three Toronto newspapers were to become two, it no longer seems likely that the *Globe* would be the one to go.

The likeliest future for newspapers as a species, not so long ago, seemed to be oblivion—and still may be, although the estimated lifespan for the healthiest of them would be better set for at least thirty years into the new century. Still, with new developments in communications technology piling up by the day, putting words on *paper*—printing, ye gods! William Caxton (1421–1491) and all that!—seems terribly anachronistic.

The product, never really attractive, has become worse, less serious-looking, with colour printing. It is unhandy to carry around, or to read at a lunch-counter or in public transport. It still costs real money, as distinct from the hidden cost of broadcast material. And it becomes a public nuisance the moment it is obsolete (which occurs immediately it is put down), because it can't be burned for environmental reasons, is only tediously recyclable and quickly fills up the municipal garbage dumps if not otherwise disposed of.

Still, print remains the best medium for the delivery of substantial information—with some emphasis on "substantial"—which perhaps should tell newspaper managements to try more of it and leave the infotainment to television, which has a family relationship with it. As long as reading is still taught in the schools, which it should be for a while, print deserves not to be dismissed as day-late television without the pictures.

But as matters stand, television news may be the greatest safeguard against newspapers quickly declining into museum exhibits. Television has never quite been able to free itself of the constraints of its own rigid format, which dictates that all any reasonable person needs to know about anything can be told in a minute and a half. That leads to the sort of interview where the interviewer comes with a prepared list of questions, none of which is ever allowed to be answered properly, because eliciting answers is not the object of the exercise, but asking. What else plagues public affairs television is its inability to escape the influence of its life partner, entertainment, which leads to confrontation for the sake of confrontation, and lack of background because background is not readily susceptible to visual presentation.

CBC television had an additional psychological problem from the start, in being born into one tradition and growing up with another. It gave up too soon the struggle to be different. Public broadcasting was begun in Canada for the express purpose of not being American broadcasting, but being better; that is what warranted its being publicly funded. The taxpayer—or the taxpayer who wanted to listen to radio—would need a licence, just as for a car. Britain's BBC was taken as the model. To ensure that the corporation would be free of commercial pressure that might affect its programming, there would be no advertising. Therefore, decisions in general programming, public affairs and entertainment alike, would be taken with a view not necessarily to attracting the largest possible audience, to be sold to advertisers, but to a standard that contained an element of raising the public taste. Elitist? Indeed. But then, "elitism" and "elite" were not dirty words at the time. That touch of elitism, in fact, was part of what warranted making the taxpayer pay for the CBC.

In news programming, the standard was founded on solidity, not flash. CBC radio has remained more or less true to that pattern, and has been praised for it. Television set out the same way but soon gave in to the notion that ratings were all—and that the U.S. networks constituted the Big Time, the only place to take lessons from. In the many sympathetic reports in print when the CBC not so long ago lost viewers after introducing "Prime Time News" at nine o'clock to replace "The National" at ten, an important point was overlooked. The time change undoubtedly was the main factor in the opting-out, but there may have been other, more substantial causes of viewers' so quickly turning away—notably that the replacement emerged in a new set which precisely depicted the content—glassier, flashier, and trashier. The revival of a U.S. "You gotta challenge" style of interviewing that had gone out of fashion about the same time as bobby sox and penny loafers also reaffirmed the value of print, as a relief from show-biz hokum if nothing else. The rise of CTV's national news to top place in a field that CBC had so long had for its own can be more correctly attributed to a better product than to a time change.

What would help all journalism in the mid-nineties would be a realistic reassessment of what it is and, even more important, what it isn't. Information, the stuff journalism trades in, is an essential consumer product, but with the rare distinction of having to meet no standard of freshness, wholesomeness, purity or absence of toxicity, either before it goes to market or while it remains there. No licence is needed to produce it and no prior examination of the product is performed, as it is with canned fish, for instance. No back label is demanded on which the natural ingredients are listed, along with all additives that may have been introduced in the processing.

Journalism, therefore, is not manufacturing in the ordinary way, but the processing, on trust, of a consumer good. Moreover, journalists are not professionals. Professionals—doctors, lawyer, engineers and all the rest—subscribe to codes of professional ethics and are accountable to the bodies that administer them. In market journalism, there is no such code. The best the trade has done is to have sponsored press councils in most provinces to hear complaints from readers about misstatements that affect them, and, here and there, to have appointed in-house ombudsmen, of whom William Morgan at the CBC is the best known. (Unfortunately for citizen confidence in the untouchability and independence of ombudsmen, he is best known for the fact that, as soon as he made a decision unfavourable to the corporation on an important matter, there were loud cries from within that the office had to be reformed.)

The result is a situation in which those of us who constitute the media are accountable for the most part only to our consciences and the law of defamation, which says, in effect, that to damage with falsehoods a person's or company's standing in the community may invite being sued.

In general, we do not like to be held accountable, and tend to look upon any perceived effort to impose accountability on us as an unwarranted and even constitutionally improper intrusion. That was what underlay the nearly universal media reaction when Senator Jack Marshall's Senate subcommittee on veterans' affairs took it upon itself to look into the facts of the *Valour and the Horror* films. Our complaint was based primarily on what most distinguishes us from the sellers of other consumer products. *We*, by direct identification, are specifically protected in the Charter of Rights and Freedoms by a degree of immunity from supervision and regulation that no mere processor of breakfast cereal can claim.

That has been an equivocal boon. As an honour, something of practical necessity, value or meaning, it is empty. It could even be argued, meanly, that its main effect has been to put some of our leading information-deliverers to the expense of going to court to seek decisions defining press rights as superior to individual rights. But it is gratifying to the ego; too much so. It has set journalists even more apart from the common horde than they already assumed themselves to be. They were elevated from being self-appointed watchdogs to being constitutionally sanctioned watchdogs. It has also permitted the term "freedom of the press" to be translated as not so much a guarantee to the *public* of an essential free flow of information, but a unique benefit, conferred for their own convenience, on the people who are called The Press.

It is not my purpose to argue that the Charter of Rights should be rewritten and a government censor implanted in every radio and television station, and every newspaper and magazine office. Rather, all that talk a bit earlier about supervision, standards and inspectors was about underlining the fact that we, the media, *are* uniquely free of outside supervision and interference—but for a larger purpose than making life easy for us.

Consequently, we need to accept—*noblesse oblige* and all that—that this constitutionally affirmed freedom incurs some corresponding responsibility. It begins with media managements recognizing that a moral obligation has been transferred to them to see that the consumer is not sold a product tainted, more than can be avoided, by dishonesty, unacknowledged bias, inaccuracy, conclusions contrived to mislead, and the neglect of facts essential to a realistic understanding—all of which overlap.

Quality control is not a term heard in newsrooms, because the word "control" itself is seen to be in conflict with "freedom", which all journalism is supposed to embody. But why *not* quality control? In any other enterprise, there must be some point from which responsibility is exercised, for the sake of the enterprise as well as the consumer, to say what goes in or on the product and what does not. The new car must leave the plant with four wheels, and no complaint about denial of free expression on the production line can be allowed to change that. Outside the business of gathering, sorting, processing and packaging information, quality control usually is highly thought of. What complicates the matter in information marketing is that, within freedom of the press, there is also freedom of expression to be reckoned with—*the writer's* freedom of expression.

Suppose the management of a newspaper said something like this: "We can't publish this. What you have here, here, and here flatly presented as facts, cannot be reconciled with what you say with equal certainty here, here and here. Therefore, your conclusion is unsustainable."

Is that an interference with freedom of expression? Yep. Is it to be avoided? Nope. Not unless the product is to become intellectually unfit for human consumption. Editing, extending even to exclusion, is a necessary and legitimate part of all information delivery. A large part of the problem with much recent journalism is that some managements have been mesmerized by freedom of expression as part of the doctrine of political correctness, to the point of being unwilling to challenge it even where it may be inappropriate, and detrimental to the quality of the product.

To managements whose concern is to be seen always as attuned to the current fetish, that restraint may generate a warm inner glow of self-satisfaction, but the merit in feeding the reader or viewer rubbish is hard to find.

Quality control in the business of processing and selling information is not to be read as the dictation of content, but as a precaution to ensure that what is sold is reasonably reliable as to fact, reasonably cohesive between premise and conclusion and reasonably attractive as words to be read or listened to. The news business is really quite an ordinary one—much less disciplined than accountancy, and somewhat more creative than selling natty gent's furnishings—and badly in need of a bout of deromanticization, demystification and deglamorization, all of which contribute to an inflated sense of self-importance.

Where media self-importance has affected Parliament is in having pushed the House of Commons and the Senate off into a sort of diplomatic limbo, as states we have decided we do not wish to recognize. Whatever Canadian readers or viewers need to know about the governance of the country, and what options are to be considered in this or that issue, they will have to get from Us. The essential elements in the system, then, are the Cabinet, the senior ranks of the public service and the media.

No American who reads a newspaper, or watches panel discussions on public affairs on television, could be left long in doubt that the country has a national legislature; consider just President Clinton's struggle with Congress over a health-care program. It would be easy, in Canada, to be unsure. Very little is ever reported of what the people in the two chambers of the legislature do or say.

Obviously, the constitutional arrangements are different in the two countries, but not so different that our Fathers of Confederation left out a national legislature. Its existence is evidenced by the fact that the proceedings of the House of Commons—committees not included—covered more than 5,500 pages of *Hansard* in just the first session of the current 35th Parliament. However, scarcely a word ever reaches print or the air, except for bits from exchanges between ministers and a handful of front-bench MPs which provide the base for an essay of the reporter's choice. In other words, the House is treated not as a vital element but as a facility. Listening to hours of debate, then having to boil all that down to a reliable and readable account of manageable length, is tedious. Consequently, the frequently cited right of the people to know has been found suspendable where Parliament is concerned.

This is not a trivial matter. When the privatization of Pearson International Airport in Toronto blew up late in the 1993 election campaign, *The Globe and Mail* was embarrassed to find it did not know as much about the subject as it would like—this long after the bill had run the full course in Parliament, and with the paper having one of the largest single-newspaper bureaus in Ottawa, and a good library.

Media inattention to Parliament is not a new thing, but one that has grown. Its roots may go back to the great Pipeline Debate of 1956, a critical point in media/political relations. Still, it was only years later that the newest bright thought in the Ottawa press gallery became "This is not where the action is, but in the departments." That was about the time of Senator Keith Davey's 1970 Senate committee on the mass media. The committee pushed along the idea that Ottawa reporters had to move—their heads, at least—out of the House of Commons to capture what was happening before it happened. As one writer subsequently put it, the Davey committee accepted as a sort of rule that "the best measure of an effective press is how well it prepares the public for the dislocations of social change." That reflected long-term thinking, but it also reinforced the idea that, even in the short run, Parliament was the end of the line in the process of policy formulation and enactment. The process begins with the Cabinet, the caucus of the governing party, and the bureaucracy—two bureaucracies, actually, the government's own political advisers and the public service advisers whose job it is to translate government objectives into constitutionally sound legislation. Only when that is complete does Parliament enter the picture.

It became the conventional wisdom that reporters would report more usefully if they were able to tell their readers and listeners what was coming before a bill was already in the House of Commons for debate—in other words, while time remained for public influence to be exerted. Two incidental effects of such thinking have been to elevate the media and interest groups in their own minds in relation to the parliamentarians, and to provide an excuse for the media to duck out of the tedious business of reporting the debates of a lot of inferior communicators.

In the Mulroney years, the two great *economic* issues—to separate those from the great constitutional issues of the Meech Lake Accord and the Charlottetown agreement and subsequent referendum—were the free trade agreement (FTA) with the United States and the Goods and Services Tax (GST). As late as April 1994, the two issues were being lumped with scandal by The Canadian Press in a routine story on election spending, to which it attached a homely moral about money not buying electoral success: "The Progressive Conservatives were the big spenders in the October vote at $10.4-million. . . . But such largesse didn't help them after nine years in office dominated by free trade, the goods and services tax, and scandals." That was to represent the three as a matched set of skeletons in the Tory closet. The taint of scandal was in the *reporting* of the FTA and the GST, not in the issues themselves. Certainly in the reporting of the negotiations over free trade, the negative side received more attention than the positive. (The ostensible debate over the GST, which we will come to, was mainly an exercise in competitive denigration.)

On Balance, a publication of the Fraser Institute in Vancouver, produces monthly analyses of how the media are performing in prominent subjects in the news. The October 1988 issue was based on a day-by-day and story-by-story study of free-trade coverage from the end of May. It focused on just two news deliverers, the CBC in its paired night-time news and public affairs shows, "The National" and "The Journal", and *The Globe and Mail*. What follow are just a few conclusions; "The Globe and Mail was consistent in its coverage in that those opposed to free trade were given almost twice as much space to provide their views [as] those supporting the deal. . . ." "Statements critical of free trade accounted for two-thirds of CBC's coverage. . . ." "While the media conferred importance to the free trade issue by prominent display . . . almost half of the statements made (44 percent) . . . focused on the negotiation process and political relations surrounding the deal." That meant the substance of the deal received just slightly more attention than the deadlocks, clashes, lacks of progress, disappointing responses and imminent failures of the negotiations—which, as bad news, always rate higher than good news.

An interesting sidelight was produced from an analysis of what CBC reporters said just in their summings-up, which to the minds of *On Balance*'s editors usually reflected more personal opinions than the reporters allowed themselves in the body of their reports. The negatives in the conclusions far exceeded those earlier in the item. "While in general," it said, "CBC reporters opposed free trade twice as often as they supported it, their concluding remarks were nine times more likely to oppose the deal."

When media coverage swings so heavily to one side, it becomes legitimate to ask: are persons who think of themselves as adversaries of governments—or even just of the government of the day—capable of taking into consideration where the national interest lies, or are the arcane pleasures of being an extra-parliamentary opposition enough? Was the preponderance of reporting against free trade attributable to reasoned judgements of the pluses and minuses of the agreement, or did it reflect a large measure of dislike of the government, and a wish to see it fail in free trade and everything else? *On Balance* recorded three members of the *Globe*'s Ottawa bureau, Geoffrey York, Hugh Winsor and Ross Howard, as having offered *only* negative viewpoints. The *Globe* editorially supported the FTA.

Canada had a two-way national interest in the agreement—one, the anticipatated benefits, and, two, the avoidance of ruinous costs that perhaps would occur from opting to stay out, a small isolationist between a unifying Europe and the world's largest trading nation. The government in Ottawa is elected to represent the national interest. Of course, there is no guarantee ever that everyone in the country is going to agree with what it is doing. But it ought to be entitled, at least, to see in those who report on government a glimmer of recognition of the practical reality that, in dealings with the government of another country, there are no political points to be gained at home from not playing the national interest, and to the hilt.

Even that practical proposition got short shrift in the free trade debate. There were allegations of "giveaways", of a loss of sovereignty being risked in negotiating free trade at all, and more specifically in stories rooted in utterances from the Liberal and NDP campaigns about the devastation that would be done in Canadian social programs if the agreement was signed. One version of the threat was that U.S. industry would say, and the administration in Washington would accept, that Canadian social programs constituted subsidies to competing Canadian companies, and would be made subject to countervailing duties; the Canadian government would then need to unravel the safety net (most notably health care) in pursuit of "harmonization", or see Canadian exporters suffer severely.

Two points neglected in that effective campaign propaganda were that social programs were not included in the negotiations, and that universal social programs—programs not specific to any company, region or trade sector but equally available—were specifically exempted from retaliatory action under the General Agreement on Tariffs and Trade (GATT), to which both Canada and the United States, and most of the rest of the world, were signatories. Hokum or not, it was effective. With just three weeks to go in the campaign, *Maclean's* was reporting: "The most intense discussion last week centred on the effect of free trade upon the nation's safety net."

A less easily documented but relevant point was that the United States already had a growing movement, not to knock down Canada's health-care program, but to create one at home. It had backing, not yet universal but growing, in business: Lee Iacocca, the very public-person president of Chrysler, was an advocate; there was support in the unions. While the returns were still coming in from the presidential election that returned George Bush for a second term in 1988, Edward Kennedy and Jesse Jackson, together on national television, said a health-care plan would have to be in the Democratic platform for 1992.

All that was knowable, and might have spared Canadians a lot of hand-wringing over the future of medicare, had the newsrooms of the country shown more interest in finding out. Instead, the most effective reproof came from the intervention of Emmett Hall, a retired Supreme Court judge, a respected figure sometimes known as the father of medicare for his leadership in 1960 of the royal commission on the health needs of Canadians. He said, although not in quite so many words, that the alarms raised were baloney.

This predicates another interesting question: do media have an obligation to try to put right what they themselves did not put wrong in the first place? The logic of the asserted "right of the public to know" seems to dictate a yes answer: if the people have an inherent right to know, it must include the right to know when they have been sold bad information, wherever it may have originated. Think of it as the Tuna Rule; the concern was not where the fish came from, but whether it was in a salubrious condition when sold.

If readers and viewers have a right to know when they should rearrange their conclusions because they have been significantly misinformed, some guidelines would be useful as to ways of informing them. One of the easiest would be to give up the old-boy understanding about maintaining silence about one another's gaffes. Along with other benefits, a little ratting would have an invigorating effect on public discourse generally.

It would also help if, whenever a story appeared that was certain to unleash the pack, the industry leaders, at least, assigned reporters not just to follow up and expand on the original trail, but to dig into the other side to see if a row-back, as it used to be called, might be warranted. Whatever was found might not overtake the pack, which would already be in full cry, but might cause it to hesitate.

In the longer term, the knowledge that back-checking was routine practice could even have the effect of raising standards—no bad thing for credibility all round.

Free trade passed. More surprisingly, a second Mulroney government was elected, again with a majority. Obviously there was more against the likelihood of that happening than just doubts over free trade, which, fortunately for the Conservatives, eased somewhat before the campaign ended. Also fortunately for them, the concentration on free trade was such that the prospective GST—which was available in a government white paper as policy for the immediate future, and vulnerable as something still in a formative stage—was never taken up. Less than a year later, the most hated tax ever, the most dreaded tax, the worst, the most inequitable tax, as it was called (along with much else), was the biggest story going.

In a story in the Ottawa *Citizen*, on December 20, 1989, by which time the GST was well advanced to becoming law, Greg Weston, a staff writer, began with this sinister look back:

About a month *before* the 1988 federal election, a group of government backroom plotters gathered at the Finance department to pore over a major public opinion survey on Canadians' feelings towards the proposed Goods and Services Tax. The message was clear. No amount of sugar-coating—nothing at all—was going to make Canadians *like a new tax on just about everything.*

Most of the political schemers and public relations wizards around the boardroom table that day reached the same gloomy conclusion. The best the government could hope was to limit public animosity to something short of an open tax revolt.

As pollster Angus Reid described the situation . . . "Basically, Canadians just don't trust the government on this issue."

Curious, curious. A known proposition, virtually ignored by opposing parties and the media through a whole general election campaign; the sponsoring party re-elected with a majority; and shortly thereafter the proposition is the subject of speculation about a possible taxpayer revolt because of the voters' distrust of the people they so recently elected. Clearly both the media and the voters had neglected a matter of vital importance during the campaign.

Scarcely less curious is the fact that once the GST was in effect—although there was no dancing in the streets—an abrupt change in tone occurred in the reporting:

"Tax provides modest boost to car dealers"—*Globe and Mail*, January 3, 1991.

"GST's impact could be less than predicted"—same paper, same day.

"Think of Sweden"—*Windsor Star*, January 5, 1991, in an editorial on similar taxes in other countries, ending with "When you consider how others live . . . 7 percent doesn't sound so bad. At least the Swedes don't think so."

"It's not all doom 'n' gloom"—*Ottawa Sun*, January 6, 1991.

"GST beefs 'low'"—*Calgary Herald*, January 24, 1991.

"GST complaints are few"—Regina *Leader-Post*, January 31, 1991.

"Most of us didn't feel GST pinch, poll reports"—Ottawa *Citizen*, February 7, 1991.

Yet, between times, there had been a sustained and vehement campaign to educate Canadians in what they might expect from the new tax—with a heavy bias towards one conclusion: pain.

That campaign, too, was curious. It could not be said that the long explanatory stories, and even series, on the tax itself were totally lacking in efforts at balance. However, the weight of argument generally was against the tax—usually with no suggestion of what the government should do instead, considering the state of the country's debt, or where it might find either compensating savings in expenditure or increases in revenues from other sources if the GST were abandoned. (It is one of the non-constitutional protections of the Charter of Rights and Freedoms that we may denounce proposals without incurring a responsibility to suggest alternatives.)

When attention turned to the effect of the tax on specific businesses or groups of Canadians, the reporting became flatly negative. When it was in a political context, the reporting varied from dismissive of a monumental blunder, to real or purported outrage, to suppressed glee at the prospective downfall of the Mulroney government.

Whether it was the fault of reporters, or of slightly befuddled government officials, some of the money facts set before the public were at best approximate:

> "The federal government will spend a little more than $500 million in the next year to administer and collect the GST."—Ottawa *Citizen*, March 1, 1991.
>
> "Running the 7 percent Goods and Services Tax this year will cost Canadian taxpayers $734 million. . . ." *Toronto Star*, same day.
>
> "Pointing to the recent budget's revised administration costs of $745 million for 1991 and 1992, the New Democrats' Lorne Nystrom said. . . ."—Ottawa *Citizen*, March 14, 1990.
>
> "[Revenue Minister] Jelinek gave a rough breakdown . . . $365 will be spent in 1991–92" in administration costs, plus a share of another "$300 million in transition costs. . . ."—*Toronto Star*, March 14, 1990.

It would be foolish to suggest that the GST was not badly handled by the government. To start with, it is difficult to sell people the idea that there can be anything to be said for erasing a tax most of them have never heard of, and substituting a tax they will pay every time they buy anything from a corn remedy to a set of solid-gold exercise weights. The GST needed more, and more persuasive, explanation. Nothing was helped when the government said the tax would be revenue-neutral—i.e., produce no more revenue than was already coming in—and only much later, and contradictorily, said the extra revenue would go to reduce the deficit. That last might have made a good blood-sweat-and-tears argument to begin with, but introduced as a sort of afterthought, it seemed only tricky, muddled or both.

But again, as in the case of the debate on the free trade agreement, there is the question: was all the rage in the media against the GST the product of detached judgement of its merits and demerits as a tax policy, or was it more a case of hostility to the government sponsoring it? And what will happen in the distant aftermath of the nineties, with a new government in power and flummoxed in its search for a way of achieving the same revenue by some means tarted-up enough to be called by another name? Can the media, which so thoroughly excoriated the predecessor government for bringing in such a retrograde, inequitable and inexcusable tax blithely accept precisely the same but with bells on, and escape accusations of being flagrantly hypocritical and unbelievable?

When, at mid-year 1994, a Liberal-dominated House of Commons committee proposed exactly that—including that the provinces be invited to join in, as the Conservatives had done and been rejected—the general response from the parliamentary press gallery was low key, understanding, explanatory; the plan was not represented as any sort of plot against the people. It is difficult for someone who believes that we need very much more of media being low-key, understanding, and explanatory to deplore that. But this moderate response, so different from the rant against the GST, suggested hypocrisy rather than a sudden outbreak of rational restraint. Such inconsistency invites the conclusion that if the reporting was not unreliable in the first instance, it must be so in the second. That damages the credibility of all journalism, but particularly print journalism, which depends for its audience more on the well informed and politically aware.

The next word here was to have been "perhaps"—as the introduction to saying it might be time to step back and reconsider. But scrap the "perhaps." More is required than stepping back on one issue.

I arrived in the newsroom of *The Globe and Mail* in 1945. Soon after, Bruce West, who had been with the *Globe* before the Second World War and had then gone off to be a Canadian information officer in London and Washington, returned from Washington. He was to become the custodian of a popular column—a light and easy daily essay on local people, happenings and idiosyncrasies that the news routinely passed over. Bruce loved stories. One of his was about a Washington correspondent of *The Times* of London—Sir Somebody—one of whose maxims of journalism was that "altogether too many good stories are ruined by over-verification." I have always liked that, because it contains a kernel of truth which most journalists privately subscribe to but prefer not to admit.

Another story was of two young men from the same home town who met by chance on the street in New York. They talked about growing up together and the town, and how old So-and-so was doing, and what had become of this one and that one. They were about to part when one said, "Look, I apologize. We've talked all this time about the old town, and about my side of things, and I haven't even asked you what you're doing here in New York." And the other said, "I live here. I'm a reporter. On a newspaper. [Long pause.] But look, if you happen to see my old mom when you get back home, don't tell her. I mean, about my being a newspaperman. She thinks I play piano in a whorehouse."

That image of newspapermen as persons in an exciting business somewhere on the borderline between the respectable and the disreputable was never true, but it had a satisfying devil-may-care ring to it. The fellow who didn't want his dear old mom to know how far he had fallen short of her hopes probably thought of himself as being "in the newspaper *game*". If his work was mainly in the city hall press room, covering municipal politics, he would be known to the mayor, and perhaps even to himself, as "one of the press room *boys*". Both of those terms are trivializing and have almost disappeared, assisted out by the fact that many of the boys nowadays are not boys and never were. As for self-depreciating humour about journalism and its practitioners—or about anything, come to that—gone, gone, gone. Journalism, we must always remember, is a serious business. Very. That is one of the things most wrong with it.

No matter what form the current media self-image takes, it always has to have that slightly puffed-up element—of steely-eyed agents of the people, unsleeping in their dedication to the task of overseeing the political process for evidence of corruption, dereliction of duty, uncaringness for the needs and entitlements of the populace, and so on, and so on, and so on.

Perhaps, in considering whither we are drifting, it would be a good idea to find a middle position between the genial but exaggerated awareness of imperfection demonstrated by Sir Whomever and the New York reporter, on the one hand, and, on the other, the intimations of infallibility and sainted purpose which have overtaken us. We could do that by accepting the role, less glamorous, perhaps, but no less worthy, of simple producers and vendors of information as a basic consumer need, like canned soup or comfortable shoes.

No offence meant. Just a suggestion, just a suggestion.

INDEX